The American History Series

SERIES EDITORS
John Hope Franklin, *Duke University*
A. S. Eisenstadt, *Brooklyn College*

Charles E. Neu

BROWN UNIVERSITY,
PROFESSOR OF HISTORY, EMERITUS

America's Lost War

Vietnam: 1945–1975

HARLAN DAVIDSON, INC.
WHEELING, ILLINOIS 60090-6000

Visit us on the World Wide Web at www.harlandavidson.com.

Library of Congress Cataloging-in-Publication Data

Neu, Charles E.
    America's lost war : Vietnam, 1945–1975 / Charles E. Neu.
        p. cm. — (The American history series)
    Includes bibliographical essay and index.
    ISBN 0-88295-232-3 (alk. paper)
    1. Vietnamese Conflict, 1961–1975—United States. 2. Vietnam—History—1945–1975. 3. United States—Foreign relations—Vietnam.
4. Vietnam—Foreign relations—United States. 5. United States—History—1945– I. Title: Vietnam, 1945–1975. II. Title. III. Series:
American history series (Wheeling, Ill.)
    DS558.N475 2005
    959.704'3373—dc22
                                2004020853

Cover photo: Men of H Company, 2nd Battalion, 7th Marines, move along rice paddy dikes in pursuit of the Viet Cong, 1965. Courtesy of the National Archives. ARC 532437.

Manufactured in the United States of America
07 06 05 04 1 2 3 4 5 MG

For Art

FOREWORD

Every generation writes its own history for the reason that it sees the past in the foreshortened perspective of its own experience. This has surely been true of the writing of American history. The practical aim of our historiography is to give us a more informed sense of where we are going by helping us understand the road we took in getting where we are. As the nature and dimensions of American life are changing, so too are the themes of our historical writing. Today's scholars are hard at work reconsidering every major aspect of the nation's past: its politics, diplomacy, economy, society, recreation, mores and values, as well as status, ethnic, race, sexual, and family relations. The lists of series titles that appear on the inside covers of this book will show at once that our historians are ever broadening the range of their studies.

The aim of this series is to offer our readers a survey of what today's historians are saying about the central themes and aspects of the American past. To do this, we have invited to write for the series only scholars who have made notable contributions to the respective fields in which they are working. Drawing on primary and secondary materials, each volume presents a factual and narrative account of its particular subject, one that affords readers a basis for perceiving its larger dimensions and importance. Conscious that readers respond to the closeness and immediacy of a subject, each of our authors seeks to restore the past as an actual present, to revive it as a living reality. The individuals and groups who figure in the pages of our books ap-

pear as real people who once were looking for survival and fulfillment. Aware that historical subjects are often matters of controversy,
our authors present their own findings and conclusions. Each volume
closes with an extensive critical essay on the writings of the major
authorities on its particular subject.

The books in this series are designed for use in both basic and
advanced courses in American history, on the undergraduate and graduate levels. Such a series has a particular value these days, when the
format of American history courses is being altered to accommodate
a greater diversity of reading materials. The series offers a number of
distinct advantages. It extends the dimensions of regular course work.
Going well beyond the confines of the textbook, it makes clear that
the study of our past is, more than the student might otherwise understand, at once complex, profound, and absorbing. It presents that past
as a subject of continuing interest and fresh investigation. The work
of experts in their respective fields, the series, moreover, puts at the
disposal of the reader the rich findings of historical inquiry. It invites
the reader to join, in major fields of research, those who are pondering anew the central themes and aspects of our past. And it reminds
the reader that in each successive generation of the ever-changing
American adventure, men and women and children were attempting,
as we are now, to live their lives and to make their way.

John Hope Franklin
A. S. Eisenstadt

CONTENTS

Photographs follow pages 70, 128, 206

PREFACE
AND ACKNOWLEDGMENTS

In the fall of 1963, when only a few Americans had died in South Vietnam, Ho Chi Minh talked to a Polish diplomat in Hanoi. "Neither you nor I know the Americans well," the great revolutionary leader reflected, "but what we do know of them, what we have read and heard about them, suggests that they are more practical and clear-sighted than other capitalist nations. They will not pour their resources into Vietnam endlessly. One day they will take pencil in hand and begin figuring. Once they really begin to analyze our ideas seriously, they will come to the conclusion that it is possible and even worthwhile to live in peace with us."[1]

Ho was correct to assume that American leaders would prosecute the war differently than had their French predecessors; he was wrong to conclude that they were wiser and would make a more realistic assessment of the dynamics of the Vietnamese revolution. Only a year and a half after he spoke the sporadic fighting in Vietnam was transformed into a big American war, and the American phase of the Vietnam conflict caused far greater destruction and loss of life than had the French phase. And many years passed before American leaders finally put pencil to paper, calculated the odds in Vietnam, and concluded that they could not prevail at a reasonable cost.

The American phase of the Vietnam War, which lasted for twenty-one years—from 1954 to 1975—was a long and bloody one. More than 58,000 Americans lost their lives, and another 153,000 were wounded, but American losses pale in comparison to those suffered by the Vietnamese. Perhaps as many as 4 million North and South Vietnamese soldiers and civilians lost their lives, roughly 10 percent of the entire population. Any traveler in Vietnam today is struck by the countless number of cemeteries and war memorials, a grim, silent testament to the length and violence of the struggle.

Americans are not accustomed to failure, and ever since the fall of Saigon on April 30, 1975, they have tried to understand how the United States and its South Vietnamese ally suffered such a humiliating defeat. On many levels, and in many different ways, the process of coming to terms with the Vietnam War continues to unfold. Veterans who fought in Vietnam are still trying to understand what happened to them; policymakers who escalated the U.S. involvement in the war are still trying to explain their miscalculations; and political leaders who came of age during the war are still trying to define its legacy and determine its influence on contemporary politics and diplomacy. As the journalist Morley Safer writes, each witness to that conflict is "still imprisoned, to one extent or another, by that place and by that time."[2]

For nearly thirty years this process of assimilation has continued, as Americans of all ages have struggled to make sense of the Vietnam War. The flood of books on the subject continues to grow, as does the list of films that seek to capture the essence—and purpose—of the conflict. And in college classrooms across the United States, students still express a keen interest in knowing more about what they sense was a pivotal event in the recent past, one that brought a sea change in the life of the nation.

From the American perspective, the central question is why the nation fought so long and so hard in such a distant place and why, in the end, it left and let Communist revolutionaries overrun South Vietnam. Recent literature has explored in great depth the decision-making process within the U.S. government and has traced how these decisions were carried out in the field. Historians of the war now know a lot about the different stages of America's involvement and the policies of the various administrations—whether the efforts of Dwight D. Eisenhower to aid the French, the advisory war under John F. Kennedy, the transformation of the war under Lyndon B. Johnson into a big, expensive war, or the long, agonizing withdrawal under Richard M. Nixon.

In recent years some scholars, along with former secretary of defense Robert S. McNamara, have argued that the conflict should and could have been ended earlier. "There were missed opportunities," McNamara suggests, "either for avoiding the war before it started or for terminating it before it had run its course."[3] It seems to me, however, that American escalation of the war was virtually inevitable, as was the failure of the United States and its South Vietnamese ally. Or, as historian Ernest R. May writes, "Given the assumptions generally shared by Americans in the 1960s, it seems probable that any collection of men or women would have decided as did members of the Kennedy and Johnson administrations."[4]

Leaders in Washington, preoccupied with the Cold War and fearful of Communist expansion into Southeast Asia, too often viewed the conflict in Vietnam as an abstraction, even after they had committed high numbers of men and materials to it. Many were insensitive to the local circumstances of the war, underestimating the Communist revolutionaries and overestimating the ability of our Vietnamese allies to govern and American forces to fight effectively. Though well equipped and led, the American troops on the ground in Vietnam faced a situation unprecedented in U.S. military history: the climate and terrain were adverse, a vast cultural gap separated Americans from all Vietnamese, whether friend or foe, and the balance of local forces was unfavorable. For their part, American officials—from presidents to cabinet members to military commanders—never truly grasped that the United States faced an enemy of strength, fanaticism, and staying power, one that had created an impressive revolutionary movement. In contrast, in South Vietnam the United States had a weak foundation on which to build. No firmly established political institutions emerged in the Republic of Vietnam, nor did a native elite willing to work with the American-backed government in Saigon. American officials could never find leaders capable of mobilizing the disparate population of South Vietnam, or create a South Vietnamese Army able to stand on its own.

In July 1965 a confident General Earl G. Wheeler, Chairman of the Joint Chiefs of Staff, assured a worried President Johnson that

North Vietnam could put no more than 25 percent of its 250,000-man army in South Vietnam. Wheeler welcomed the prospect of North Vietnamese Army troops crossing south of the seventeenth parallel, for it would "allow us to cream them."[5] It was a beguiling, if naïve, vision, one that made the escalation of U.S. involvement in the war easier to justify, but one that also, once the war became a bloody stalemate, made U.S. withdrawal painful to contemplate. Having made such a large-scale commitment on the basis of so many faulty assumptions, the leaders of the United States government—from one administration to another—found it extremely difficult to reassess their beliefs and devise an exit strategy. Instead they persevered, pushing for changes in the military or political situation, and hoping that somehow the will of the North Vietnamese would crumble.

The United States also found itself outmaneuvered in the international arena. While America's major allies—with the exception of France—did not openly oppose its involvement in Vietnam, the British, German, Italian, and Japanese governments were skeptical of America's commitment to a non-Communist South Vietnam and gave little assistance. In contrast, North Vietnam skillfully exploited its two major allies, China and the Soviet Union, extracting from them diplomatic support and large amounts of economic and military aid. And the leaders in Hanoi, along with their allied revolutionary force in South Vietnam—the National Liberation Front—undertook a worldwide propaganda campaign against the American war effort, portraying an imperialist power bullying a small, impoverished nation. "The international dimension," historian George C. Herring concludes, ". . . [was] a major reason for America's failure in Vietnam."[6]

This book seeks to explain, to those too young to remember the war as well as to those who lived through it, why the United States embarked on its journey to Vietnam and why it committed so many resources, human and material, to such a small, remote, and seemingly insignificant part of the world. Studying the United States' involvement in the Vietnam War has never been easy, for it was a protean conflict, one that underwent many phases and transformations during its twenty-one years. Over this time the level of American commitment to the government in South Vietnam changed enormously, as did that of the government in Hanoi to the revolutionaries in the South.

Clearly, for those with no memory of the war, understanding it presents many challenges. The Cold War, which provided a lens through which Americans viewed Vietnam, ended more than a decade ago; long gone is the unique mood of the early and mid-1960s, when Americans possessed so much optimism about what the nation could accomplish both at home and abroad. Names and places once mentioned nightly on the evening news—Vo Nguyen Giap, Ngo Dinh Diem, Khe Sanh, Da Nang—have been relegated to history books. But if the task of coming to terms with this tragic war is difficult, it is also essential. For those who lived through the Vietnam War, the controversy surrounding the war in Iraq has raised familiar issues, such as the credibility of American leaders, their ability to understand a distant society and culture, the paucity of international support for a foreign intervention, the conduct of American troops, and the lack of an exit strategy for a bloody and troubled occupation. We cannot possibly hope to understand the foreign policy crises of our own time without analyzing the Vietnam War.

* * *

In the early 1960s, as a graduate student at Harvard University, I began to follow the Vietnam War. It seemed a distant struggle in an exotic land; I never imagined that it would become America's longest war and create so much turmoil at home. After I completed my Ph.D. in the history of American foreign relations I moved to Houston to take a position on the faculty of Rice University, where the war soon became a major issue for me and many of my students. While I was too old for the draft, those I taught were not so fortunate, and they were bitterly divided over the rights and wrongs of the conflict.

From the start, I was skeptical about American involvement in Vietnam, and over the years my opposition to the war deepened; yet I knew that I did not understand many aspects of it. After going to Brown University in 1970, I followed the literature closely and finally, in 1980, began to teach a seminar on the war. Nine years later I started teaching a lecture course on Vietnam, one that proved to be among the most popular courses the university offered.

Teaching the war to a younger generation of students was a constant challenge, as was keeping up with the widening stream of scholarship about the conflict. My desire to understand, and to write about, the war was strengthened by three trips I took to Vietnam in the 1990s. As I traveled throughout this extraordinarily beautiful country, talking with young people, veterans of the South Vietnamese Army, and North Vietnamese leaders, I gained a deeper understanding of the Vietnamese side of the struggle. My trips to Vietnam also reminded me that I was part of a generation marked by the war, one that had embarked in the 1960s on a long and sad journey that is still far from over.

Many people have helped me in the writing of this book. Pham Van Manh, my guide during my 1995 trip to Vietnam, taught me much about Vietnamese society; James G. Blight, director of Brown University's Vietnam War Project, introduced me to a perspective on the war I had not previously considered; my friend Ambassador Nguyen Xuan Phong set an example of courage and survival; James R. Reckner, director of the Vietnam Center at Texas Tech University, organized many conferences from which I have learned a great deal; and the Vietnam veterans who visited my courses left a lasting impression on me and my students. Two distinguished scholars of the war, Robert K. Brigham and Ernest R. May, read the manuscript with care and suggested ways to improve it. I am especially grateful to Ernest May for his friendship over the years and for the inspiration of his scholarship. During the six years I chaired Brown's History Department, Karen Mota and Cherrie Guerzon, two superb administrators, eased the burdens of my position and allowed me to find time for my own work, while the publisher Andrew J. Davidson waited patiently for this project to be completed and guided it skillfully through the production process. My wife Sabina, a companion for all seasons, helped by giving me her love and support, as did my brother Art, generous in so many ways, to whom I have dedicated this book.

Charles E. Neu
Miami, Florida
August, 2004

1 Mieczyslaw Maneli, *War of the Vanquished* (New York, 1971), pp. 154–55.

2 *Flashbacks: On Returning to Vietnam* (New York, 1990), xix.

3 Quoted in Robert S. McNamara, James G. Blight, and Robert K. Brigham, *Argument without End: In Search of Answers to the Vietnam Tragedy* (New York, 1999), p. 1.

4 *"Lessons" of the Past: The Use and Misuse of History in American Foreign Policy* (New York, 1973), pp. 120–21.

5 Quoted in George C. Herring, *LBJ and Vietnam: A Different Kind of War* (Austin, Tex., 1994), p. 35.

6 "Fighting without Allies: The International Dimensions of America's Defeat in Vietnam," in Marc Jason Gilbert, ed., *Why the North Won the Vietnam War* (New York, 2002), p. 78.

Readers will note that I have not provided a phonetic pronunciation key. Because of the way in which the Vietnamese language developed, there is no accurate way to use Western phonetics correctly; English lacks the right combination of letters to allow Viet diacritical marks to make sense. Rather than provide an inherently inaccurate guide, I have decided to let readers devise their own solution to the puzzle of how to deal with the pronunciation of Vietnamese names and phrases.

Indochina, 1908–1954. Adapted from Stanley Karnow, *Vietnam: A History* (Penguin Books, 1997) p. 123. Used by permission of WGBH Educational Foundation.

CHAPTER ONE

The First Indochina War, 1945–1954

In late August 1945 the Communist revolutionary leader Ho Chi Minh left his guerrilla base in the mountains of north Vietnam and traveled to the city of Hanoi. As Ho and his escort entered the capital, they found the streets decorated with Viet Minh flags—a gold star in the middle of a field of red. In the center of the city banners draped from tree to tree spanned the boulevards, denouncing French imperialism and proclaiming "Independence or death" and "Viet Nam for the Vietnamese." French colonial officials, stripped of their power and under guard in the palace of the governor-general, watched apprehensively as Vietnamese revolutionaries took control of the city and proclaimed on September 2 the Democratic Republic of Vietnam (DRV). Ho, standing on a high wooden platform and wearing a khaki suit with a high-collared jacket, announced that "Viet Nam has the right to enjoy freedom and independence and in fact has become a free and independent country. The entire Vietnamese people are determined to mobilize all their physical and mental strength, to sacrifice their lives and property in order to safeguard their freedom and independence."[1] It seemed as if the old colonial order in Vietnam had suddenly and irreversibly collapsed.

Origins of the Revolution

No one had expected such a turn of events. Prior to World War II, the façade of French colonial rule had been imposing. The core of Indochina's major cities, especially Hanoi and Saigon, resembled French provincial capitals, with their wide, tree-lined boulevards and ochre-colored public buildings. In the countryside French tea and rubber plantations stretched for miles, while in the highlands of Vietnam the French built the hill town of Dalat, a place to escape from the oppressive heat of the coastal regions. The French colonial elite, housed in comfortable villas and occupying the pinnacle of Indochinese society, intended to stay forever.

Beneath the surface, however, lay an ugly and complex reality. The French conquest of Vietnam, which began in 1858, had been a long, arduous, and violent one. When finally completed in 1883, the French had divided Vietnam into three segments, the protectorates of Tonkin and Annam in the north and the colony of Cochin China in the south. By the end of the nineteenth century, these three territories had been joined with the protectorates of Laos and Cambodia into the Indochinese Union, ruled by a French governor-general. While the French focused their efforts on the economic and cultural transformation of Cochin China, in both north and south French control fell harshly on the masses of the Vietnamese people. A small Vietnamese elite prospered, but French policies impoverished the peasantry, driving many of them off the land in order that they might provide cheap labor for rubber and rice plantations in the south and coal mines in the north. In time, the French created a society of landless, illiterate, and oppressed peasants ruled by a colonial bureaucracy and a small group of Vietnamese landlords and administrators.

The brutality of French rule sparked Vietnamese resistance. During more than one thousand years of Chinese dominance (from 111 BC to AD 938), the Vietnamese had rebelled often and developed a strong sense of national identity. Like the Chinese before them, the French confronted periodic rebellions; their uncompromising policies drove the Vietnamese toward violence. In the first three decades of the twentieth century, even many educated Vietnamese embraced nationalism and joined a variety of movements dedicated to independence. Eventually Vietnamese from all walks of life would rally behind the movement led by Ho Chi Minh.

Ho Chi Minh became one of the great revolutionary leaders of the twentieth century. Born in central Vietnam in 1890, he left Vietnam in 1911, when he was only twenty-one-years old, and did not return to his homeland for thirty years. Inspired by Marxism-Leninism and consumed with a passion to free his people, he became a professional Communist revolutionary. Ho wandered the world, visiting the United States, living for six years in Paris, studying in Moscow at the University of Oriental Workers (an academy for Asian insurgents), and training with Communist revolutionaries in China. A prolific pamphleteer and skilled polemicist, Ho's writings (smuggled into Vietnam) opened a new world for those of his countrymen dissatisfied with French rule, while his dedication and gentleness converted to his cause many Vietnamese living abroad. "He was," one colleague recalled, "taut and quivering, with only one thought in his head, his country, Vietnam."[2]

The Impact of World War II

After 1939, as the expansionist Japanese occupied part of China and swept through Southeast Asia seizing British, Dutch, and French colonial possessions (Indochina fell in 1940), Ho realized that French rule had been fatally undermined. The time had come, he concluded, to form a broad front of Vietnamese patriots to fight both the Japanese and the French and, at the end of the Pacific War, claim independence for their nation. In early 1941 he traveled from southern China into the mountains of northern Vietnam, where in May he and his confederates organized the Viet Minh, or League for the Independence of Vietnam. Ho became the unquestioned leader of the new movement. During the war years he and his colleagues built up a small guerrilla force and began the momentous task of organizing the Vietnamese people. "A revolution," he advised impatient comrades, "is like the rising tide, and the reliable elements are like the pilings sunk in a riverbed; it is they who will maintain the soil at low tide."[3]

Viet Minh guerrillas gathered intelligence, harassed Japanese garrisons, and rescued American airmen (flying missions over China) shot down over northern Vietnam, while Viet Minh cadre spread Ho's message throughout Vietnam. In July 1945 American agents of the Office of Strategic Services (OSS)—the forerunner of the Central Intelligence Agency (CIA)—parachuted into the Viet Minh's jungle camp. Seeking intelligence on Japanese activities in Indochina, they began to train and assist Ho's small force. The Viet Minh's dedication and organizational skills impressed these young OSS officers. They also liked Ho, who questioned them about American history and especially about the Declaration of Independence. One remembered him as "an awfully sweet guy. If I had to pick out the one quality about that little old man sitting on his hill in the jungle, it was his gentleness."[4] Ho's real attitudes toward the United States, even in retrospect, are hard to gauge, but he foresaw that American power in Asia would be great at the end of World War II.

In 1940, confronted with Japanese demands, the rulers of French Indochina had decided to collaborate, giving up real power but retaining the façade of colonial rule. Now, French administrators carried out the orders of the Japanese, brutally exploiting the Vietnamese people until March 1945, when the Japanese military suddenly imprisoned French authorities and assumed direct rule over Indochina. With the end of the Pacific War in sight the Japanese formed a weak Vietnamese government and waited for the Allies to work out arrangements for the liberation of Indochina. Their wartime occupation had destroyed the invincibility of French rule and created a vacuum of authority in which Vietnamese nationalism flourished.

At the Potsdam Conference in July 1945, Allied leaders settled on a plan for the liberation of Indochina. British troops would occupy Saigon and accept the surrender of the Japanese south of the sixteenth parallel; north of that line, troops of the Chinese Nationalist government led by Jiang Jieshi (Chiang Kai-shek) would supervise the disarming of the Japanese. In the south British troops, with the help of recently released French soldiers and Japanese forces, quickly took control of Saigon. In the north, where Chinese forces arrived in Hanoi after it had been temporarily occupied by the Viet Minh, an uneasy truce held between Vietnamese and Chinese troops pending a final decision on the fate of Indochina.

In the fall of 1945 Ho's courtship of the U.S. government continued. In talks with OSS officers and in letters to President Harry S. Truman, Ho asked for American aid and recognition of Vietnam as an independent nation. French colonial rule, he argued, should not be restored, both because of the principles of the Atlantic Charter and because France had "ignominiously sold Indochina to Japan and betrayed the allies."[5] Realizing that his movement had aroused little interest among Chinese and Soviet leaders, he sought to end his international isolation by reaching out to the American government. Only American intervention, he knew, could prevent the return of the French.

In the south, where the Viet Minh was weaker than in the north, British occupying forces helped restore French authority. In October the 35,000 French troops that had assembled in Saigon took the offensive, pushing the Viet Minh into the countryside and setting up a new, French-dominated administration.

In the north, where Ho's popularity went uncontested, the position of the Viet Minh remained stronger. Even so, Ho realized the vulnerability of his new government. Lacking international backing and eager to expel the Chinese Nationalists, he sought to save at least a portion of his power. In early 1946 he began negotiations with the French, conceding some of the autonomy of his Democratic Republic of Vietnam and actually agreeing to let the French army return to Hanoi and the port city of Haiphong. He even traveled to Paris seeking a compromise with French leaders. By September, however, Ho was pessimistic. "It will be a war," he told an American reporter, "between an elephant and a tiger. If the tiger ever stands still the elephant will crush him with his mighty tusks. But the tiger does not stand still. He lurks in the jungle by day and emerges by night. He will leap upon the back of the elephant, tearing huge chunks from his hide, and then he will leap back into the dark jungle. And slowly the elephant will bleed to death. That will be the war of Indochina."[6]

The French government, unstable and eager to restore its nation's battered prestige, was in no mood to bargain with Vietnamese revolutionaries. In December 1946 fighting between French and Viet Minh troops broke out in Haiphong, and the violence soon spread to Hanoi. French troops, supported by armor and artillery, pushed the lightly armed Viet Minh guerrillas back into the countryside and mountains of northern Vietnam. The first Indochina war had begun.

America's Response

The fate of Ho Chi Minh and his revolution formed a small drama played out against the imposing backdrop of World War II. During the war President Franklin D. Roosevelt was preoccupied with the demands of global coalition warfare, seeking to keep the grand alliance together and coordinate the assault on the German empire in Europe and the Japanese empire in Asia. As he pondered the shape of the postwar world, he knew that the role of the United States and the Soviet Union would increase while that of the traditional European powers would diminish. Roosevelt believed that the war had released powerful nationalist forces in the non-Western world and that the colonial empires of the British, Dutch, and French were doomed. Disappointed by the collaboration of France's Vichy government with Germany, Roosevelt held strong convictions about France's role in Indochina. The French, he argued, have "had the country . . . for nearly one hundred years, and the people are worse off than they were at the beginning."[7] Occasionally FDR talked about a trusteeship for Indochina that would grant some power to local nationalists and prevent the return of the French. Southeast Asia, however, remained a sideshow, and as the war drew to a close Roosevelt found that pressing political, military, and strategic concerns forced him to agree to the reassertion of British, Dutch, and French sovereignty over former colonies in the region.

Roosevelt's successor in April 1945, Harry S. Truman, had little interest in what to him seemed an obscure part of the world. Truman and his advisers ignored the pleas of Ho Chi Minh, and the United States stood aside as the French, using American lend-lease military equipment, reoccupied Indochina and pursued policies that led to the outbreak of their war with the Viet Minh.

In late 1946, when the first Indochina war broke out, American leaders were absorbed in the vast changes taking place in the international system, changes that had moved the United States to the center of the world stage and had brought a confrontation with the Soviet Union. Convinced that the Soviet Union was a powerful and ruthless foe, Truman and his advisers concluded that the United States must take the lead—through a patient, flexible defense—in checking or containing its political and territorial expansion. Or, as the president announced to Congress in March 12, 1947, the United States must "support free peoples who are resisting attempted subjugation by armed minorities or by outside pressures."[8]

Which "free peoples" to support, however, was difficult to determine. Initially American officials sought to differentiate between vital and peripheral interests and defend strongpoints in Europe and Asia rather than commit American resources to a perimeter defense along all the extensive boundaries of the Cold War. George F. Kennan, at the time the State Department's chief planner, argued that there were "only five centers of industrial and military power in the world which are important to us from the standpoint of national security."[9] Thus in 1947 and 1948 the United States intervened in the civil war in Greece, devised bold plans for the recovery of Western Europe, gradually disengaged from the civil war raging in China between the Communist forces of Mao Zedong (Mao Tse-tung) and the Nationalist forces of Jiang Jieshi, and decided that a reconstructed (with American help) Japan was the key to the stabilization of Asia. Events in Indochina were thus subordinated to larger concerns.

As the war in Indochina settled into a stalemate, Truman and his advisers had mixed feelings about French efforts to reimpose colonial rule. They wanted the French to pursue more enlightened policies, delegating more power to non-Communist nationalists and creating a Vietnamese National Army to assist the French Expeditionary Corps. But they also wanted the French to persevere because of their view of Ho Chi Minh and his Viet Minh. Despite Ho's intense nationalism, his admiration for the United States, and his apparent neutrality in the early Cold War, most American officials believed that the Vietnamese were politically immature and highly susceptible to outside manipulation. They viewed Ho and his comrades as part of a monolithic Communist conspiracy, one directed from Moscow, and they believed that his triumph would bring major risks for the United States. In February 1947 Secretary of State George C. Marshall criticized France's "dangerously outmoded colonial outlook" but also warned that "we do not lose sight [of the] fact that Ho Chi Minh has direct Communist connections and it should be obvious that we are not interested in seeing colonial empires [and] administrations supplanted by [the] philosophy and political organizations emanating from and controlled by [the] Kremlin."[10] Marshall clearly had no solution to America's dilemma.

Officials in Washington worried, however, about the way in which the war was draining the French economy and curtailing the French contribution to the recovery of Europe. In the early years of the conflict, the United States did not provide any direct military or economic aid for the French, although Marshall Plan funds undeniably enabled the French to use other resources to prosecute the war in Indochina. But the political situation in France was so fragile that American leaders felt they had no choice but to pursue a policy of benevolent neutrality. Given the importance they attached to the reconstruction of Western Europe, and France's critical role in this effort, they had little leverage with the government in Paris.

The Expansion of the Cold War

In 1948 and 1949 a series of unsettling events abroad—the Berlin blockade, the triumph of communism in China, and the Soviet development of an atomic bomb—intensified the Cold War. As the perceived threat from communism grew, American policymakers were convinced that they faced a crisis every bit as dangerous as the one they had confronted in World War II, and that many nations around the world were up for grabs. They were increasingly less content to rely on economic and political instruments to contain the Soviet Union and its surrogates and increasingly more inclined to rely on U.S. and allied military might. Therefore, those who forged America's Cold War strategy moved away from the concept of defending Europe and Japan toward a perimeter defense that expanded the geographical boundaries of the Cold War. As declared by National Security Council document 68 (NSC-68), a key planning statement issued in April 1950, "The issues that face us are momentous, involving the fulfillment or destruction not only of this Republic but of civilization itself."[11]

The spread of the Cold War raised the stakes in Indochina. Initially American leaders had established a link between the fate of Indochina and the fate of France and Western Europe. In 1949 and 1950 they began to worry more about the Cold War in Asia. In October 1949 Mao Zedong proclaimed the People's Republic of China and soon thereafter Jiang Jieshi and his Nationalist government fled to the island of Formosa (Taiwan). The triumph of communism in

China opened up a new and more dangerous phase of the war in Indochina. In January 1950 both China and the Soviet Union recognized the Democratic Republic of Vietnam, providing Ho with the international support essential for the defeat of the French. Now Stalin urged Mao to take the lead in promoting revolution in Asia and, in conversations with Ho, China's new leader promised that "Whatever China has and Vietnam needs, we will provide." China's aid, including both advisers and heavy weapons, gave the divisions of General Vo Nguyen Giap, the Viet Minh's military commander, greater striking power, raising the possibility of the collapse of the French war effort. But the support of Beijing and Moscow linked Ho and his cause to the global Cold War; as U.S. Secretary of State Dean Acheson warned, it "reveals Ho in his true colors as the mortal enemy of native independence in Indochina."[12]

By the close of 1949 the U.S. government concluded that "The extension of communist authority in China represents a grievous political defeat for us. . . . If Southeast Asia is also swept by communism, we shall have suffered a major political rout, the repercussions of which will be felt throughout the rest of the world. . . . The colonial-nationalist conflict provides a fertile field for subversive movements, and it is now clear that Southeast Asia is the target for a coordinated offensive directed by the Kremlin."[13] Concerned about instability throughout Southeast Asia, Truman and his advisers worried about the security of the offshore island chain extending all the way from Indonesia and the Philippines to Japan. In Indonesia the new republic led by President Archmed Sukarno promised stability, but in Malaya and the Philippines Communist rebels challenged Western-oriented governments. The defense of Asia, however, continued to center on Japan, the most advanced industrial nation in the region. With the China market closed off to it, Japan had to develop close economic ties with the nations of Southeast Asia if it hoped to prosper. The so-called domino theory had emerged, which held that a failure in any one of these nations could lead to more momentous failures elsewhere in the region.

In early 1950 American leaders began to act on their conviction that Indochina, a key domino in Southeast Asia, was threatened by a Communist insurgency. The previous year the French had created native governments in Cambodia, Laos, and Vietnam, all alleged "free states" within the French Union. Designed as a gesture to local nationalists, none of these puppet governments exercised any real authority. The State of Vietnam was led by the ex-emperor Bao Dai, who had collaborated with the French for over two decades and who spent more time on the French Riviera than in his own nation. Despite the artificiality of these creations, officials in Washington believed they could serve as a starting point for rallying non-Communist nationalists in Indochina, and in February 1950 the United States recognized all three governments. American leaders also decided to become more directly involved in the French war effort, in May extending economic and military assistance to Bao Dai's government. Then the Americans set up the Military Assistance and Advisory Group (MAAG) in Saigon. Consisting of fifteen American military officers, MAAG was charged with monitoring the flow of American equipment and observing the French conduct of the war. In addition, a number of American civilian experts began to appear in Saigon to offer various kinds of assistance to the Vietnamese government. This transition from indirect to direct support marked a crucial escalation of U.S. involvement in the war.

The Deepening Commitment

The outbreak of the Korean War on June 25, 1950, confirmed the worst fears of American leaders. Previously the Truman administration had placed South Korea beyond America's defense perimeter in Asia, but once North Korean forces crossed the 38th parallel virtually everyone in Washington agreed that the United States must intervene. Notified of the invasion, Truman's shock soon gave way to moral outrage. "Korea," he told one adviser, "is the Greece of the Far East. . . . If we just stand by, they'll move into Iran and they'll take over the whole Middle East. There's no telling what they'll do, if we don't put up a fight now."[14] He and his advisers assumed that the Communist powers were acting in concert and that, should Stalin sense any irresoluteness in the U.S. response, the Soviet leader might gamble elsewhere in the world. Thus the defense of South Korea suddenly became vital to America's credibility.

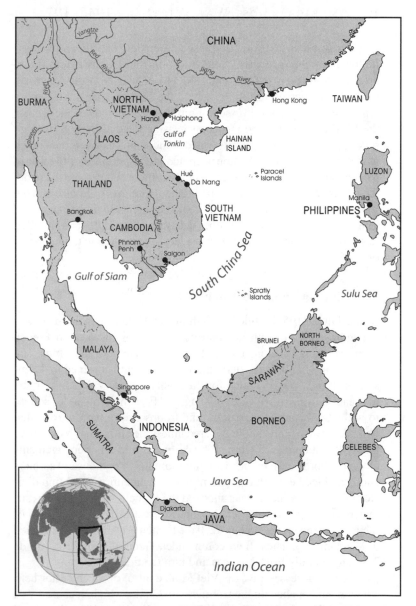

Southeast Asia, 1954. From Edward J. Marolda, *The U.S. Navy in the Vietnam War: An Illustrated History* (Brassey's, Inc., 2002). Used by permission.

The war in Korea only heightened the anxiety of officials in Washington about the security of Southeast Asia and led, by extension, to greater involvement in the French–Viet Minh war. Now the American government increased military aid to the French, dispatching more arms, ammunition, naval vessels, aircraft, and armored vehicles across the Pacific. In July 1950 a special mission headed by U.S. foreign service officer John E. Melby traveled to Indochina to assess the French war effort. The Melby Mission accepted the importance of the war in Vietnam but was critical of French policies there and pessimistic about the outcome, concluding that "the political interests of France and the Associated States are not only different, they are mutually exclusive."[15] The Melby report generated some debate in Washington, but it failed to shake the resolve of American leaders to persevere in their support of the French.

The Elephant and the Tiger

In the fall of 1950, while the fighting in Korea intensified, newly strengthened Viet Minh units struck at a series of fortified French outposts strung out along the border between Vietnam and China. The French army in northern Vietnam, road bound and confined to defensive positions, was no match for the highly mobile Viet Minh. In the evacuation of the town of Cao Bang, the French commander sought to withdraw his artillery, trucks, and troops over a narrow road that wound between high, jungle-covered limestone cliffs. His forces drove into a devastating Viet Minh ambush. In this and other engagements along the border, the French lost approximately six thousand soldiers and abandoned enough equipment to equip an entire Viet Minh division. These stunning defeats shocked the French, who had underestimated the strength of the enemy and overestimated the abilities of their own army. In December 1950 the French government dispatched to Vietnam its greatest field commander, General Jean de Lattre de Tassigny, to rally French forces and turn the tide of the war.

These successes gave the Viet Minh control of much of northern Vietnam and opened up the frontier with China, which became a vast rear area. The French still held, however, Hanoi and Haiphong and the heavily populated areas surrounding them. In January 1951 General Giap launched a broad offensive against French positions in the Red River Delta. Radio Viet Minh announced that the Communist army would be in Hanoi by Tet, the Vietnamese New Year observed in late January. The liberation of Hanoi was "the gift that it [the army] will give President Ho for Tet."[16] This time Giap badly miscalculated. De Lattre was a far more imaginative commander than was his predecessor; he exploited his superior mobility and firepower and inflicted heavy losses on enemy units that had finally come out in the open to fight. Even so, the war remained a stalemate, with the French in control of the cities and portions of the Red River and Mekong deltas, while the Viet Minh controlled much of the countryside and slipped into the cities at night to spread terror.

Time, however, was on the side of the Viet Minh. The French needed a quick victory before the political will of the French government and people weakened, while the Viet Minh would benefit from a protracted war. Ho Chi Minh, drawing on the deep-rooted nationalism and xenophobia of the Vietnamese people, had organized a sacred war against the white foreign invaders and their native clients. Early in the conflict he warned a French visitor: "You would kill ten of my men for every one I kill of yours. But even at that rate, you would be unable to hold out, and victory would go to me."[17]

For a Western army, Vietnam was a difficult place to fight a war. Hills and heavily forested mountains covered more than half of its territory, while the large delta formed by the Mekong River in the south—a vast maze of canals and streams—lay submerged during the long monsoon season from May to October. The monsoons restricted military operations; mangrove swamps, limestone caves, and triple-canopied jungles made it easy for the native forces to conceal troops and supply depots. And the Viet Minh devised ingenious ways to move men and equipment across this formidable terrain—using thousands of porters to handle supplies—while the French, dependent on mechanized equipment, had to rely on Vietnam's roads, many of which were no better than dirt tracks and became virtually impassable during floods. The physical geography gave Giap's mobile guerrilla forces a decisive advantage over the road-bound French armored columns.

It was a curious war, one in which remnants of France's colonial empire clashed with revolutionary nationalism. The French Expeditionary Corps, numbering about 200,000 men, included 69,000 Frenchmen, 20,000 Foreign Legionaires (Germans, Poles, Hungarians, Spaniards, and other nationals), 51,000 Africans and North Africans (drawn from French possessions there), and 60,000 pro-French Indochinese (Vietnamese, Cambodians, Laotians, and tribal peoples). A typical operation might include a French tank unit, Moroccan, Vietnamese, or Senegalese infantry, and a Legion mortar company.

In January 1952 a young American diplomat, newly assigned to the American embassy in Saigon, observed a military operation in territory between Saigon and the Cambodian border, an area dominated by large rubber plantations. Howard Simpson found himself with a small North African armored cavalry unit commanded by French officers. Per orders, the armored cars were to sweep through the plantation, driving Viet Minh believed to be in the area toward a river, where Vietnamese troops would be waiting for them in a blocking position. As the armored vehicles lumbered along in the stifling heat, the French officers spotted no enemy soldiers. Nor did they find the Vietnamese blocking force in its proper position; instead they found the soldiers relaxing and cooling off in the river they were supposed to be defending. Simpson was struck by the strangeness of the war. "I couldn't help but wonder," he remembered, "if the Moroccans, Algerians, Tunisians, and black Africans of the Expeditionary Corps weren't taking part in some huge charade. What were they really thinking, fighting under the tricolor so many thousands of miles from home?"[18]

America's Dilemma

Even from the sidelines American leaders realized that the French Indochina war was a quagmire, with no victory in sight. Searching for a way to break the stalemate, they urged the French to pursue a more aggressive military strategy, to expand the Vietnamese National Army, and to cede more authority to Bao Dai's government in Saigon. Only by relinquishing real power and convincing the Vietnamese people to rally around Bao Dai's regime, Americans reasoned, could the French hope to prevail and retain some influence in what would eventually become a non-Communist, independent Vietnam.

The French did not, however, share the American vision of the future of Vietnam. Set in their old colonial ways, contemptuous of the people they sought to rule, and convinced that the success of Ho Chi Minh's forces would undermine their entire overseas empire, they made only token concessions to the American point of view. Rather than bow to American demands, French political and military leaders asked the United States for ever-higher levels of military and economic aid —by 1953 the U.S. was paying more than 40 percent of the cost of the war—and they also pressed for American participation in a regional collective security treaty and promise to commit U.S. ground combat troops should the Chinese army intervene in the war, as it had done in Korea. "Do not," General de Lattre reprimanded Defense Department officials, "say *my* theatre. It is not my theatre; it is *our* theatre." On one level, the French asked for greater American involvement; on another, they bitterly resented the increasing American presence in Vietnam and obstructed the efforts of American officials to observe the war. Americans, they believed, were not only dangerously naïve about the "dirty war" in Vietnam but also were spreading foolish ideas about freedom and independence among the local population.[19]

Officials in Washington, in no mood for a confrontation, would not agree to move toward a collective security treaty or promise to commit troops should the Chinese invade. But neither would they risk provoking a French withdrawal. All segments of the American government agreed that holding the line in Vietnam was crucial to the success of the Cold War in Asia. In June 1952 a key planning document concluded that "Communist domination, by whatever means, of all Southeast Asia would seriously endanger in the short run, and critically endanger in the longer term, United States security interests."[20]

Truman and his advisers desperately wanted to keep the French and their Vietnamese allies fighting, but they realized that neither the political nor military aspects of the war were going well. "Fact is," the senior American diplomat in Indochina cabled Washington, "that Ho Chi Minh is the only Viet who enjoys any measure of national prestige."[21] By late 1952 the French had suffered 90,000 casualties and been pushed back into enclaves surrounding the major cities of Vietnam. Bao Dai's government was corrupt and ineffective, while Ho Chi Minh's hold on the Vietnamese people had grown as the Viet Minh introduced reforms in areas under its control. The war had grown dramatically in scale, having drawn three to four thousand Chinese advisers to the side of the Viet Minh, and spilled over into Laos and Cambodia. What had begun as a rebellion against the French in late 1946 had become a major conflict, one with far-reaching international implications.

Eisenhower Takes Charge

Dwight D. Eisenhower came to the American presidency through what by the mid-twentieth century had become an unusual path, a career in the military. The five-star general had gained international fame as the supreme commander of Allied forces in Europe during World War II; after the war he had served the Truman administration as Army Chief of Staff and the first head of the North Atlantic Treaty Organization (NATO) before resigning to run for the presidency. Before taking office Eisenhower had worked with many world leaders and had acquired great confidence in his judgment of people and events. During his two terms in the White House most Americans admired and trusted Eisenhower; for eight years he overshadowed all other figures on the nation's political stage.

Eisenhower and his advisers shared the general Cold War assumptions of the Truman administration: they believed that the United States faced the danger of Communist expansion throughout the world and were especially concerned about the designs of the new rulers of China on Southeast Asia. Eisenhower, however, was more cautious than his predecessor, arguing that "we're not in a moment of danger, we're in an age of danger," and that the United States must be prepared to sustain a long struggle with the Soviet Union and its surrogates.[22] A conservative on domestic issues, Eisenhower worried about the costs of containment and the impact of the Cold War on the life of the nation. "Every gun that is made," the president warned, "every warship launched, every rocket fired signifies in the final sense, a theft from those who hunger and are not fed, those who are cold and not clothed."[23] On the one hand, "Ike" had a sense of the limits of the nation's resources; on the other, he wanted to combat communism everywhere in the world. Since Eisenhower never resolved this contradiction, it was by no means certain how he would balance one conviction against the other in a crisis.

Eisenhower inherited a major commitment to the French war effort in Indochina. The president and his secretary of state, John Foster Dulles, agreed with Truman and Acheson that the stakes in Indochina were high. In his first State of the Union Address to Congress, Eisenhower proclaimed that France was holding "the line of freedom" in Indochina against the "calculated assault" of "Communist aggression throughout the world," while Dulles told the president that the crisis in Indochina "had probably the top priority in foreign policy, being in some ways more important than Korea, because the consequences of loss there could not be localized, but would spread throughout Asia and Europe."[24] While the boundaries of the Cold War had stabilized in Europe, they were far more fluid in Asia, where the West faced Communist-led insurgencies in Malaya, the Philippines, and Indochina.

Like their predecessors, Eisenhower and Dulles were unhappy with the course of the war. The French war effort, they believed, was weakened by faulty military strategy, uninspired leadership, and, most of all, the refusal of the French government to admit that the era of European colonialism had ended. Thus American officials continued to urge their ally to give greater independence to Bao Dai's State of Vietnam, and also to prosecute the war more aggressively. They posited that an expanded Vietnamese National Army, fighting for a truly independent government, could with French assistance prove more than a match for the Viet Minh. Unless leaders in Paris moved in this direction, Eisenhower told his advisers, "nothing could possibly save Indochina, and that continued United States assistance would amount to pouring our money down a rathole."[25]

But, as always, the French government was not easily influenced. Weariness over the war was widespread, the parliament was restive, and it was by no means certain that the French would cooperate in U.S.-backed plans for the defense of Western Europe, embodied in the concept of a European Defense Community (EDC). Franco-American relations, therefore, remained delicate. Although the United States had signed an armistice ending the Korean War in July 1953, it did not want to see the war in Indochina end in a negotiated settlement. Eisenhower and Dulles urged the French to persevere in their war effort, but, at the same time, allow the United States a far greater say in both the political and military aspects of the struggle. Dulles would have liked the French to behave as the British had in early 1947, when, lacking the resources to deal with the escalating civil war in Greece, they asked the U.S. government to take charge of the anti-Communist cause there.

By the spring of 1953 the French faced a desperate military situation. In the northern part of Indochina, French forces were largely confined to the densely populated Red River Delta, while in central and southern Indochina they were entrenched in the cities, with the Viet Minh dominating the rural areas. The French Expeditionary Corps was a polyglot colonial army, a mechanized, road-bound force with a fragile logistical system and an air force much smaller than the one the United States would later deploy. It was not, in fact, a match for the Viet Minh, who by 1953, thanks to massive Chinese aid, fielded many well-equipped units. Ho Chi Minh's army no longer consisted of lightly armed guerrilla bands.

In May 1953 the new commander in Indochina, General Henri Navarre (a career soldier who replaced de Lattre's successor Raoul Salan), developed a plan, with Washington's approval, to seize the military initiative. While Navarre and French leaders had no illusions about inflicting a decisive defeat on the Viet Minh, they did hope to improve their military position and set the stage for a negotiated end to the war.

The Battle of Dien Bien Phu

As Navarre gathered his troops for an offensive in the Red River Delta, General Giap moved Viet Minh forces into northern Laos in order to overextend the French. In November 1953 Navarre responded by parachuting some of his best troops into Dien Bien Phu, a remote village in the northwest corner of Vietnam. Eventually nearly 12,000 French troops under the command of the flamboyant Colonel Christian de Castries were in Dien Bien Phu, busily constructing a fortress in a broad valley twelve miles long and six miles wide and surrounded by rugged terrain and hills as high as 1,000 feet. The French fortress, more precisely an interlocking series of fortified strongpoints, included an airfield, since Dien Bien Phu could only be supplied from the air.

French calculations in concentrating so many troops in such a distant outpost were confused. In part Navarre wanted to close off enemy invasion routes into Laos and create a base deep in the interior, from which his patrols might harass the Viet Minh. He also hoped to draw enemy units into an unequal battle in which they would be decimated by superior French firepower. Shortly after the first French troops landed at Dien Bien Phu, the American diplomat Howard Simpson flew in and spent three days visiting the various strongpoints. "I couldn't claim expertise as a tactician," he recalled, "but to me the dark ridges of the nearby mountains seemed ominous and threatening. . . . There was little talk of the 'high ground' at Dien Bien Phu; it had already been ceded to the enemy by default."[26]

By the early spring of 1954 Giap had moved nearly 50,000 troops into the hills overlooking Dien Bien Phu. "This campaign," Ho wrote his general, "is a very important one, not only militarily, but also politically, not only for domestic reasons, but for international ones as well. So all of our people, all of our armed forces, and the entire Party must entirely unite to get the job done."[27] Through a massive logistical effort, involving thousands of porters, heavy artillery pieces were broken down into their component parts then carried and pulled up the surrounding hills, where, with the help of Chinese advisers, the weapons were reassembled, deeply dug in, and carefully camouflaged. On March 13, 1954, when the Viet Minh unleashed into the valley a massive bombardment, the French garrison suddenly discovered that it was outgunned and that Giap's well-placed artillery was largely impervious to air attack.

French commanders had made a series of fatal miscalculations. They had underestimated Giap's ability to move a large force a long distance through rugged terrain, to sustain it through an elaborate logistical system, and to put artillery in the hills overlooking the fortress. Therefore they had failed to anticipate that flights in and out of the valley would be cut off, making it extremely difficult to resupply the garrison and impossible to evacuate the wounded. Finally, they had assumed that Giap would throw his troops against fortified French positions, taking so many casualties that he would be forced to order a retreat. Initially Giap did use human-wave assaults, but heavy losses forced him to rethink his strategy. Instead he decided slowly to strangle

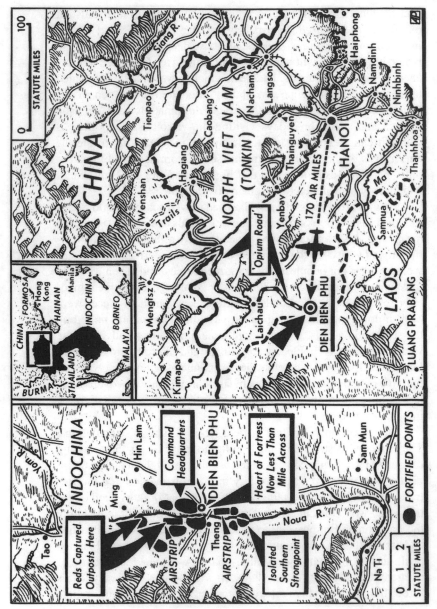

The Battle of Dien Bien Phu. AP/Wide World

the fortress, encircling it with tunnels and trenches that drew closer and closer, all the while pounding French defenders with his howitzers.

The French had been outgeneraled. Given their limited air-transport capacity, they had been unable to bring in sufficient matériel to construct bunkers able to withstand the enemy's artillery fire, while their own artillery had been deployed in open, uncovered pits. French artillerymen, one American observer noted, "were living in a dream world."[28] Early in the battle French commanders realized that their days in defense of Dien Bien Phu were numbered. Nevertheless, they and their men fought bravely to save the garrison, parachuting in both supplies and additional troops, but in April one strongpoint after another fell. Finally, on May 7, 1954, the occupants of the French command bunker surrendered. Giap's forces took de Castries, along with the remaining defenders, prisoner; soon the Viet Minh flag, the yellow star on a sea of red, flew over the fortress. The French had suffered a stunning military and psychological defeat.

Washington's Response

As the Battle of Dien Bien Phu intensified, Eisenhower had faced a stark choice. How far would he go to save the French position in Indochina? What, if any, sacrifices would he ask the American people to make to prevent the triumph of communism in Indochina? Would he, in short, use American military power to save the French and prevent a political settlement of the war?

The president was deeply concerned about the fate of Indochina. At a press conference on April 7, 1954, when asked about Indochina's strategic significance, he gave a classic summation of the "domino thesis." "Finally," he patiently explained, "you have broader considerations that might follow what you would call the 'falling domino' principle. You have a row of dominoes set up, you knock over the first one, and what will happen to the last one is the certainty that it will go over very quickly. So you could have a beginning of a disintegration that would have the most profound influences." Eisenhower then applied this general theory to all of Southeast Asia. "But when we come," he continued, "to the possible sequence of events, the loss of Indochina, of Burma, of Thailand, of the Peninsula, and Indonesia following . . . now you are talking really about millions and millions and millions of people." The president's conclusion was nothing short of alarmist: "So, the possible consequences of the loss are just incalculable to the Free World."[29]

Despite Eisenhower's fears, he remained wary of any kind of direct American military intervention. In late March, when French chief of staff General Paul Ely visited Washington, Eisenhower agreed to supply more aircraft and technicians. From the start of the crisis, however, he had ruled out the use of American ground troops, telling his advisers that "There was just no sense in even talking about United States forces replacing the French in Indochina. If we did so, the Vietnamese could be expected to transfer their hatred of the French to us. I can not tell you . . . how bitterly opposed I am to such a course of action. This war in Indochina would absorb our troops by divisions!" In conversations he and Dulles had with Ely, both men would not agree even to American air strikes—either from aircraft carriers in the Gulf of Tonkin or bases in the Philippines—unless, as Eisenhower put it, he "got a lot of answers" from Paris.[30]

Before committing any more men or munitions to Vietnam, the president insisted on a wide range of conditions, including congressional approval, British participation in any military venture, involvement of at least some of the nations of Southeast Asia, a full and clear grant of independence to the State of Vietnam, French agreement to turn the military command of the war over to the United States but keep their own troops in combat, and a French promise to fight on, not just use American intervention as a cover for withdrawal or a way to improve their bargaining position. Eisenhower knew that many of these conditions were unlikely to be met. The French government was not prepared to grant independence to the Vietnamese, British prime minister Winston Churchill and foreign secretary Anthony Eden wanted the Indochina war to end in a negotiated settlement, and many members of Congress—their memories of the Korean War still vivid— opposed any American involvement in a land war in Asia. If the United States did intervene, however, Eisenhower was determined to take charge of the conflict. As Dulles told Ely, the American government could "not afford to send its flag and its own military establishment and thus to engage the prestige of the United States" unless it expected to win.[31]

Some of Eisenhower's advisers advocated American military intervention in Vietnam. Vice President Richard M. Nixon, a fervent anti-Communist, supported the use of both American air power and ground combat troops, informing the president that "it might not be necessary to have more than a few conventional air strikes . . . to let the Communists see that we are determined to resist."[32] Admiral Arthur W. Radford, chairman of the Joint Chiefs of Staff (JCS), approved a joint American-French plan, code-named Operation VULTURE, for massive air strikes against Viet Minh positions in the hills above Dien Bien Phu. Radford's plan for air strikes, however, generated little enthusiasm among other members of the JCS. Army Chief of Staff Matthew B. Ridgeway, who had brilliantly led American forces in Korea, adamantly opposed any kind of American military intervention. He warned of "the problems and difficulties which would be encountered by a large modern force operating in Indo-China."[33] And most of Eisenhower's other military advisers doubted that an air strike would decisively affect the outcome of the battle, realizing that even American troops would face formidable obstacles fighting in Indochina.

Had all his conditions been met, Eisenhower might have authorized American intervention to save Dien Bien Phu. It seems more likely, however, that the president would never have moved in that direction. He and Dulles did, to be sure, try to secure British participation in and prior congressional approval of any such campaign, but these efforts were largely for the record, designed to appease hawks within and outside the administration and to protect themselves against right-wing critics in Congress.

Still, in early April, as the situation for the French at Dien Bien Phu became critical, Eisenhower tried to convince Churchill of the dangers of appeasement, cabling him that, if Indochina fell, "the ultimate effect on our and your global strategic position with the consequent shift in the power ratio throughout Asia and the Pacific could be disastrous."[34] He also had Dulles and Radford meet with key congressional leaders. Emphasizing the gravity of the crisis, they asked for a congressional resolution giving the president discretionary authority to use American air and sea power to prevent the expansion of communism in Southeast Asia. Two powerful senators, Richard B. Russell (Democrat, Georgia) and Majority Leader Lyndon B. Johnson (Democrat, Texas), expressed alarm at the thought of American military intervention. Russell asserted that "Once you commit the flag, you've committed the country. There's no turning back. If you involve the American air force, why, you've involved the nation." Johnson argued that "we want no more Koreas with the United States furnishing 90 percent of the manpower."[35] Such a resolution could be obtained, the senators insisted, only if the French promised independence to the State of Vietnam and Great Britain and other allied nations joined in the effort.

Thus any American attempt to rescue the French fortress at Dien Bien Phu faced formidable if not insurmountable obstacles. Moreover, as Eisenhower and Dulles pondered the crisis, they realized that the fall of Dien Bien Phu would constitute only a limited setback. While it would lead to the loss of some of Indochina to Communists, it would also reduce if not eliminate the French role there and clear the way for a new era of American leadership. As Dulles noted, "it should be possible to salvage something from Southeast Asia, free of the taint of French colonialism."[36] Anticipating the division of Indochina, with American support for a non-Communist South Vietnam, they pushed for the creation of a Southeast Asia Treaty Organization (SEATO) as part of a fall-back position to limit the damage brought about by a French collapse. They were convinced that the non-Communist Vietnamese in the southern half of the nation were no different than the South Koreans, and that once freed from French obstructionism and energized by independence they would fight as hard for their freedom as had the Viet Minh. Or, as Eisenhower put it, "there are plenty of people in Asia, and we can train them to fight."[37]

The Geneva Settlement: The Emergence of Two Vietnams

On April 26, less than two weeks before the fall of Dien Bien Phu, a Big Power conference convened at Geneva to seek a more permanent settlement of the Korean War and a settlement of the war in Indochina. From late April to July 21, 1954, delegations from China, France, Great Britain, the Soviet Union, and the United States, along with representatives of Cambodia, Laos, the State of Vietnam, and the Viet Minh, struggled to bring the long war in Indochina—now in its eighth year—to an end. The United States came to the negotiations as a reluctant participant, torn between its desire to convince the French to persevere and its realization that, for better or worse, the French phase of the war had come to an end. The Viet Minh delegation, hoping to capitalize on its military and political successes, saw the conference as a way, at long last, to bring about the unification of Indochina under the leadership of Ho Chi Minh. The French government, after June 18 under the leadership of Premier Pierre Mendès-France, sought to negotiate a dignified retreat, while British, Chinese, and Soviet leaders maneuvered to extract concessions from all sides in effecting an end to the war.

Thus forces outside of Indochina had a decisive impact on the outcome of the conference. Neither China nor the Soviet Union wanted to push France so hard that the talks would fail, thereby creating a volatile situation that might prompt American military intervention. China, exhausted by the Korean War and eager for a period of peace, sought to keep U.S. forces away from its southern frontier. The Soviet Union, far more concerned with Western Europe than with Southeast Asia, hoped to prevent the French from joining the U.S.-backed European Defense Community. In short, neither of the great Communist powers was willing to run any risks for the unification of Indochina under Ho Chi Minh's rule.

In fact, Chinese and Soviet leaders pressed the Viet Minh for concessions. Isolated and fearful of American power, the Viet Minh finally gave way, accepting military disengagement and the division of Vietnam into two military regroupment zones at the seventeenth parallel. The division, however, was to be only temporary, for the accord stated that in two years elections for the reunification of the country would be held under the supervision of an International Control Commission (ICC). The agreement further prohibited the introduction of outside military forces or the establishment of foreign military bases in either portion of Vietnam, and also forbade the State of Vietnam in the south or the Democratic Republic of Vietnam in the north to enter into any sort of a military alliance with a third-party nation. Indochina had ceased to exist and peace had been achieved, but the settlement reached at Geneva was a military truce rather than a permanent solution to the Vietnamese people's ordeal. The only documents actually signed were a cease-fire between the French and the Viet Minh, while the political aspects of the accord were verbally endorsed by the participants. Trying to maintain some distance from the settlement, the United States did not endorse the agreement but "took note" of the accords and pledged to "refrain from the threat or use of force to disturb them." The new prime minister of the State of Vietnam, Ngo Dinh Diem, rejected them outright, predicting "another more deadly war."[38]

Leaders in Hanoi agreed. Chinese Prime Minister Zhou Enlai (Chou En-lai) had promised them a substantial increase in economic aid and assured North Vietnamese premier Pham Van Dong that "With the final withdrawal of the French, all of Vietnam will be yours." A few days before the Geneva Accords were signed, Ho Chi Minh explained that some of his comrades, "intoxicated with our repeated victories, want to fight on at all costs, to a finish; they see only the trees, not the whole forest. . . . They are unaware that we are struggling in international conferences as well as on the battlefields in order to attain our goal." By the summer of 1954, Ho believed that Vietnamese revolutionaries had made great strides toward the independence of all of Indochina, but that the struggle for peace would be "a hard and complex one."[39] The United States had emerged as the new enemy of the Indochinese people, and a new strategy would be needed to defeat its imperialist schemes.

During the final phase of the French war, Eisenhower had avoided American military intervention. He had never been inclined to deploy American military power, even carrier-based aircraft, for he was too skeptical of the French, too conscious of the military realities of the situation, and too aware of American popular and congressional opinion. Eisenhower's decision to let Dien Bien Phu fall and accept a negotiated end to the conflict was, in retrospect, less significant than his decision to preserve the southern half of Vietnam as a bastion of anti-communism. If ever there was a time to stand aside and let events in Indochina take their course, it was the spring and summer of 1954. Without American intervention to prop up the new South Vietnamese regime of Prime Minister Diem, Vietnam, as Eisenhower and Dulles readily admitted, would have been swiftly unified under Ho Chi Minh. But Eisenhower's hatred of communism was so strong and indiscriminate, and his understanding of the revolution in Vietnam so flawed, that he committed the United States to a course that would have fateful consequences.

Notes

1 Quoted in William J. Duiker, *Ho Chi Minh* (New York, 2000), 322–23.

2 Quoted in Stanley Karnow, *Vietnam: A History* (New York, 1991), 137.

3 Quoted in Duiker, *Ho Chi Minh*, 261.

4 Quoted in Robert Shaplen, *The Lost Revolution* (New York, 1965), 29.

5 Quoted in William J. Duiker, *U.S. Containment Policy and the Conflict in Indochina* (Stanford, Calif., 1994), 38.

6 Quoted in Duiker, *Ho Chi Minh*, p. 379.

7 Quoted in Cordell Hull, *Memoirs,* 2 vols. (New York, 1948), II, 1597.

8 Quoted in Alonzo L. Hamby, *Man of the People: A Life of Harry S. Truman* (New York, 1995), 387.

9 Quoted in John Lewis Gaddis, *Strategies of Containment: A Critical Appraisal of Postwar American National Security Policy* (New York, 1982), 30.

10 Quoted in Mark Philip Bradley, *Imagining Vietnam and America: The Making of Postcolonial Vietnam, 1919–1950* (Chapel Hill, N.C., 2000), 163.

11 Quoted in John Lewis Gaddis, *Russia, The Soviet Union, and the United States: An Interpretive History,* 2nd ed. (New York, 1990), 203.

12 Quoted in Duiker, *Ho Chi Minh*, 422; quoted in Robert Mann, *A Grand Delusion: America's Descent into Vietnam* (New York, 2001), p. 73.

13 Quoted in Gary R. Hess, *The United States' Emergence as a Southeast Asian Power, 1940–1950* (New York, 1987), 206.

14 Quoted in Hamby, *Man of the People,* 537.

15 Quoted in Ronald H. Spector, *Advice and Support: The Early Years of the United States Army in Vietnam, 1941–1960* (New York, 1985), 114.

16 Quoted in William J. Duiker, *Sacred War: Nationalism and Revolution in a Divided Nation* (New York, 1995), 73.

17 Quoted in A. J. Langguth, *Our Vietnam: The War, 1954–1975,* (New York, 2000), 63.

18 *Tiger in the Barbed Wire: An American in Vietnam, 1952–1991* (New York, 1994), 29.

19 Quoted in William Conrad Gibbons, *The U.S. Government and the Vietnam War: Executive and Legislative Roles and Relationships, Part I, 1945–1960* (Princeton, N.J., 1986), 99; Simpson, *Tiger in the Barbed Wire,* xvi.

20 Quoted in Gibbons, *The U.S. Government and the Vietnam War,* 116.

21 Ibid., 89.

22 Quoted in Stephen E. Ambrose, *Eisenhower: Volume Two, The President* (New York, 1984), 89.

23 Quoted in Gaddis, *Strategies of Containment,* 133.

24 Quoted in David L. Anderson, *Trapped By Success: The Eisenhower Administration and Vietnam, 1953–1961* (New York, 1991), 17.

25 Quoted in Gibbons, *The U.S. Government and the Vietnam War,* 126.

26 Quoted in Simpson, *Tiger in the Barbed Wire,* 109.

27 Quoted in Duiker, *Ho Chi Minh,* 453.

28 Quoted in Simpson, *Tiger in the Barbed Wire,* 109.

29 Quoted in Lloyd C. Gardner, *Approaching Vietnam: From World War II through Dienbienphu, 1941–1954* (New York, 1988), 196–97.

30 Quoted in Gibbons, *The U.S. Government and the Vietnam War,* 153; quoted in Ambrose, *Eisenhower,* 177.

31 Quoted in Ambrose, *Eisenhower,* 177.

32 Quoted in Stephen E. Ambrose, *Nixon: The Education of a Politician, 1913–1962* (New York, 1987), 346.

33 Quoted in Gibbons, *The U.S. Government and the Vietnam War,* 237.

34 Ibid., 196.

35 Quoted in Mann, *A Grand Delusion,* 146–47.

36 Quoted in Gibbons, *The U.S. Government and the Vietnam War,* 251.

37 Quoted in Ambrose, *Eisenhower,* 182.

38 Quoted in George McT. Kahin, *Intervention: How America Became Involved in Vietnam* (New York, 1986), p. 61; quoted in Karnow, *Vietnam: A History,* 221.

39 Quoted in Duiker, *Ho Chi Minh,* 459–60.

CHAPTER TWO

The Emergence of South Vietnam, 1954–1961

October 9, 1954, the day on which the Geneva Accords mandated the takeover of Hanoi by Communist forces, dawned cold and damp. Through the early morning the city stood empty and silent. A few French armored cars sat at the main intersections, while offices and shops had not opened, their doors and windows shuttered. Finally, at 10:00 AM, from the edge of the city arose a distant hum, one that grew more distinct as the soldiers of General Giap's army appeared. They were, as one American observer noted, "small men in drab uniforms wearing leaf-woven, cloth-covered helmets fitted with camouflage nets. . . . Their approach was heralded by the soft shuffling of hundreds of feet in tennis shoes. The Viet Minh entry into Hanoi was destined to be one of the most silent victory marches in the history of the world's conquering armies." Gradually windows and shutters opened and red flags with yellow stars appeared; the people of Hanoi, responding to the urgings of propaganda workers, began to shout "Free Vietnam!" and "Ho Chi Minh—one thousand years!"[1] After nine years of bitter warfare, Vietnamese revolutionaries had reoccupied Hanoi.

In the south the atmosphere surrounding the arrival of the new prime minister, Ngo Dinh Diem, was far different. More than three months earlier, on June 25, 1954, Diem, who had been abroad for four years, arrived at Saigon's Tan Son Nhut Airport. Greeted by a small crowd of Catholic supporters, French officials, and foreign diplomats, Diem sped in a closed car through a quiet city to Norodom Palace, his residence and the seat of government. Unknown to most of his own people, Diem had returned home to rule.

The Rise of Ngo Dinh Diem

The new prime minister was fifty-three years old. A French-educated Catholic from Central Vietnam, as a young man Diem had briefly served as a provincial governor and in 1933 as Bao Dai's minister of the interior, but had soon resigned over the refusal of his French masters to give him more authority. For years Diem lived in Hué—the old imperialist capital in Central Vietnam—with his mother and younger brother and followed at a distance all of the vicissitudes of Vietnamese politics in the 1930s and 1940s. A fervent nationalist and anti-Communist, Diem went into exile in 1950, traveling first to the United States, where he met prominent Americans such as Francis Cardinal Spellman of New York and Senators John F. Kennedy (Democrat, Massachusetts) and Mike Mansfield (Democrat, Montana), and then to Belgium and France. In June 1954 the emperor Bao Dai, sensing the end of the French era in Vietnam, and calculating that Diem might be able to draw the United States onto the Vietnamese scene to help create an effective non-Communist government in the south, appointed Diem his new prime minister.

Diem was a short, rotund man with dark hair and ivory skin; he nearly always dressed in immaculate white suits, as had French colonial administrators. He was courageous and patriotic, but also eccentric and mistrustful of all except members of his own family. In some ways the new prime minister—a Catholic in a largely Buddhist country—already was a dated figure, a man who had lived on the margins of Vietnamese society for too long with only a limited understanding of the revolutionary passions that had transformed his country. In other ways he was a modern nationalist who had his own ideas about how to move South Vietnam forward. Diem believed that he was "predestined for leadership," that he understood far better than

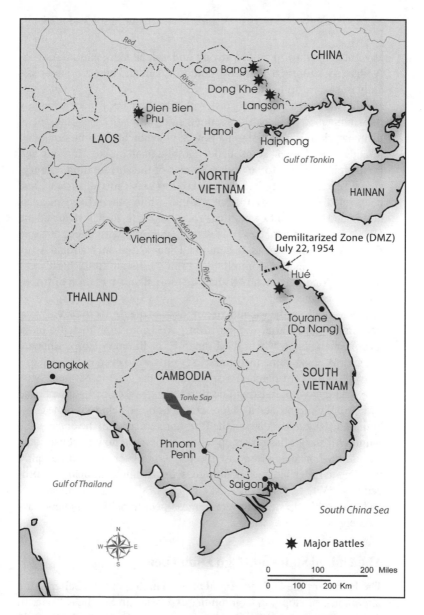

North and South Vietnam, 1954. Adapted from Stanley Karnow, *Vietnam: A History* (Penguin Books, 1997) p. 219. Used by permission of WGBH Educational Foundation.

any outsiders how to build a strong and independent nation. As U.S. Ambassador Elbridge Durbrow noted, "Diem and others do not basically trust most foreigners."[2]

Diem faced a staggering task in South Vietnam, a place which by the summer of 1954 had descended into political chaos and social disintegration. Within Saigon a powerful syndicated crime organization, the Binh Xuyen, controlled a gambling and prostitution ring and ran the city's police force. In large areas of the surrounding countryside, French authority had long ceased to exist; many peasants had been ruled for years by the Viet Minh, while others lived in areas dominated by one of two political-religious sects, the Cao Dai and the Hoa Hao, both of which exercised their authority with impugnity and fielded substantial armies. In contrast, Diem's Vietnam National Army was poorly trained and unreliable; initially his authority hardly extended beyond Saigon, and he had no more than a battalion of troops under his command.

Nevertheless, the vacuum of authority in the southern part of Vietnam immediately after the partition gave Diem time to settle in, at least in the capital, where the French Expeditionary Corps lingered on, guaranteeing some measure of stability. And even before Diem's arrival, the CIA dispatched a small team, the Saigon Military Mission, charged with assisting Diem to form a viable government. Led by Edward G. Lansdale, a CIA operator who had achieved fame combating the Huk insurgency in the Philippines earlier in the decade, the Saigon Military Mission group advised Diem on how to consolidate his power. Lansdale often saw the prime minister at night patiently listening to his exhaustive monologues, explaining administrative procedures ("What," Diem once asked, "does floating a loan mean?"),[3] and urging him to rally the Vietnamese people behind his new government.

The United States and Ngo Dinh Diem

The leaders of the U.S. government were united in their belief in the importance of stopping Communist expansion in Southeast Asia. In the mid-summer of 1954, Secretary of State John Foster Dulles told reporters that "the important thing from now on is not to mourn the past, but to seize the future opportunity to prevent the loss of northern Viet-Nam from leading to the extension of communism throughout Southeast Asia and the Southwest Pacific."[4] On September 8, 1954, the United States, along with Australia, France, Great Britain, New Zealand, Pakistan, the Philippines, and Thailand, signed the accords creating the Southeast Asia Treaty Organization (SEATO). In contrast to NATO (formed in 1949), SEATO was a loose regional alliance that did not require an automatic response from all its member nations should one of them come under attack. Nevertheless, it did serve as a pointed warning to the Soviet Union and the People's Republic of China that the United States had extended the boundaries of the Cold War to the seventeenth parallel dividing North and South Vietnam.

In October 1954 President Eisenhower, overruling doubts among some of his advisers, decided to support Diem; gradually American civilian and military officials assumed duties once performed by the French. The U.S. Navy helped in the resettlement of 800,000 refugees—mostly Catholic—from north to south Vietnam, and the Military Assistance and Advisory Group (MAAG) in Saigon—created in September 1950—expanded and took over the training of the South Vietnamese Army. With Lansdale at his side, Diem maneuvered to gain control of the army and buy off the leaders of the influential sects. After a visit to Saigon in February 1955, Dulles reported to Eisenhower that Diem "was much more of a personality than I had anticipated. He is not without defects but his merits seemed greater than I had thought."[5]

Some domestic groups rallied behind Diem's regime. South Vietnam's Catholics, especially the hundreds of thousand who had fled North Vietnam in the aftermath of the Geneva Accords, were his most loyal followers. And as American funding of Diem's government grew, he could rely more on the army and bureaucracy. Even so, his government remained fragile, and some American officials continued to have doubts about Diem's ability to govern. In November 1954 General J. Laughton Collins arrived in Saigon as Eisenhower's special representative and ambassador to assess the situation in South Vietnam. Collins was appalled by the confusion in Saigon and what he viewed as Diem's weaknesses as a leader. Or, as he cabled Washington in early April 1955, "Diem does not have the capacity to achieve the necessary unity of purpose and action from his people which is essential to prevent his country from falling under communist control."[6] Upon returning to Washington in late April, Collins convinced a reluctant Eisenhower and Dulles that the United States should replace Diem with someone else. Before the cable naming a prospective successor could be implemented, however, bloody fighting broke out in the center of Saigon between Diem's troops and those of the Binh Xuyen and the Cao Dai and Hoa Hao sects. Much to everyone's surprise, Diem's troops triumphed, silencing discussions in Washington about replacing the prime minister with another non-Communist nationalist. Diem, Dulles now declared, was a "popular hero." "Diem rightly or wrongly," the secretary of state continued, "is a living symbol of Vietnamese nationalism struggling against French colonialism and corrupt backward elements."[7] Assured of American backing, Diem could finally consolidate his position in South Vietnam.

The Consolidation of Diem's Rule

The contours of Diem's regime quickly emerged. Deploying his army to break the power of the Cao Dai and the Hoa Hao, Diem rejected the possibility of elections to reunify Vietnam (as had been called for in the Geneva Accords) and in October 1955 held a referendum on the monarchy. By an overwhelming majority (more than 98 percent of the votes cast) Bao Dai was deposed and Diem became president of the new Republic of Vietnam (RVN). While this republic had a democratic façade, with a constitution and National Assembly, it was in fact an authoritarian regime run by Diem and members of his family. One of his brothers, Ngo Dinh Nhu, lived with his family in the presidential palace and served as a presidential adviser. A French-educated intellectual who was fascinated with totalitarian ideology and organizational techniques, Nhu was the regime's resident philosopher as well as the director of the Can Lao, a secret party that infiltrated the bureaucracy and army and gave the Ngo family a separate source of information and control. Nhu's wife, Madame Nhu, a flamboyant woman who had grown up in a prominent Vietnamese family, was an outspoken, aggressive defender of the regime (critics called her the

"Dragon Lady") and a moralist (she banned sentimental songs and dancing) who headed one of the government's mass organizations, the Women's Solidarity Movement. Another brother, Ngo Dinh Can, lived in Hué and directed political and military affairs in the central provinces, while still another one, Archbishop Ngo Dinh Thuc, led South Vietnam's Catholic Church.

Diem and his family ruled over a nation of 16 million people, two-thirds of whom lived in Saigon and territory stretching to the south and west to the Mekong Delta, and one-third of whom lived along the narrow coastal plain north of the capital stretching up to the seventeenth parallel. The rugged, mountainous interior of South Vietnam was sparsely populated by Montagnards (mountain people). Divided by regional, ethnic, and religious antagonisms, the peoples of the new nation lacked a cohesive political community, even unifying institutions. The French had left an impressive material legacy: imposing villas, churches, and public works; extensive irrigation and drainage systems; and a vast number of rubber and tea plantations. They had not, however, prepared the Vietnamese for self-rule, and they had long denied them the basic freedoms of press, speech, and assembly. French colons had dominated leadership positions in the civil service, leaving the Vietnamese with little experience in managing the affairs of the nation. And the French-trained Vietnamese army lacked modern weapons and skilled leaders. In short, the Republic of Vietnam was a shell, lacking any strong sense of national identity. Even the most gifted leader would have found the task of creating a new nation daunting.

And Diem was not a democratic consensus builder; he was far better at attacking real or fancied opponents than in reaching out to his nation's disparate and dispirited people. In the summer of 1955 Diem began a Denunciation of Communists Campaign aimed at the systematic repression of remnants of the Viet Minh (which remained in the countryside) and of other, non-Communist groups or individuals who opposed his regime. Lasting through 1956 and 1957, this bloody campaign inflicted serious damage on Communist cadres, reducing their number from 15,000 to 5,000, and jailing close to 50,000 opponents of his regime. Diem also moved to extend his control into the countryside, when in 1956 he abolished elected village councils and appointed in their place outside administrators—mostly Catholics from Central Vietnam—to rule villages across the nation. Reversing land-reform measures carried out by the Viet Minh during the French war, he returned land to wealthy landlords or sold it to supporters of his regime. In the short run, Diem had brought stability to South Vietnam; in the long run, he had sown the seeds of a whirlwind.

Progress in South Vietnam

Speaking before the American Friends of Vietnam in June 1956, Senator John F. Kennedy summed up his perception of the significance of South Vietnam: "Vietnam represents the cornerstone of the Free World in Southeast Asia, the keystone to the arch, the finger in the dike. Burma, Thailand, India, Japan, the Philippines and obviously Laos and Cambodia are among those whose security would be threatened if the red tide of Communism overflowed into Vietnam. . . . If we are not the parents of little Vietnam, then surely we are the godparents. . . . This is our offspring—we cannot abandon it, we cannot ignore its needs."[8] If South Vietnam was a key domino, its leader, Ngo Dinh Diem, had become, as *Life* magazine proclaimed, "The Tough Miracle Man of Vietnam."[9] In May 1957 Diem made a triumphal state visit to the United States. Flown to Washington on Eisenhower's presidential airplane, he addressed a joint session of Congress, paraded through the streets of New York City, and visited other parts of the nation. The *New York Times* hailed Diem as "an Asian liberator, a man of tenacity of purpose, a stubborn man . . . bent on succeeding, a man whose life—all of it—is devoted to his country and his God."[10]

As Diem stabilized his rule, high-level officials in Washington paid less attention to South Vietnam. In the late 1950s Eisenhower and Dulles (who would die in 1959) were preoccupied with a series of Cold War crises, so U.S. policy toward South Vietnam lacked any firm guidance from the top. By this point U.S. economic aid covered two-thirds of the government's budget, bringing prosperity to at least the urban areas of the nation. Most American dollars found their way to the South Vietnamese military; little was spent on economic development or on long-term projects that might have created a self-sustaining economy. In reality, South Vietnam was a heavily subsidized U.S. protectorate, with the form but not the substance of a nation.

In the fall of 1955 the troops of what was now officially titled the Army of the Republic of Vietnam (ARVN) were pulled together into larger units and the new head of MAAG, General Samuel T. Williams, concentrated on rebuilding and retraining the South Vietnamese military. With the support of his superiors in Washington, he transformed ARVN into a seven-division force of 150,000 men, a road-bound army with the heavy weapons and logistical capabilities necessary to take on the North Vietnamese Army (NVA). Williams and other American officers had little understanding of counterinsurgency warfare; it was difficult for them to imagine a peasant-based insurgency that could become a serious challenge to ARVN. "Communist guerrillas," Williams reassured Diem, "have been destroyed in Greece, Korea, the Philippines and Iran. They can be destroyed in Vietnam."[11]

Diem, too, wanted a large, conventional military force. Equally preoccupied with the security of his regime and that of his nation, he needed an army that could crush his domestic opponents as well as confront North Vietnamese invaders. But Diem had little understanding of modern military organization; from his perspective, the primary purpose of the army was to guarantee the survival of his regime. Thus his main criteria for promotion within the military was loyalty, not necessarily competence. In addition, he created duplicate chains of command to ensure control over his military forces, and he communicated directly with military units through his own radio net. His senior officers, most of whom had been trained by the French, had been on the losing side of the long Vietnamese struggle for independence. They had no way of infusing ARVN with a sense of national purpose. Rife with favoritism, insubordination, and a low level of combat skills, ARVN, for all of its modern weaponry, was a loose coalition of units rather than a cohesive military force.

In the late 1950s the MAAG (which had grown from around 340 officers in July 1954 to around 685 when Eisenhower left office) labored to transform ARVN. American advisers established training schools in South Vietnam, sent some senior officers to the United States for instruction, put ARVN's logistical system on a sound footing, and worked closely with senior South Vietnamese commanders. General Williams saw Diem often, listening patiently to his seemingly endless speeches and trying to influence his decisions. In the protocol office of the presidential palace, Williams and his interpreter sat on Diem's right, while Diem rambled on, chain-smoking Vietnamese cigarettes, each of which the harried interpreter had to light. On the surface, much progress was made, as American weapons arrived and ARVN took on the look of the U.S. military, even down to the uniforms worn by its soldiers. Beneath the surface, however, structural problems remained unresolved and often undetected by General Williams and his staff. Most members of MAAG served only eleven-month tours in South Vietnam, and they arrived in that nation without any knowledge of its history, culture, or language. Confronted by a formidable cultural and language barrier, they had trouble communicating with Vietnamese in all walks of life and fell back on stereotypes to explain weaknesses in ARVN. As one official study of the U.S. Army put it, ARVN's flaws stemmed from "the long-standing nature of the Vietnamese people; passive, submissive, fatalistic, accustomed to being led . . . pastoral and non-mechanical."[12]

Mounting Discontent

In 1957 and 1958 popular discontent with Diem's rule slowly began to emerge. In the cities of South Vietnam, many feared and resented the president's repressive measures. In the rural areas, remnants of the Viet Minh, stunned by the severity of Diem's anti-Communist campaign, began to organize the peasantry, assassinate local officials, and even ambush patrolling ARVN units. The South Vietnamese government labeled these insurgent guerrillas the Viet Cong (VC), a derogatory term that was to endure.

Initially General Williams and his staff were unconcerned by mounting unrest in the countryside. They viewed the ambushes and assassinations there as distractions, acts designed to disrupt their training of ARVN for large-unit, conventional warfare. Williams believed the Vietnamese peasantry to be a highly traditional and passive people; he had no conception of the ways in which many years of warfare had disrupted traditional patterns among the peasantry and created the conditions for a broad-based revolutionary movement. For his part, Diem viewed the increasing guerrilla activity as a military and administrative problem, deploying ARVN units to suppress it and launching the agroville program to gather peasants into fortified villages that could be defended more easily. In September 1959 he told Williams that "the strategic battle against the VC has been won; now remains the tactical battle, which means the complete cleaning out of many small centers of Viet Cong activity."[13]

Understandably, American officials were slow to detect the extent of the organized resistance in the countryside. Lacking independent sources of intelligence, they relied on a regime that was itself out of touch with the peasantry. In contrast to Williams, however, Ambassador Durbrow was critical of Diem's leadership and of the family-based regime he had built. The ambassador and other officials in Saigon described Diem as a leader who "overrides most of his Ministers, reduces their authority, and assumes personal responsibility for the smallest details of government. He is inclined to be suspicious of others; he lacks an understanding of basic economic principles."[14] They wanted Diem to rely less on his family, reach out to his non-Communist opposition, and place less emphasis on military security and more on economic development.

But Diem and his American critics lived in different worlds. American officials urged the president to move toward a democratic, capitalist society and expected him to follow their advice. As one presidential adviser recalled, most Americans regarded Vietnam "as a 'young and unsophisticated' nation, populated by affable little men, unaccustomed to the modern world, who, if sufficiently bucked up by instruction and encouragement, might amount to something."[15] Diem and his brother Nhu, however, were suspicious of capitalism and individualism and rejected Western models of development. They found Americans arrogant and overbearing, and they doubted the steadfastness of the U.S. commitment to the long-term welfare of South Vietnam. The French, Nhu remarked, at least understood Vietnam, while the United States "helps us with a lot of money but doesn't know anything about Vietnamese affairs." Diem and Nhu realized they needed American support, yet they worried about becoming too dependent on American money and advice. "If you order Vietnam around like a puppet on a string," Diem told an American journalist, "how will you be different—except in degree—from the French?"[16] Diem believed he knew how to lead his nation and that his vision of modernization—a hazy third way between capitalism and communism—would rally his people behind efforts to develop a sound South Vietnam.

On January 26, 1960, at the town of Trang Sup, northeast of Saigon, Viet Cong units attacked the headquarters of the ARVN's Thirty-second Regiment, easily overrunning outlying sentry posts, penetrating to the heart of the base, killing or wounding sixty-six South Vietnamese troops, and making off with large quantities of U.S.-supplied weapons. Both Diem and his American advisers were shocked by the scale of the debacle. At long last concerned over security in the countryside, Williams proceeded to lecture Diem about the need to observe the chain of command and end favoritism in his army. Later that year, as the breakdown of ARVN became even more apparent, Ambassador Durbrow met alone with Diem. Convinced that "drastic action" was necessary,[17] Durbrow read South Vietnam's president a formal memorandum listing ways in which he must reform his regime and broaden his base of popular support, and suggesting that he send Nhu and his unpopular and outspoken wife into temporary exile. Diem's response was evasive; he had no way, after more than five years in power, of lessening his reliance on his family or breaking down the isolation of his regime.

The seriousness of the crisis in South Vietnam was highlighted on November 11, 1960, when both Diem and American officials in Saigon were surprised by a rebellion of elite paratroopers. Before dawn these rebels, who had been among Diem's most loyal supporters, attacked the presidential palace, trapping Diem, Nhu, and Madame Nhu inside. The leaders of the coup, daring but naïve and disorganized, sought to force reforms on Diem, not to remove him from power. Diem shrewdly engaged them in negotiations, promising changes, while he summoned loyal ARVN units from outside Saigon to come to his rescue. By the end of the day Diem had been saved, but the coup attempt had revealed the shakiness of his government and left American officials in Saigon and Washington scratching their heads, more uncertain than ever of how to assess the situation in South Vietnam or how to proceed—either in dealing with Diem or in dealing with the growing rebellion in the countryside.

Hanoi's Quest for Unification

In the late 1950s the center of Saigon, the "Pearl of the Orient," still had the look and the feel of a provincial town in southern France.[18] Its wide tree-lined boulevards, majestic public buildings, and quiet residential streets lined with elegant villas all conveyed to the newcomer a sense of familiarity and stability. It was difficult for most American officials to look beyond Saigon to the countryside, where most of the population lived and where in the late 1950s a new revolutionary force was gathering momentum.

In 1954, in the aftermath of the Geneva settlement and the division of Indochina, most of the Viet Minh who had fought the French in the south went north to join the new regime of Ho Chi Minh. Around 15,000 civilian and military cadres, however, buried their weapons and stayed behind. In 1955, when Diem began his campaign of repression, many guerrillas were killed, while others fled into the remote areas of the countryside and began to organize opposition to his government. As they did so, they appealed to leaders in Hanoi for aid.

The government in Hanoi, or Democratic Republic of Vietnam, was a Marxist-Leninist state, with all power concentrated in the executive directorate (Politburo) of the Communist Party (Lao Dong), led by Ho Chi Minh and his senior colleagues. At all levels of North Vietnamese society, a Communist ruling elite held power, filling government offices, overseeing the armed forces, banning opposition groups and parties, and imposing its policies on the people. Ho and his advisers, bitter over the division of Vietnam in 1954 and the broken promise to hold elections in 1956, were determined one day to unify their nation and complete their revolution. Initially, however, they responded cautiously to the pleas of their southern comrades. North Vietnam had been devastated by the French war, with much of its transportation infrastructure in ruins and much of its population on the edge of starvation. Ho and his associates needed time to rebuild their economy, modernize their army, and develop a Communist-party apparatus that would impose discipline on the rural masses. In 1956 a brutal program for the collectivization of agriculture ignited a large peasant rebellion. After intense debate, leaders in Hanoi chose to concentrate on building socialism in the north rather than on unifying Vietnam under Communist rule. Ho wrote his "southern comrades" that the struggle would be long and hard, and that the south could not be liberated until the north itself was strong. With the government in Hanoi temporizing, Diem's aggressive measures seriously damaged Communist forces in the south, reducing their number to the aforementioned 5,000 members. As one Vietnamese historian wrote, it was the "darkest hour" of the revolution.[19]

The attitude of the Soviet Union and China also restrained those who ruled North Vietnam. In the late 1950s both Communist giants, concerned with domestic reconstruction, sought a peaceful international environment. The new Soviet leader, Nikita Khrushchev, emphasized peaceful coexistence with the West, urging Hanoi to "reunify the country through peaceful means on the basis of independence and democracy," while Mao Zedong believed that it would require a protracted struggle to resolve the issue of a divided Vietnam. "If ten years is not enough," he warned North Vietnamese officials, "it may take one hundred."[20] Given North Vietnam's heavy reliance on its patrons in Moscow and Beijing for economic and military aid and diplomatic support, its leaders dared not defy their benefactors by taking too aggressive an approach to national unification.

Revolutionaries in Hanoi, however, viewed South Vietnam's government as corrupt and repressive, and believed that as Diem tried to extend his rule into the countryside he would further alienate the peasantry. As General Giap put it, Diem and his supporters operated a "fascist dictatorial political regime, ferociously oppressing and exploiting the people, using every barbarous means to suppress the patriotic movement." South Vietnam had become, Giap and his colleagues concluded, an American colony. "The Vietnamese people," Ho Chi Minh proclaimed, "should not forget that their principal enemies are the American imperialists and their agents who still occupy half the country and are feverishly preparing for war."[21]

Despite fears of prompting direct American military intervention, the North Vietnamese government could not resist for long the clamor of southern revolutionaries for support. In early 1959 it decided to take control of the movement in the south and authorize a shift to an armed rebellion. In the first half of 1959, Ho's government made three additional decisions. First, it ordered the construction of revolutionary base areas in the Central Highlands of South Vietnam. Second, it created a new, secret organization charged with building a system of trails running from North Vietnam through the mountainous regions of neighboring Laos and into South Vietnam (the network that would become known as the Ho Chi Minh Trail). Third, it set up a maritime supply route along the coast. In June 1959 leaders in Hanoi dispatched the first shipment of arms to the south. Along with the munitions went native southerners who had gone north in 1954; now these seasoned revolutionaries—both men and women—were returning to their homeland to strengthen emerging rebel forces. Progress along these lines was so rapid that in December 1960, on secret orders from Hanoi, delegates met in the jungle near the Cambodian border to form an organization to comprise all of Diem's opponents in South Vietnam, the National Liberation Front (NLF). Diem no longer faced scattered opposition; he now had to deal with a united movement dedicated to the overthrow of his government.

Changes in the international environment also encouraged Hanoi's deepening involvement in the rebellion in the south. While Khrushchev disliked the growing violence in South Vietnam and Southeast Asia, Mao moved toward confrontation both with the Soviet Union and the West. Despite his fear of American power, the Chinese leader saw China as the leader of oppressed people throughout the world, and he supported national liberation movements. As the war in South Vietnam intensified, Mao promised assistance to North Vietnam; in 1963, during visits to Hanoi, prominent Chinese officials assured their North Vietnamese comrades that "We are standing by your side, and if war breaks out, you can regard China as your rear." And at a conference of regional Communist-party leaders, Foreign Minister Zhou Enlai proclaimed that China would support the "revolution in Southeast Asia."[22]

From the start the relationship between the government in Hanoi and those who directed the rebellion in South Vietnam was close, if paradoxical: it was an indigenous rebellion, but one shaped and directed from the north, a subtle blending of north and south Vietnamese revolutionaries. The rank and file of the NLF came from the south, as did many of its officials, but the key positions were held by members of the Vietnamese Communist party. Thus the NLF was never a fully independent organization. Its hard core of Communist leaders carefully veiled their objectives and cleverly manipulated their non-Communist comrades. The NLF's program emphasized the struggle against colonialism and called for land reform and democracy in the south. Pointing to the alleged economic miracle in the north, it promised that once the revolution triumphed the people could look forward to the expulsion of "U.S. imperialists," the creation through elections of "a broad national democratic coalition administration," a general amnesty for supporters of the Saigon government, and a period of separate governance for the south before its reunification with the north.[23] In short, the NLF's program appealed to the ideals and longings of a broad range of the South Vietnamese people.

A New War

In the late 1950s the NLF spread rapidly, gaining supporters in both urban and rural areas. In the cities it never developed a mass base, but it did draw into its ranks a fair number of influential, well-educated South Vietnamese. Many members of this small elite despised the oppression and corruption of Diem's rule as well as his dependence on the United States. In contrast, they found Ho Chi Minh a genuine, charismatic figure. Truong Nhu Tang, a member of a wealthy Saigon family who became a prominent figure in the southern revolution, remembered, as a student in Paris, meeting Ho in 1946. Overwhelmed by Ho's warmth, simplicity, and vision of Vietnam's past and future, Truong recalled years later that "from that afternoon I was Ho Chi Minh's fervent partisan. . . . The force of Ho's personality had by itself created a turning point in my life."[24] Tang and others involved in the insurgency harbored grave reservations about the Communist experiment in North Vietnam, and they preferred a middle path between the foreign-backed Diem regime and all-out Communist revolution. But the real choice was between Diem and the NLF. Whatever their doubts about its ultimate goals, it was a Vietnamese organization that championed the unification and independence of their nation.

The real base of the NLF, however, lay in the countryside, where much of the peasantry had lived under Viet Minh rule for years. In the Mekong Delta, an immense watery floodplain shimmering with rice paddies divided by low dikes, lived one-half of South Vietnam's peasants. In this region south of Saigon, the French had never held more than the small cities and towns and the few roads that connected them, and Diem's officials and soldiers were similarly isolated in this sea of peasant hostility. Not just in the delta but throughout rural South Vietnam, the peasantry held a list of grievances against the government in Saigon, ranging from the lack of land and the high rents charged by exploitive landlords, to resentment against appointed district and village officials with no local ties, to anger at the depredations of ARVN units as they moved through the countryside, often helping themselves to whatever foodstuffs they wanted and treating the residents with disrespect—or worse. Closely knit and intensely suspicious of outsiders, the peasantry blamed Diem for his reliance on another group of hated, white foreigners. Many referred to him contemptuously as "My-Diem," or "American-Diem." A Communist organizer remembered that "the [rural] people were like a mound of straw, ready to be ignited."[25]

One peasant girl, who grew up in a contested village near Da Nang, remembered learning about the war from NLF cadre. The cadre played upon her fear of outsiders and love of ancestors by teaching her songs and stories about Ho Chi Minh, "Uncle Ho." "Like an unbroken thread," she remembered, "the path from our ancestors and legends seemed to lead inevitably to the Northern leader—then past him to a future of harmony and peace."[26] Soon thereafter, at the age of thirteen, Le Ly Hayslip began to fight for the Viet Cong.

NLF organizers shrewdly exploited and redirected these grievances, using them to create revolutionary base areas and a disciplined community at the village level. First they moved to murder or intimidate local officials through a careful use of violence, curtailing their freedom of movement and in effect isolating the Saigon government from the rural population. Then they began the long process of political education and psychological reorientation. Their goal was to transform entire villages, through a combination of persuasion and coercion, into secure centers of revolutionary activity.

To achieve these goals, the NLF had to break down some traditional attitudes and replace them with those necessary to build an effective army and a functioning revolutionary organization. The Vietnamese peasantry had long lived in the slow rhythms of time and space of a primitive agricultural society. Most of these people were unfamiliar with clocks, machines, or precision instruments, even with schools or factory-work routines. Initially some Viet Cong soldiers neglected to maintain their weapons, forgot to return to their units on time, or panicked when attacked. Thus the NLF had to transform the peasantry into hardened soldiers and collaborators who would not only fight but pay taxes, supply medicine, report on the enemy, or build tunnels, trenches, booby traps, and small arms.

Building a revolutionary apparatus in a remote countryside was a slow, time-consuming process, but as early as 1957 and 1958 small insurgent groups had gone into action, assassinating local officials and clashing with government forces. Some areas saw spontaneous local uprisings against Saigon's authority. By the end of 1959 the increased level of enemy activity was evident throughout South Vietnam. Insurgents ambushed ARVN units, attacked outposts and watchtowers, and sometimes boldly entered larger towns. In July 1959 a VC squad attacked American advisers attached to the ARVN's Seventh Infantry Division stationed at the city of Bien Hoa, close to Saigon. Easily avoiding South Vietnamese army guards, the six VC slipped through a barbed-wire fence and sprayed the mess hall with automatic weapons fire. One American was wounded and two others were killed—the first Americans to die by enemy action in South Vietnam. Viet Cong forces remained relatively small, numbering around 12,000 by the end of 1960, but the ability of the rebellion to shift from propaganda, intimidation, and assassination to effective military action took both South Vietnamese and American officials by surprise. Clearly, a new war had begun.

Notes

1 Howard R. Simpson, *Tiger in the Barbed Wire: An American in Vietnam, 1952–1991* (New York, 1994), 139–40.

2 Quoted in Philip E. Catton, *Diem's Final Failure: Prelude to America's War in Vietnam* (Lawrence, Kans., 2002), 25, 27.

3 Quoted in Cecil B. Currey, *Edward Lansdale: The Unquiet American* (Washington, D.C., 1998), 154.

4 Quoted in David L. Anderson, *Trapped by Success: The Eisenhower Administration and Vietnam, 1953–1961* (New York, 1991), 66.

5 Quoted in Ronald H. Spector, *Advice and Support: The Early Years of the United States Army in Vietnam, 1941–1960* (New York, 1985), 248.

6 Quoted in Anderson, *Trapped by Success,* 105.

7 Ibid., 115.

8 Quoted in William Conrad Gibbons, *The U.S. Government and the Vietnam War: Executive and Legislative Roles and Relationships, Part I: 1945–1960* (Princeton, N.J., 1986), 303–04.

9 Quoted in Anderson, *Trapped by Success,* 246.

10 Quoted in Chester L. Cooper, *The Lost Crusade: America in Vietnam* (New York, 1970), 153.

11 Quoted in Spector, *Advice and Support,* 273.

12 Ibid., 286.

13 Ibid., 334.

14 Ibid., 304.

15 Arthur M. Schlesinger, Jr., *A Thousand Days: John F. Kennedy in the White House* (Boston, 1965), 543.

16 Quoted in Catton, *Diem's Final Failure,* 26, 29.

17 Quoted in Gibbons, *The U.S. Government and the Vietnam War, I,* 341.

18 Simpson, *Tiger in the Barbed Wire,* 1

19 Quoted in William J. Duiker, *Sacred War: Nationalism and Revolution in a Divided Vietnam* (New York, 1995), 112, 120.

20 Quoted in Qiang Zhai, *China and the Vietnam War, 1950–1975* (Chapel Hill, N.C., 2000), 77; quoted in William J. Duiker, *Ho Chi Minh* (New York, 2000), 508.

21 Quoted in Cecil B. Currey, *Victory at Any Cost: The Genius of Viet Nam's Gen. Vo Nguyen Giap* (Washington, D.C., 1997), 227; quoted in Duiker, *Ho Chi Minh,* 494.

22 Quoted in Zhai, *China and the Vietnam War,* 117; quoted in Chen Jian, *Mao's China and the Cold War* (Chapel Hill, N.C., 2001), 208.

23 Quoted in George McT. Kahin, *Intervention: How America Became Involved in Vietnam* (New York, 1986), 115.

24 Truong Nhu Tang, *A Vietcong Memoir* (New York, 1985), 16.

25 Quoted in Neil Sheehan, *A Bright Shining Lie: John Paul Vann and America in Vietnam* (New York, 1988), 192–94.

26 Le Ly Hayslip, *When Heaven and Earth Changed Places: A Vietnamese Woman's Journey from War to Peace* (New York, 1989), xi.

CHAPTER THREE

The New Frontier in Vietnam, 1961–1963

The mood of the new administration was tough and energetic. President John F. Kennedy, more than a generation younger than Eisenhower, believed that in the late 1950s the nation had drifted and promised to "get this country moving again." His inaugural address on January 20, 1961, devoted almost entirely to Cold War issues, was a stirring call to action and sacrifice. "Let every nation know," the young president proclaimed, "whether it wishes us well or ill, that we shall pay any price, bear any burden, meet any hardship, support any friend, oppose any foe to assure the survival and the success of liberty. . . . Since this country was founded, each generation of Americans has been summoned to give testimony to its national loyalty. The graves of young Americans who answered the call to service surround the globe."[1]

JFK and the World

Kennedy acted on this rhetoric, launching ambitious programs such as the Peace Corps, Food for Peace, the Alliance for Progress, a space program charged with landing a man on the moon, and confronting the Soviet Union in a series of crises. In pursuing these initiatives at home and abroad, Kennedy carried the American people with him. They were willing to support his administration in the "long twilight struggle" that had no end in sight.[2] The war in Vietnam was a part of that struggle, a war in which Americans confronted a savage enemy in a wilderness landscape and where, it seemed, they could test their character and fulfill their special destiny. In the early 1960s the scale of the war remained small, allowing room for individuals to make their mark. One American general, in a talk to advisers attached to the South Vietnamese army, summed up the prevailing attitude then he remarked: "It isn't much of a war, but it's the only war we've got, so enjoy it."[3]

Kennedy had been critical of Eisenhower's military policies and his attitude toward the Third World. Convinced that his predecessor had relied excessively on nuclear weapons, JFK quickly set out to multiply military options by enlarging and modernizing conventional forces and developing both a theory and capability for counterinsurgency warfare. Kennedy believed that the battle for Western Europe had been fought and won in the late 1940s and the early 1950s, and that the geographical focus of the Cold War had shifted to the non-Western world. "The great battleground for the defense and expansion of freedom today," he noted soon after entering the White House, "is the whole southern half of the globe—Asia, Latin America, Africa, and the Middle East—the lands of the rising peoples. Their revolution is the greatest in human history. More than an end, they seek a beginning."[4]

Kennedy's key advisers—special assistant for national security affairs McGeorge Bundy, Secretary of Defense Robert S. McNamara, and Secretary of State Dean Rusk—shared his mood and outlook. Young and self-confident (Bundy was forty-two, McNamara forty-four, Rusk fifty-two), they saw themselves and the man they served as representatives of a new generation, and they entertained no doubts about the role that the United States should play in world affairs. Bundy characterized the nation as the "locomotive at the head of mankind, and the rest of the world the caboose." McNamara, looking back years later, concluded that "it is very hard . . . to recapture the innocence and confidence" with which Kennedy's advisers approached both Vietnam and other international crises.[5] Of these three advisers, McNamara became the most influential. A brilliant executive at the Ford Motor Company, he was a man of boundless energy and self- confidence, a master of numbers and the techniques essential for the management of large organizations. The new secretary of defense was impatient and hardworking; over the course of his more than seven years in office he would travel to South Vietnam nine times. McNamara's assertiveness, his faith in American power, and his capacity to absorb information, gave his opinions in the inner circle around the president unusual authority.

Challenge in Southeast Asia

Kennedy's first year in office saw a series of foreign policy crises ranging from the ill-fated Bay of Pigs invasion of Cuba in April 1961 to a dangerous confrontation over Berlin, which culminated in August when the Soviet Union began to build a wall between the two halves of the city. In Southeast Asia, Kennedy initially showed more concern with Laos than with South Vietnam. In the former, a mountainous, landlocked country that shared lengthy borders with North Vietnam and South Vietnam (to its east), and Cambodia (to its southwest), war had broken out between the Pathet Lao (the Laotian Communist movement) and the forces of the Royal Lao government. While Kennedy engaged in belligerent rhetoric, he realized the weaknesses of the Royal Government and decided to seek a diplomatic rather than a military solution to the conflict there. In May a conference on Laos opened at Geneva, with ambassador-at-large W. Averell Harriman as the U.S. representative.

Kennedy's decision to negotiate in the case of Laos made the taking of a firm stand in Vietnam even more important. Shortly after assuming office, he received a report from Edward G. Lansdale on a recent trip to Saigon. Lansdale still admired Diem, but he warned Kennedy that South Vietnam was in a critical condition and should be handled "as a combat area of the cold war, as an area requiring emergency treatment."[6] Worried, Kennedy moved to increase support to the Diem regime. In early May, Frederick Nolting Jr. arrived in Saigon to replace Ambassador Durbrow, and a few days later Vice President Lyndon B. Johnson showed up there too. Both men showered Diem with renewed assurances of American support; Johnson publicly praised him as "the Winston Churchill of Asia."[7]

By the fall of 1961 events in South Vietnam had Kennedy perplexed. He continued to receive varying assessments of Diem and his regime—some critical, some optimistic—and conflicting recommendations for American policy, ranging from the neutralization of South Vietnam to the commitment there of U.S. combat troops. Finally, in early October, Kennedy decided to cut through the confusion by dispatching to Saigon a special fact-finding mission headed by his personal military adviser, General Maxwell D. Taylor, and White House adviser Walt W. Rostow. The two men and their staff spent two weeks on their mission, returning to Washington on November 2 convinced of the vital importance of the struggle in South Vietnam. They proposed to JFK a crucial shift in America's role as adviser "to [a] limited partnership and working collaboration" with Diem's government.[8] In addition to this joint administrative effort, Taylor and Rostow recommended that the United States expand aid for South Vietnam's military forces, put more American advisers in the field, and send more U.S. helicopters to improve ARVN's mobility. Most important, they urged the dispatch of 8,000 U.S. combat troops and retaliation against North Vietnam (direct bombing) should it continue to infiltrate men and equipment into the south. To reinforce his tough recommendations, Taylor cabled the president that "As an area for the operations of U.S. troops, SVN is not an excessively difficult or unpleasant place to operate."[9]

Kennedy rejected the most extreme advice in the Taylor and Rostow report; the crisis in South Vietnam did not seem critical enough to justify the deployment of American combat troops or the bombing of North Vietnam. At the same time, he rejected another option, a negotiated end to the conflict, one urged on him by Harriman, who doubted that Diem's government could survive if it continued to be "repressive, dictatorial and unpopular."[10] He wanted to expand the conference then in progress for the neutralization of Laos to include South Vietnam. If only the United States would negotiate with Com-

munist revolutionaries, he suggested, it might find a way to imple-
ment the 1954 Geneva Accords.

Kennedy and most of his close advisers had no interest in either
dramatic escalation of the war or negotiating with the enemy. Instead, in late 1961 the president chose a middle course, increasing
the number of American military advisers in South Vietnam and the
flow of military equipment to ARVN. And most of the members of
Kennedy's inner circle supported a larger military commitment and
a limited partnership with Diem. In short, the arguments for modest
escalation in South Vietnam seemed more compelling than those
for withdrawal.

The Kennedy administration, along with most Americans interested in international affairs, viewed the war in South Vietnam
in terms of the regional struggle with China and the global struggle
with the Soviet Union. For Kennedy and his associates, South Vietnam was a test of the nation's ability to support non-Communist
regimes in Southeast Asia and of its credibility around the world.
Failure in South Vietnam, aside from undermining America's international position, might also precipitate a bitter domestic debate over who was responsible for the loss of that nation to communism. Kennedy and other leading Democrats remembered vividly the fall of Jiang Jieshi's Nationalist government in 1949 and
how Republicans had blamed the Truman administration for the
loss of China to communism. Now JFK worried about similar attacks from conservatives should he appear to falter in the face of
Communist aggression, especially after the debacle at the Bay of
Pigs, the decision to negotiate in Laos (which resulted in a coalition government in July 1962), and the passive response of the
administration to the erection of the Berlin Wall. These decisions,
at least as far as domestic politics was concerned, had increased
the importance of firm stands elsewhere; otherwise the administration might be weakened by assaults from the right and Kennedy
might fail to win reelection in 1964. As Rusk and McNamara
warned in November 1961: "The loss of South Viet-Nam to Communism . . . would stimulate bitter domestic controversies in the
United States and would be seized upon by extreme elements to
divide the country and harass the Administration."[11]

Seeming Progress in South Vietnam

One morning in December 1961, an American newspaper correspondent was drinking coffee on the terrace of Saigon's Majestic Hotel when, to his amazement, the *U.S.S. Core* turned a bend in the river and steamed toward the port of Saigon with the first shipment of forty-seven helicopters on its deck. The new shift in the war, recommended by Taylor and Rostow, had begun.

As American equipment and advisers (the number rose from around 2,000 at the end of 1961 to more than 11,000 at the end of 1962) poured into South Vietnam, results quickly followed. ARVN units now flew into battle aboard American-made helicopters piloted by Americans, and accompanied by American advisers. American aircraft began to drop napalm bombs (a jellied gasoline that sticks to and deeply burns human flesh) on enemy units; others began Operation RANCH HAND, a defoliation program aimed at clearing areas along key roads and denying natural cover and food to the enemy. The United States government upgraded Military Advisory and Assistance Group to Military Assistance Command, Vietnam (MACV) and hardened its commitment to South Vietnam, both in a series of statements by senior officials and a special report entitled *A Threat To The Peace: North Viet-Nam's Effort To Conquer South Viet-Nam.* At a press conference in early March 1962, Secretary of State Rusk announced that "there can be peace overnight in Vietnam if those responsible for the aggression wish peace,"[12] while the State Department's document claimed that the war in the south was primarily the result of aggression from the north. Both the scale and the nature of the nation's commitment to South Vietnam had dramatically changed.

As 1962 progressed, JFK and his advisers became more optimistic about the course of the war. On his first trip to South Vietnam in May 1962, Secretary of Defense McNamara, after having spent only forty-eight hours talking to officials and traveling in the field, informed reporters that he had seen "a great deal of South Vietnam . . . and . . . acquired a 'good feel'" for conditions in the nation. Asked what impression he would carry back to the president, McNamara responded that he had "seen nothing but progress and hopeful indications of further progress in the future." After the press conference had ended and

McNamara was getting into his car, one reporter asked him off the record how he could be so sanguine about a war that the United States had just begun to fight. The secretary of defense shot back: "Every quantitative measurement we have shows that we're winning this war."[13] For most American leaders, failure against such a poorly armed enemy seemed inconceivable.

Additional grounds for hope came with the South Vietnamese government's unveiling of its strategic hamlet program. In 1959 Diem had begun his agroville program, which sought to gather peasants into fortified villages. The agroville scheme was small in scale and, due to peasant resistance, abandoned in early 1961. In early 1962, however, Diem, with American encouragement, launched the far more ambitious strategic hamlet program, a large and expensive enterprise designed to build new bases for the government in the countryside. In theory, the "hamleted" peasantry would be protected from the demands of the NLF; no longer able to extract men and food from the villages, the rebellion in the countryside would fade away. In practice, however, the strategic hamlet program never functioned as an effective bulwark to the insurgency, for the Saigon government never had genuine support among the peasantry, most of whom never regarded its authority as legitimate.

Diem's brother, Ngo Dinh Nhu, took charge of the strategic hamlet program, giving it a high priority. Nhu fantasized about inspiring a counter-revolution in the countryside that would undermine the NLF, but in fact he was a French-educated intellectual who knew little about the rural people of his own nation. Nhu was obsessed with numbers; he wanted to erect hamlets as quickly as possible. The first pilot project, Operation Sunrise, opened in March 1962 in a province north of Saigon. With American approval and financing, Nhu pressed forward, announcing in September 1962 that 4.3 million peasants, or about one-third of the rural population, had been relocated.

Nhu issued instructions on the basis of his theories, while the government's bureaucracy routinely carried them out, often reporting half-completed projects as finished. In an effort to prevent small groups of guerrillas from entering villages, the program relocated peasants, forcing them to walk long distances from their new living quarters to their fields. The peasants furthermore resented being made to work without pay to dig moats, implant sharpened bamboo stakes, and erect fences to deter an enemy that, in many cases, was already a part of their lives. The appointed local officials, often aloof and corrupt outsiders, embezzled money allocated for improvements. In short, rather than draw the peasantry to the government's side, the strategic hamlet program helped push them further toward the NLF.

These flaws were, of course, more apparent in retrospect than at the time. Senior American officials in Washington and Saigon, who could not see beyond the imposing fortifications and smart formations of local troops standing at attention, were impressed. Preoccupied with the global Cold War, they found it hard to focus on the nature of the revolution in the South Vietnamese countryside. Some lower-level American soldiers and civilians in South Vietnam, however, saw through the smoke and mirrors and were sharply critical of the strategic hamlet program. As one American on the scene remarked, Diem's and Nhu's officials "haven't the faintest idea what makes peasants tick—and how can they? They're city boys who earned promotions by kissing the asses of their bosses, and all they care about is getting back to Saigon to get promoted again."[14]

At a high-level conference in Honolulu in July 1962, General Paul D. Harkins—the new head of MACV—assured McNamara that "there is no doubt that we are on the winning side." In response to McNamara's question about how long it would take to defeat the NLF, Harkins predicted that once ARVN became "fully operational" by early 1963, victory would take about a year.[15] The secretary of defense, worried about appearing too optimistic, preferred a more cautious three-year victory scenario.

Despite all the apparent signs of progress, some high-level American observers had doubts. In December, Senate Majority Leader Mike Mansfield (Democrat, Montana), who had toured South Vietnam at the president's request, sent JFK a pessimistic report on that nation's prospects. In a discussion with the senator, Kennedy asked: "You expect me to believe this?" "Yes, you sent me," Mansfield replied, but the president continued: "This isn't what my people are telling me."[16] Still confronted with contradictory information about South Vietnam, Kennedy was cautious in his last news conference of 1962. When asked about progress since the implementation of the Taylor-Rostow report, he answered: "As you know, we have 10 or 11 times as many men there as we had a year ago. . . . So we don't see the end of the tunnel, but I must say I don't think it is darker than it was a year ago, and in some ways lighter."[17]

The New Advisory War

As American advisers spread out across South Vietnam, attached to ARVN units operating in the field, they acquired a vivid, low-level view of the war. In March 1962 one of these advisers, Lieutenant Colonel John Paul Vann, arrived in Saigon. A thirty-seven-year-old career soldier who had served in Korea, Vann, like other U.S. Army advisers assigned to South Vietnam, knew nothing about Vietnamese culture or history. But he was eager to learn about the war. In May 1962 he drove thirty-five miles south of Saigon to the provincial town of My Tho to join the headquarters of ARVN's Seventh Infantry Division, which was assigned to the northern half of the Mekong Delta. Quickly assessing the situation there, Vann concluded that the Viet Cong held the military initiative as well as the sympathy of most of the peasantry. His task was to convince the commander of the Seventh Division, Colonel Huynh Van Cao, to fight in a more aggressive and intelligent way.

The efforts of the Seventh Division's American advisory group rapidly paid off. ARVN had an enormous superiority over the Viet Cong in both equipment and firepower, if only it would use it. The enemy was lightly armed and still accustomed to fighting the kind of warfare it had waged against the French, when it could find shelter in the natural fortresses of the region—the vast swamps and mangrove forests that no roads penetrated. But American technology and aggressiveness changed the nature of the war. Helicopters shrank the barriers of time and space, making the Viet Cong vulnerable to surprise attack even in its sanctuaries. Few guerrilla hideouts were more than twenty minutes away from ARVN bases, so by flying at treetop level, thereby muffling the sound of their helicopters against the thick jungle canopy, American pilots allowed the enemy a scant few minutes warning. And American advisers monitored VC radio transmissions and employed electronic intelligence to locate enemy units.

ARVN units also enjoyed the support of fighter-bombers and M-113 armored personnel carriers (APCs)—the M-113 was a ten-ton amphibious vehicle with caterpillar tracks and topped with a swiveling, 50-caliber heavy machine gun.

Understandably these new American weapons had great shock effect on the insurgent guerrillas, people who had never encountered anything like them before. In the spring and summer of 1962, even as the Seventh Infantry Division moved into position, guerrilla units often panicked and ran, and were either killed from the air or on the ground by APCs. *Time* magazine, reflecting official reports, asked what chance did the enemy have? "The typical VietCong soldier is a thin, unkempt young man hardly reaching a G.I.'s armpit and weighing scarcely 100 lbs."[18]

Initially Vann, like many of his fellow advisers, was optimistic, convinced that he could run ARVN's Seventh Infantry Division just as he would a division of the U.S. Army. The longer he worked with Colonel Cao and his troops, however, the more Vann realized that his first impressions had been misleading, and that ARVN, like the war itself, was shaped by the peculiar history and politics of Vietnam. Colonel Cao, only thirty-four years old when Diem had appointed him division commander, was a case in point. Cao had been awarded the position largely because he was a Central Vietnamese Catholic whose family had known Diem's. Concerned about retaining the loyalty of his army and fearful of another coup attempt, Diem viewed Cao's and all his officers' first duty as the protection of the regime. Cao had a direct line to the presidential palace, and he was to be prepared to rush his troops to Saigon to save the president and his family from rebellious elements within the army.

Cao was a political general with little talent for command and virtually no understanding of modern warfare. So long as the guerrillas fled, he was enthusiastic, but Vann soon concluded that Cao was not interested in engaging the enemy—when Vann urged him to send his troops out on night patrol, the colonel responded: "It is not safe to go out at night."[9]—in properly training his men for combat, or in insisting that they treat captured Viet Cong and the local peasantry humanely. While Vann knew that the VC was suffering badly, he also realized that the enemy had ample reserves of manpower. It was only a matter of time, he reasoned, before the Viet Cong learned not to panic and how to fight ARVN more skillfully. Then the days of easy killing would be over.

And as Viet Cong commanders began to adjust to new battlefield conditions, the Seventh Division began to take more casualties. Now President Diem was displeased, warning Cao that he was taking too many risks and that, if he wished to be promoted, he would have to be more cautious. Diem feared that heavy casualties would increase discontent within the army and encourage another coup. Cao quickly responded to Diem's displeasure, making sure that his troops patrolled only where he believed no guerrillas to be present and, just in case Seventh Division units happened to stumble on the enemy, to always leave open a path of escape.

The Battle of Ap Bac

On January 2, 1963, the Seventh Division went back into action at the small village of Ap Bac, about forty miles southwest of Saigon, in what would become the most important engagement of the advisory phase of the American war in Vietnam. American intelligence had located a Viet Cong battalion of 350 men at Ap Bac. Vann and other American advisers, who had longed for the chance to have ARVN engage the enemy in a set-piece battle, convinced the new commander of the Seventh Division (Colonel Cao had already managed to get promoted) to commit his troops. This time, however, VC commanders ordered their men to stay and fight rather than fade away after the initial contact. They believed it was essential to defeat ARVN in order to restore the confidence of their troops and their peasant supporters. Furthermore, these enemy commanders, many of whom were veterans of the Viet Minh's war against the Japanese and the French, had been studying the new American machines they faced and had retrained their soldiers accordingly. At Ap Bac they dug their troops deeply into the tree-shaded dikes and waited, looking out across the rice paddies where ARVN troops were sure to touch down in American "choppers."

One thousand four hundred South Vietnamese troops were committed to the battle, most brought in by helicopter. As the copters descended into the rice paddies, five of the fifteen were shot down. Those ARVN troops on the ground, unaccustomed to close combat, quickly grew demoralized. Ignoring the pleas of their American advisers, they refused to close on the enemy. Eventually thirteen APCs joined the battle, but as the heavy vehicles moved through the rice paddies, Viet Cong riflemen took aim for the machine gunners, exposed to fire from the waist up, and the drivers, whose heads stuck up out of small hatches. As some of the gunners and drivers fell dead, the APCs, with bullets and grenades ricocheting off their sides, either stopped in their tracks or retreated. When night fell, the VC slipped away.

The Viet Cong had accomplished the impossible. Against staggering odds, it had humbled the South Vietnamese army, suffering only eighteen killed and thirty-nine wounded. Meanwhile, it had killed eighty ARVN soldiers, wounded one hundred more, and taken the lives of three American advisers. The Battle of Ap Bac revealed the inadequacies of ARVN's leadership, of the tactics Americans had taught the South Vietnamese, and of the relationship between the American advisers and their South Vietnamese counterparts—they could only advise, not command, and since few spoke more than a few words of Vietnamese, they had to communicate through interpreters, not all of whom were competent or trustworthy. Vann and other advisers of the Seventh Division knew firsthand how bad the defeat had been. In Vann's pithy summation: "It was a miserable damn performance."[20] They now began to realize that the advisory phase of America's war in Vietnam was more than a matter of supplying machines: it was also a struggle of wills against an adaptable and intelligent enemy.

The Illusion of Victory

Despite the disaster at Ap Bac, the top American officials in Saigon, Ambassador Nolting and General Harkins, remained deeply committed to the Diem regime and optimistic about the course of the war. Harkins was furious about the pessimistic reports of American advisers after Ap Bac. Since the enemy had withdrawn, he claimed that ARVN had prevailed. In fact, Harkins lacked curiosity about the war as well as about the enemy that the United States and its ally in Saigon faced. He preferred to view the lush South Vietnamese countryside from the air; as the journalist Neil Sheehan phrased it, "His mind never touched down in Vietnam."[21] And Harkins trusted Diem. When the general asked the president if, as some American advisers claimed, he had ordered his officers to avoid the enemy, Diem lied, claiming that in fact he had ordered them to be more aggressive. Harkins did not pursue the issue further; nor did he question the fake body counts that ARVN units regularly reported from the field.

By early 1963, as all the programs of the American military advisers came together, Harkins calculated that in February the ARVN would be prepared to launch a nationwide offensive to break the back of the enemy. The destruction of the Viet Cong, he figured, would take about a year, at worst three, and in the meantime Harkins's command began to draw up plans for the phasing out of the American expeditionary corps by the end of 1965.

The gap between the official American and the North Vietnamese view of the war was vividly revealed in a conversation in 1963 between Premier Pham Van Dong and the Polish delegate to the international commission set up by the Geneva Accords. "Tell me something," the premier asked the diplomat. "The American generals are always boasting of how they are winning the war in the South. Do they believe it?" The Pole responded: "As far as I can discover they do." Pham Van Dong was incredulous. "You're joking. Perhaps they boast for propaganda, but the CIA must tell them the truth in its secret reports." "I don't know," the Pole responded, "what the CIA tells them. All I can find out is that they seem to believe what they say." The premier concluded the conversation by remarking, "Well, I find it hard to believe what you say. Surely the American generals cannot be that naïve."[22]

In fact, the leaders of the American military, despite their impressive expertise in modern warfare, had not focused on the low-level reality of the struggle. Shaped by their great triumph in World War II, many older officers had grown complacent over the postwar decades. Their approach to warfare had become managerial; they assumed that a large enough investment of men and equipment was bound to overwhelm what they termed "those raggedy-ass little bastards."[23] A Joint Chiefs of Staff fact-finding group, dispatched to South Vietnam in January 1963 and headed by Army Chief of Staff Earle G. Wheeler, reported that "We are winning slowly on the present thrust, and . . . there is no compelling reason to change. . . . The 'first team' is in the game."[24]

The Challenge to Diem

In the early months of 1963 discontent with Diem's rule spread, not just among the peasantry, who had long been dissatisfied with his elitist regime, but also among ARVN officers and urban South Vietnamese. Critics were repelled by the repression and corruption Diem and his narrow family oligarchy tolerated. As the foundations of the government weakened, Diem and Nhu drew inward and became even more difficult to deal with. Diem had always been a merciless monologist, using his verbosity to punish subordinates or prevent American officials from asking unwelcome questions. He talked for hours, ignoring any attempt to interrupt him, convinced that since Americans knew so little about his country it was his duty to instruct them. While Diem held forth in the daytime, his brother Nhu held forth at night, lecturing American officials on the nature of Vietnamese society or the differences between East and West. On a hot, humid day in the spring of 1963, John Mecklin, the chief of the United States Information Service in South Vietnam, endured a two-and-a-half-hour monologue by Diem, who droned on, ignoring Mecklin's attempts to speak. Later Mecklin dreamed about a play in which an American diplomatic mission "gradually discovered that it had been dealing for years with a government of madmen, whose words were meaningless, where nothing that was supposed to have happened had really happened, yet there was no escape from continuing to try to deal with the madmen forever."[25] Mecklin's reaction may have been extreme, but it indicated that the circle of disillusionment was widening.

Now the optimism of high-level officials in Washington and Saigon began to be challenged, and not only by lower-level officials, but also by some American journalists. Young, energetic reporters such as Malcolm Browne, David Halberstam, and Neil Sheehan talked to skeptical Americans and South Vietnamese, sometimes even accompanying ARVN units on their operations, trying to learn more about the nature of the war. Especially after the battle of Ap Bac, their criticisms of ARVN and Diem's government grew stronger and their reports on the conflict increasingly diverged from the public statements of American and South Vietnamese officials.

The doubts of these reporters and of other Americans were reinforced by the eruption of the Buddhist crisis in the spring of 1963. Although a large majority of South Vietnamese were Buddhists, they found themselves ruled by Catholics, who composed only 10 percent of the population and remained tainted by their close collaboration with the French. In the old imperial city of Hué, where his brother Ngo Dinh Thuc was archbishop, preferential treatment of Catholics and discrimination against Buddhists led on May 8, 1963, to a bloody clash with local police in which eight demonstrators died. Outraged Buddhist leaders, led by the charismatic monk Thich Tri Quang, now publicly challenged the regime, demanding that it address Buddhist grievances. But Diem and Nhu regarded the Buddhists as just another sect, and they believed that concessions to them would further weaken the central government. Clearly they failed to see the gathering storm of the new Buddhist militancy.

Soon Buddhist leaders moved the struggle into Saigon, where further demonstrations culminated on June 11 in the self-immolation of a Buddhist monk in the center of the city. Associated Press correspondent Malcolm Browne, tipped off in advance of the protest, was present to photograph the elderly monk who, soaked with gasoline, lit the match himself and sat in the classic Buddhist attitude of prayer as the flames consumed him. Browne's photographs shocked Americans; they had no knowledge of the long traditions of protest in South Vietnam against unjust authority. But no one could miss the fact that the Buddhists had become a rallying point for all the discontents of urban South Vietnam against the Diem government. Even high school and university students joined in anti-government demonstrations in the spring and summer of 1963.

Reassessment in Washington

The Buddhist uprising caused worry and confusion among Kennedy and his inner circle of advisers. "Who are these people?" Kennedy impatiently asked an adviser. "Why didn't we know about them before?"[26] As American officials scrambled to learn about religion in South Vietnam and the significance of the Buddhist protests, they continued to differ sharply in their assessments of Diem and his regime. Senior military leaders, along with McNamara and Vice President Johnson, saw no alternative to Diem. The Director of the CIA, John McCone, agreed. As he told Kennedy: "Mr. President, if I was manager of a baseball team, I had only one pitcher, I'd keep him in the box whether he was a good pitcher or not."[27] But State Department officials, led by Undersecretary of State Harriman, argued that Diem was hopeless and that the U.S. government should encourage ARVN generals to organize a coup.

Confronted with so much conflicting advice, the president vacillated, unable to decide on a clear course of action. He wanted to get tougher with Diem and force reforms in his regime, but not necessarily to overthrow him. On August 22, 1963, with the arrival of Henry Cabot Lodge Jr. as the new American ambassador to the Republic of Vietnam, the administration, despite Kennedy's hesitations, moved closer toward support of a coup.

Lodge was no ordinary ambassador. A member of a prominent New England family, the tall, aloof patrician had entered the Senate in 1936, interrupted his political career to serve in World War II, and had returned to his Senate seat in Massachusetts, which he held until 1952, when he was defeated by Kennedy. Lodge had been one of the leading Republicans of the postwar era, managing Eisenhower's campaign for his party's nomination and serving as his ambassador to the United Nations. In 1960 Lodge had once again run against Kennedy, this time as Richard Nixon's vice presidential candidate. Lodge possessed great self-confidence and an independent political base.

The new ambassador arrived in Saigon convinced that the war could not be won so long as Diem stayed in power. He set out to commit the United States to a coup and undercut the opposition within the U.S. government. Raids by South Vietnamese forces on Buddhist pagodas throughout South Vietnam angered Lodge, who concluded, after his initial meetings with Diem and Nhu, that "They are essentially a medieval, Oriental despotism of the classic family type, who understand few, if any, of the arts of popular government. . . . They are interested in physical security and survival against any threat whatsoever—Communist or non-Communist."[28] After receiving a cable from Washington authorizing American support for a coup, Lodge directed Lucien Conein, a CIA operator and old Indochina hand, to get in touch with dissident ARVN generals. At the end of August Lodge reported to JFK that "we are launched on a course from which there is no *respectable* turning back: the overthrow of the Diem government."[29]

Kennedy was inclined to let the new ambassador in Saigon have his way, as long as he could guarantee the success of a coup. On September 2, 1963, in an interview with CBS news anchorman Walter Cronkite, the president sent his own warning to Diem and Nhu. "I don't think," Kennedy told Cronkite, "that unless a greater effort is made by the government to win popular support that the war can be won out there. In the final analysis, it is their war. They are the ones who have to win it or lose it. . . . And in my opinion, in the last two months, the government has gotten out of touch with the people."[30] A week later, in an interview with NBC anchormen Chet Huntley and David Brinkley, Kennedy reaffirmed the American commitment to South Vietnam. Asked if he believed in the domino theory in Southeast Asia, he replied, "China is so large, looms so high just beyond the frontiers, that if South Vietnam went, it would not only give them an improved geographic position for a guerrilla assault on Malaya, but would also give the impression that the wave of the future in Southeast Asia was China and the communists. So I believe it."[31]

As before, the president sought to resolve differences among his advisers by sending more fact-finding missions to South Vietnam. In early September he dispatched Marine General Victor H. Krulak and diplomat Joseph A. Mendenhall to Saigon. After spending thirty-six hours in South Vietnam, Krulak told the president that "the shooting war is still going ahead at an impressive pace. . . . The war will be won . . . irrespective of the grave defects in the ruling regime." In contrast, Mendenhall reported, "I was struck by the fear that pervades Saigon, Hué, and Da Nang. These cities have been living under a reign of terror. . . . Nhu must go if the war is to be won." An understandably frustrated Kennedy finally asked: "Did you two gentlemen visit the same country?"[32]

The second, and more important, mission to Saigon was led by McNamara and Taylor. After a ten-day stay, both men, while conceding that the political situation was "deeply serious," reassured Kennedy that "the military campaign has made great progress and continues to progress," and that by the end of 1965 the insurgency would be reduced "to little more than sporadic itching."[33] They urged the president to pull out 1,000 American advisers by the end of 1963, in order to demonstrate that victory was in sight. After a heated debate among his advisers, Kennedy agreed, and the White House announced the withdrawal of the 1,000 men.

The Fall of Diem

In October 1963 Diem's government organized a parade in the center of Saigon to commemorate his election to the presidency in 1955. After weeks of preparation, Diem watched impassively as troops marched by his reviewing stand. The entire area surrounding the reviewing stand, however, had been blocked off, so that the public was kept at a distance from its increasingly aloof and insecure ruler. As the crisis of political legitimacy in South Vietnam intensified, the U.S. government continued to distance itself from Diem, even applying selective economic sanctions. Diem and Nhu responded to Washington's coolness and the rumors of a military coup with several maneuvers. First, they sought to outwit, once again, dissident generals, faking a plot against the regime by neutralist forces within the military. Once order was restored and the real plotters were identified, they planned to murder some of their newly exposed military opponents as well as some of the American critics of their regime. Second, Diem and Nhu, offended by American encroachments on South Vietnamese sovereignty, actually reached out to leaders in Hanoi. Premier Pham Van Dong told the third party who relayed Nhu's overture: "Go and listen intently. One thing is sure: the Americans have to leave." Finally, while Nhu probed Hanoi's intentions, Diem sought to appease Ambassador Lodge, inviting him on a trip to Dalat and, on the morning of November 1, the day of the coup, giving him a message for Kennedy. "Please tell President Kennedy," Diem said, "that I am a good and frank ally. . . . Tell President Kennedy that I take all his suggestions very seriously and wish to carry them out but it is a question of timing."[34] Even as the end neared, Diem and Nhu tried to find some way out of the deepening crisis.

But the two brothers had run out of time; the weight of opinion in Washington had long since shifted against them. Kennedy and his senior officials were alarmed to learn of their overtures to Hanoi and angered by the possibility of betrayal. The depth of the administration's commitment to South Vietnam had been revealed earlier when Paul Kattenburg, a State Department expert on Vietnam, attended a meeting of presidential advisers. After listening for an hour, Kattenberg intervened, describing America's Vietnam policy as "a garden path to tragedy." "At this juncture," he continued, "it would be better for us to make the decision to get out honorably. . . . In from six months to a year, as the South Vietnamese people see we are losing the war, they will gradually go to the other side, and we will be obliged to leave." The president's advisers were shocked. "That's just your speculation," snapped Secretary of State Rusk. "We will not pull out of Vietnam until the war is won." Secretary of Defense McNamara observed: "We are winning the war"; Vice President Johnson agreed, arguing that "from both a practical and political viewpoint, it would be a disaster to pull out; that we should stop playing cops and robbers . . . and that we should go about winning the war once again."[35] Whatever the frailties of Diem's regime, most of the members of Kennedy's inner circle could not imagine a U.S. withdrawal from South Vietnam.

On November 1 the coup against Diem unfolded. As ARVN troops assaulted the presidential palace, Diem and Nhu discovered that friendly military units nearby were immobilized, unable to come to their rescue. They fled from the palace and ended up in a Catholic church in the Chinese section of Saigon, where they surrendered on the morning of November 2 to the coup leaders on the condition that they be given safe passage out of the country. Some of the ARVN generals, however, had no intention of allowing Diem and Nhu to survive, possibly maneuvering from abroad to undermine their new regime. With their hands tied behind their backs, they were shot and stabbed to death as they rode in the armored personnel carrier transporting them from the church to coup headquarters. Neither Ambassador Lodge nor Lucien Conein, who was with the generals at their headquarters and had a direct telephone line to the American embassy, had made more than a perfunctory effort to guarantee the safety of the president and his brother. In fact, Lodge was relieved by the turn of events. "What would we have done with them if they had lived?" he asked David Halberstam. "Every Colonel Blimp in the world would have made use of them." Lodge concluded that he had accomplished his mission to South Vietnam. "I believe prospects of victory," he cabled Washington, "are much improved."[36]

Reactions to the Coup

In many ways Diem was a poor ruler, but he was also a genuine patriot and nationalist, a leader of deep convictions with whom the United States had been allied since 1954. It made little sense to overthrow him unless U.S. policymakers were convinced a better alternative existed. "In my contacts here," Harkins reported to Washington shortly before the coup, "I have seen no one with the strength of character of Diem, at least in fighting communists. Certainly there are not [sic] Generals qualified to take over in my opinion." Or as Diem himself had warned, "I hope . . . that your government will take a realistic look at these young generals plotting to take my place. . . . I am afraid there are no George Washingtons among our military."[37] In fact, Kennedy and his senior advisers knew little about the military leaders with whom they now were involved, and they had no assurance that they could rule any better, or even as well as Diem. Tired of Diem's resistance to their constant advice, the American leaders turned to ARVN generals who would, they were convinced, be more pliable. For their part, the leaders in Hanoi were surprised that the United States had supported a coup that disrupted the South Vietnamese government. Reflecting on the event in early 1965, Mao Zedong told American journalist Edgar Snow that both he (Mao) and Ho Chi Minh "thought Ngo Dinh Diem was not so bad. . . . After all, following his assassination, was everything between Heaven and Earth more peaceful? . . . Diem had not wanted to take orders."[38]

Personally, Kennedy was shocked and saddened by the death of Diem and Nhu. "I had never," McNamara remembered, "seen him so moved."[39] The president had not realized where American involvement in the coup might lead, and now he worried about being drawn into an open-ended war. In the few weeks before his own assassination on November 22, Kennedy gave no sign of any major shift in

U.S. policy toward South Vietnam. The day before he left for Texas, he told a White House aide, Michael V. Forrestal, "to organize [early in 1964] an in-depth study of every possible option we've got in Vietnam, including how to get out of there. We have to review this whole thing from the bottom to the top."[40] It is not likely, however, that such a study would have altered the president's middle-of-the-road approach. Had Kennedy lived, he would have received recommendations from his senior advisers, who met in Honolulu on November 20, urging him to increase the level of military and economic aid to the new South Vietnamese government, stick by the earlier decision to withdraw 1,000 advisers by the end of the year, and conduct covert actions in North Vietnam.

In the years since his death, some of Kennedy's associates have speculated on what, had he lived and remained in the presidency, he would have done in South Vietnam. David F. Powers and Kenneth P. O'Donnell, close political advisers of the president, claim that Kennedy told them he planned to withdraw from Vietnam after his reelection, and Robert McNamara, who identified strongly with the president, thinks "it highly probable that . . . [Kennedy] would have pulled us out of Vietnam."[41] These efforts to defend Kennedy's historical reputation, however, ignore the fact that prior to his death he remained, as did his senior advisers, optimistic about progress in South Vietnam. Like most political leaders, John F. Kennedy was absorbed in the rush of events and did not anticipate difficult decisions he might never have to make. Historians only know what Kennedy did in South Vietnam, not what he might have done. Over the course of his less than three years in office, he greatly expanded American military and economic aid to the South Vietnamese government, increased the number of military advisers there from less than 700 to more than 16,000, and embraced the war both in private and in public, making it more difficult for his successor to walk away from it. Puzzled by the war in South Vietnam until the end, he sent one fact-finding mission after another, hoping that some combination of advisers would resolve his doubts. It is fitting that Kennedy's last instructions commissioned still another study on what he should do about Vietnam.

Notes

1 Quoted in Theodore C. Sorensen, *Kennedy* (New York, 1965), 178, 246–47.

2 Ibid., 248.

3 Quoted in Neil Sheehan, *A Bright Shining Lie: John Paul Vann and America in Vietnam* (New York, 1988), 58.

4 Quoted in Sorensen, *Kennedy,* 529–30.

5 Quoted in George C. Herring, *America's Longest War: The United States and Vietnam, 1950–1975* (New York, 1979), 74;   Robert S. McNamara, *In Retrospect: The Tragedy and Lessons of Vietnam* (New York, 1995), 39.

6 Quoted in William Conrad Gibbons, *The U.S. Government and the Vietnam War: Executive and Legislative Roles and Relationships, Part II, 1961–1964* (Princeton, N.J., 1986), 12.

7 Quoted in Robert Dallek, *Flawed Giant: Lyndon Johnson and His Times* (New York., 1998), 13.

8 Quoted in George McT. Kahin, *Intervention: How America Became Involved in Vietnam* (New York, 1986), 135.

9 Quoted in Richard Reeves, *President Kennedy: Profile of Power* (New York, 1993), 255.

10 Quoted in McT. Kahin, *Intervention,* 137.

11 Quoted in Gibbons, *The U.S. Government and the Vietnam War, II,* 90.

12 Quoted in Fredrik Logevall, *Choosing War: The Lost Chance for Peace and the Escalation of War in Vietnam* (Berkeley, Calif., 1999), 37.

13 Quoted in Deborah Shapley, *Promise and Power: The Life and Times of Robert McNamara* (Boston, 1993), 151; quoted in Sheehan, *A Bright Shining Lie,* 289–90.

14 Quoted in Stanley Karnow, *Vietnam: A History* (New York, 1991), 274.

15 Quoted in Sheehan, *A Bright Shining Lie,* 290.

16 Quoted in Reeves, *President Kennedy,* 443.

17 Quoted in Robert Dallek, *An Unfinished Life: John F. Kennedy, 1917–1963* (Boston, 2003), 666.

18 Quoted in Reeves, *President Kennedy,* 281.

19 Quoted in Sheehan, *A Bright Shining Lie,* 56.

20 Ibid., 277.

21 Ibid., 285.

22 Ibid., 307–08.

23 Ibid., 204.

24 Quoted in Reeves, *President Kennedy,* 448.

25 John Mecklin, *Mission in Torment: An Intimate Account of the U.S. Role in Vietnam* (New York, 1965), 205.

26 Quoted in Reeves, *President Kennedy,* 490.

27 Quoted in John Ranelagh, *The Agency: The Rise and Decline of the CIA* (New York, 1986), 435.

28 Quoted in Reeves, *President Kennedy,* 590.
29 Quoted in Anne E. Blair, *Lodge in Vietnam: A Patriot Abroad* (New Haven, Conn., 1995), 45.
30 Quoted in David Kaiser, *American Tragedy: Kennedy, Johnson, and the Origins of the Vietnam War* (Cambridge, Mass., 2000), 246.
31 Quoted in Robert Mann, *A Grand Delusion: America's Descent into Vietnam* (New York, 2001), 290.
32 Quoted in Reeves, *President Kennedy,* 595.
33 Quoted in Gibbons, *The U.S. Government and the Vietnam War, II,* 184; quoted in Howard Jones, *Death of a Generation: How the Assassination of Diem and JFK Prolonged the Vietnam War* (New York, 2003), 380.
34 Quoted in Ellen J. Hammer, *A Death in November: America in Vietnam, 1963* (New York, 1987), 223, 283.
35 Quoted in Reeves, *President Kennedy,* 576–77 and Gibbons, *The U.S. Government and the Vietnam War, II,* 161.
36 Quoted in Sheehan, *A Bright Shining Lie,* 371; quoted in Reeves, *President Kennedy,* 651.
37 Quoted in Reeves, *President Kennedy,* 642; quoted in Francis X. Winters, *The Year of the Hare: America in Vietnam, January 25, 1963–February 15, 1964* (Athens, Ga., 1997), 49.
38 Quoted in Hammer, *A Death in November,* 310.
39 McNamara, *In Retrospect,* 84.
40 Quoted in Dallek, *An Unfinished Life,* 685–86.
41 McNamara, *In Retrospect,* 96.

Top: Saigon, 1948.
Courtesy of the National Archives.
Middle: A French Foreign Legionnaire goes
to war in the Red River Delta, ca. 1954.
Courtesy of the National Archives.
ARC 541967.
Bottom: French Foreign Legion questioning
Viet Minh suspect, ca. 1954. Courtesy of the
National Archives. ARC 541969.

Opposite top: President Dwight D. Eisenhower and Secretary of State John Foster Dulles greet President Ngo Dinh Diem, 1957. Courtesy of the National Archives. ARC 542189.
Opposite bottom: John F. Kennedy gives a press conference on the situation in Laos, 1961. Courtesy of the National Archives.
Above: North Vietnamese leaders celebrate the twenty-first anniversary of North Vietnam, 1966. From left, Vo Nguyen Giap, Truong Chin, Le Duan, Ho Chi Minh, and Ton Doc Thang. AP/Wide World.

Top: Some of the first U.S. Marines arrive at a beach near Da Nang in South Vietnam, 1965. U.S. Marine Corps.
Bottom: Vietnamese refugee couple, 1965. Courtesy of the National Archives. ARC 532436.

Top: A Buddhist monk burns himself to death in protest against persecution of Buddhists by the South Vietnamese government, 1963. Photo by Malcolm Browne, AP/Wide World. Bottom: U.S.S. Maddox *on surveillance of the North Vietnam coast. The destroyer was attacked by North Vietnamese torpedo boats in 1964. U.S. Navy.*

North Vietnam's Ho Chi Minh (left) seeks support from China's Mao Zedong in Beijing in November 1964. Library of Congress. LC-U9-12776-4.

Top: LBJ with troops in Vietnam, 1966. Courtesy of the National Archives. ARC 542077.
Bottom: Secretary of Defense Robert McNamara (left) and General Westmoreland in conference with General Tee, 1965. Courtesy of the National Archives. ARC 532429.

Top: President Lyndon Johnson discusses Vietnam policy with Secretary of State Dean Rusk (left) and Secretary of Defense Robert McNamara (right) in July 1965. Courtesy Library of Congress, LC-U9-14278-8A.
Bottom: Chairman Nguyen Van Thieu, LBJ , and Prime Minister Nguyen Cao Ky during a ceremony, 1967. Courtesy of the National Archives. ARC 542079.

CHAPTER FOUR

The Transformation of the War, 1963–1965

On December 19, 1963, Secretary of Defense McNamara arrived at Saigon's Tan Son Nhut Airport to assess the situation in South Vietnam. On his previous journey in late September he had been optimistic; now he confirmed the bad news reaching Washington. The statistics on which he had based his earlier recommendation to withdraw military advisers were, he concluded, "grossly in error." The strategic hamlet program was in disarray, and the NLF's hold on the rural population was growing stronger. The new military junta that had replaced Diem, headed by General Duong Van Minh, was "indecisive and drifting." "Current trends," McNamara warned President Lyndon B. Johnson, "unless reversed in the next 2–3 months, will lead to neutralization at best and more likely to a Communist-controlled state."[1] His final recommendation was sobering: "We should watch the situation very carefully, running scared, hoping for the best, but preparing for more forceful moves if the situation does not show early signs of improvement."[2]

LBJ Settles In

In late 1963 South Vietnam was not one of President Johnson's top priorities. He knew the situation there was serious and the American commitment deep. As he told Ambassador Lodge, "I am not going to lose Vietnam. I am not going to be the President who saw Southeast Asia go the way China went."[3] But Johnson reasoned that he could temporize in South Vietnam while focusing on his ambitious domestic agenda. His mind was filled with plans for what, in the next year, he would term his "Great Society," a sweeping reform program that included a war on poverty, medical insurance for the elderly, civil rights legislation, and federal aid to education. LBJ would avoid making any big decisions on Vietnam until he had met many of the legislative goals of his Great Society and won reelection in November 1964.

The new president relied heavily on McNamara, as well as Kennedy's other senior advisers, to guide his foreign policy. As vice president, Johnson had traveled to South Vietnam and to many other nations, but he had been on the margins of foreign policy debates in the Kennedy administration and had only a shallow knowledge of the war in South Vietnam. In contrast to Kennedy, Johnson cared more about domestic than foreign affairs; he was, as one observer noted, "King of the river [but a] stranger to the open sea."[4]

Johnson was a sentimental patriot with conventional views of the Cold War. He accepted the domino theory, believed that the United States must combat communism around the world, and, during the 1950s, occasionally had criticized Truman and Eisenhower for not being aggressive enough in confronting Communist foes. But this master of domestic politics lacked a reflective, skeptical intellect and often felt insecure in dealing with foreign diplomats and foreign policy issues. "Foreigners," he told one aide, "are not like the folks I am used to." For all his intelligence and shrewdness, Johnson did not have an independent way of thinking about foreign policy and was, as one scholar notes, "culture-bound and vulnerable to cliches and stereotypes about world affairs."[5]

Despite these limitations, Johnson worked hard to master America's relations with its European allies, becoming an effective leader of the Atlantic Alliance and maneuvering skillfully within its multi-lateral structures. European issues and leaders, however, were relatively familiar; those in Southeast Asia were far more elusive. And no American president, from Truman through Nixon, had any good solution to the dilemmas presented by the war in Vietnam. As Johnson told his national security adviser McGeorge Bundy in May 1964, "I don't think it's [Vietnam] worth fighting for and I don't think that we can get out. It's just the biggest damned mess that I ever saw"[6]

Deterioration in South Vietnam

In late 1963 an American journalist drove south from Saigon into the Mekong Delta, where 40 percent of the South Vietnamese population lived. He visited Hoa Phu, one of the strategic hamlets build under Diem. It looked like "it had been hit by a hurricane," with its barbed wire fence torn apart and its watchtowers gone.[7] Only a few of its original one thousand residents remained. One night, the journalist learned, Viet Cong troops had entered the hamlet and told the peasants to leave. Lacking protection from government troops, and resentful of relocation from the start, they readily complied. Throughout the nation, what had once appeared as a highly successful program was, it turned out, only a shell, one that revealed the enormous gap between administrators in Saigon and peasants in the countryside.

The junta led by General Minh proved, if anything, less competent in ruling South Vietnam than Diem and Nhu. Minh and his colleagues expended much energy in shifting administrative positions, but they had no program to broaden the base of their government. Representing an older generation of South Vietnamese military leaders that identified with the French, they sensed the war weariness among the urban population and resisted a larger U.S. military presence or any greater American role in the direction of the war. At a time when many officials in Washington wanted deeper American involvement, Minh's group of generals contemplated a friendly competition with the NLF for political power.

The initial optimism of American leaders about the new regime in Saigon soon turned to fears of its flirtation with neutralism, and in January 1964 Washington encouraged a coup by a more compliant, pro-American faction within the South Vietnamese military. The new government of General Nguyen Khanh took power on January 30, 1964.

Khanh led a group of American-trained ARVN officers who were bitterly opposed to negotiations with the insurgents, favored an intensification of the war, and wanted more, not less, American involvement in South Vietnamese affairs. Khanh impressed Ambassador Lodge as more of an American-style professional soldier with modern administrative skills. Lodge praised him for "his eagerness to accept American advice and help" and urged him to give Fireside Chats to the Vietnamese people similar to those of President Franklin D. Roosevelt.[8]

The peak of American enthusiasm for Khanh's regime came in March 1964, when McNamara once again traveled to Saigon, in part to promote Khanh to his own people. Barnstorming on a tour arranged by the American Embassy, McNamara revealed his awkwardness as a campaigner, especially in the exotic world of South Vietnamese politics. American observers noticed his woodenness on the platform, while Vietnamese noticed his tin ear for their difficult tonal language. At one stop he used a Vietnamese phrase without the proper intonation, so that instead of saying "Long Live Vietnam," his Vietnamese audience understood him to say "Vietnam wants to lie down."[9]

Khanh, too, proved to be a disappointment. He and his allies in the military, more absorbed in political maneuvering than in running their nation, had no notion of how to unify their people or prosecute the war more effectively. Even as he was promoting Khanh, McNamara reported to Johnson that the situation had "unquestionably been growing worse" since his last trip.[10] Back in Washington, an exasperated Secretary of State Rusk asked: "Is there any way in which we can shake the main body of leadership by the scruff of the neck and insist that they put aside all bickering and lesser differences in order to concentrate upon the defeat of the Viet Cong?" "Somehow," Rusk concluded, "we must change the pace at which these people move and I suspect that this can only be done with a pervasive intrusion of Americans into their affairs."[11]

The View from Hanoi

As the generals squabbled in Saigon, Ho Chi Minh and his senior comrades plotted their future strategy in South Vietnam, arguing bitterly over what course to pursue. Some wished to escalate rapidly, others worried about provoking direct U.S. intervention. All realized that support for the NLF was strong but not overwhelming and calculated that the prospect for a rapid victory, as the balance of forces stood in late 1963 and early 1964, was remote. It seemed likely that Johnson would maintain the American commitment in South Vietnam and possibly send combat troops. How long, they wondered, could the Viet Cong deal with the challenge in the south alone?

In late 1963 the North Vietnamese government sent a small team of military specialists and civilian cadre south to assess the situation. The group traveled by foot down the Ho Chi Minh Trail, the network of jungle paths that threaded through southern Laos and northeastern Cambodia, spilling out at various points into South Vietnam. Even for experienced revolutionaries, the trip was an arduous one, as they walked through triple-canopy jungles and over mountain passes, plagued by malaria-bearing mosquitoes and leeches in ponds and dropping from branches. Since the areas traversed by the Ho Chi Minh trail were remote and contained few villages, the group had to carry most of what it needed for its survival—food, clothing, medicine—and sleep in jungle clearings. It took them five weeks to reach their destination in South Vietnam.

After studying NLF resources and leadership, these North Vietnamese experts returned to Hanoi with the conclusion that the southern revolutionaries could not achieve victory on their own—the deployment south of units of the North Vietnamese Army (NVA) was essential. After more debate, leaders in Hanoi accepted these recommendations and decided to reorder their economic and social priorities and mobilize the North Vietnamese population for an expanded conflict. They began to dispatch NVA units south, and by the end of the year 10,000 North Vietnamese troops were in South Vietnam assisting around 170,000 Viet Cong guerrillas. These North Vietnamese soldiers fused into the elite battalions of the Viet Cong, giving them additional fighting power and adding a new dimension to the struggle.

The North Vietnamese also decided to improve the Ho Chi Minh Trail, to add rest stations, build roads and bridges along certain segments, erect anti-aircraft defenses at points, and, in general, do whatever was necessary to speed the passage of men and arms into South Vietnam. Such improvements, however, took time, and early in the war the most efficient way to move heavy weapons and ammunition into the south was on ocean-going fishing trawlers. These 120-foot steel-hulled boats sailed from North Vietnam to night-time rendezvous points with guerrillas at any one of hundreds of small bays and river outlets along South Vietnam's 1,500 miles of coastline. There the Viet Cong would unload mortars and heavy machine guns, hiding them nearby until the need to use them arose.

As this buildup progressed, leaders in Hanoi planned to use NVA units along with greatly strengthened Viet Cong units to chew up the South Vietnamese army. As ARVN weakened and confusion mounted in South Vietnam, they hoped to foment a general uprising in the cities that would dissolve the government in Saigon and put in its place a neutralist regime—dominated by the NLF—that would throw out the United States. As General Giap proclaimed: "The stubborn U.S. imperialist warmongers do not [yet] accept the need to forsake their armed plot of intervention."[12]

Even with the progress at hand, all the factions in Hanoi agreed that an expanded war in the south would require assistance from China and the Soviet Union. The Sino-Soviet dispute, which had grown bitter by the early 1960s, had forced the North Vietnamese into a tense balancing act between their two allies, both of whom sought to draw North Vietnam into their orbit. Khruschev's overthrow in October 1964 and his replacement by a collective leadership headed by Leonid Brezhnev and Alexei Kosygin brought promises of increased military assistance; meanwhile Mao Zedong encouraged an aggressive strategy in South Vietnam. The Americans, Mao assured one North Vietnamese visitor, "do not want to fight a war" in Indochina. If, however, the United States did intervene more deeply in South Vietnam, Mao asserted that "our two parties and two countries must cooperate and fight the enemy together."[13] By the end of 1964 North Vietnam had assurances of support from both of its big allies.

The View from Washington

As 1964 progressed, officials in Washington realized that, despite Khanh's new government, the tide of battle was running against the United States in South Vietnam. Frustrated by the ineffectiveness of America's ally in Saigon, the Joint Chiefs of Staff (JCS) wished to take over the direction of the war and launch air strikes against North Vietnam, while civilians in the Defense Department pushed for the graduated use of force against North Vietnam and a congressional resolution supporting future military actions.

The president sent mixed signals to his advisers. On the one hand, Johnson wished to bend the conflict in South Vietnam to his will, pressing McNamara to come up with a plan to win the war, or, as he put it to his secretary of defense: "Let's get some more of something, my friend, because I'm going to have a heart attack if you don't get me something. . . . We're not getting it done. We're losing. So we need something new."[14] Still, Johnson wanted no major decisions until after the November 1964 elections. With bills pending in Congress and his own run for reelection nearing, he had no desire to stir up a public that seemed unconcerned about the war in Vietnam. In the spring of 1964 polls showed that 63 percent of the American people had given little or no attention to the fighting there, while 25 percent had heard nothing about the war.

Despite his caution, the president encouraged McNamara to reaffirm the administration's position and prepare the public for military intervention. At the end of March, McNamara described South Vietnam and Southeast Asia as having "great strategic significance in the forward defense of the United States." The war there was "a test case for the new Communist strategy"—wars of national liberation. Impatient with the deteriorating situation in South Vietnam, McNamara was becoming an enthusiastic proponent of greater American intervention. "Bit by bit," his biographer writes, "he became a believer in a cause."[15]

The administration's preparations for the long haul were revealed in June, when General William C. Westmoreland replaced Paul D. Harkins as the commander of American forces and General Maxwell D. Taylor replaced Henry Cabot Lodge Jr. as ambassador. Westmoreland, who had arrived in Saigon in January as Harkins's deputy, was widely regarded as one of the most talented generals in the U.S. Army. A tall, handsome graduate of West Point, Westmoreland had served with distinction in both World War II and Korea and seemed, both in appearance and attitude, the model professional soldier. While eager to take over his new command, he had no illusions about achieving rapid success: as he told the secretary of defense, "this is going to be a long war. . . . And its going to be a war that will try the patience of the American people."[16]

The second member of this formidable new team in Saigon was Maxwell Taylor, a soldier who had had a brilliant career, both in World War II and Korea and as Army Chief of Staff under President Eisenhower. Taylor had resigned in protest because of what he perceived as Eisenhower's neglect of conventional warfare, but he had become close to Kennedy, serving as his personal military adviser and chairman of the Joint Chiefs of Staff. Long involved with the war in South Vietnam, Taylor, like Westmoreland, appreciated fully the magnitude of the task before him. Soon after arriving in Saigon, he described Khanh's regime as an "ineffective government beset by inexperienced ministers who are also jealous and suspicious of each other."[17] As Taylor and Westmoreland began to reorganize the American effort in South Vietnam, Johnson and his advisers in Washington waited for the right moment to transform their plans into more decisive policies.

The Gulf of Tonkin Incident

Since the mid-1950s, the CIA had sent South Vietnamese commando teams into North Vietnam. These operations, designed to disrupt North Vietnamese society, had met with little success, and by early 1964 the U.S. government devised a new program to detect North Vietnamese coastal defense installations. South Vietnamese commandos were to harass enemy radar stations, thereby activating them so that American electronic intelligence vessels off the coast could chart their locations and frequencies. These so-called DeSoto missions were begun in the mid-summer of 1964, with the U.S. Navy destroyer *Maddox* eavesdropping along the coast, backed up by the aircraft carrier *Ticonderoga* at the entrance of the Gulf of Tonkin.

On August 2 the *Maddox* cruised about fifteen miles off the main-
land of North Vietnam. Two days earlier, South Vietnamese commandos had raided defense installations on North Vietnamese islands
nearby. Linking the presence of the *Maddox* with the South Vietnamese raids, the North Vietnamese decided to retaliate, sending out small
patrol boats to attack the *Maddox* . In the ensuing engagement, which
lasted no more than twenty minutes, the destroyer damaged two of
the North Vietnamese boats and sank a third. While Hanoi and Washington related different versions of the event, no one denied that a
serious clash had occurred.

Johnson and his senior advisers, preoccupied with the presidential campaign, were puzzled by North Vietnamese behavior and inclined to play down the incident. Convinced that North Vietnam would
not repeat such an attack, the president rejected retaliatory measures
but kept the *Ticonderoga*'s task force in the Gulf of Tonkin and dispatched a second destroyer, the *C. Turner Joy* to join the *Maddox*.
The two ships now maneuvered farther offshore, some sixty miles off
the North Vietnamese coast. Volatile summer weather conditions in
the Gulf of Tonkin distorted radar beams and caused sonar to mal-
function. On the evening of August 4, Captain John Herrick of the
Maddox, convinced that his and the other destroyer were under attack
by torpedo boats, ordered both ships to fire and engage in evasive
maneuvers. Only in the aftermath of the alleged firefight did Herrick
and his crew, along with the pilots who had been circling overhead in
jets at the time, have doubts about the whole incident. No one, they
realized, had actually seen a Communist patrol boat.

Even as Herrick sent his doubts up the chain of command, the
president, in no mood for a leisurely investigation of the incident and
worried about attacks from right-wing Republicans, declared that he
was "being tested" and ordered retaliatory air strikes against North
Vietnam. Then he immediately moved to push a resolution through
Congress. On August 5, American planes bombed North Vietnamese
patrol boat bases and an oil storage depot, and that evening the president appeared on television, justifying the first American bombing
mission against North Vietnam as a response to "repeated acts of violence against the armed forces of the United States."[18]

Although Johnson knew the facts surrounding the incident lay in
doubt, he cited it to get a resolution through Congress that would free

his hand militarily. With overwhelming support in the Senate and House, LBJ convinced the chair of the Senate Foreign Relations Committee, J. William Fulbright (Democrat, Arkansas), to push through the legislature what became known as the Gulf of Tonkin Resolution. Fulbright portrayed the resolution as a moderate measure, one "calculated to prevent the spread of war," and allayed the fears of liberal Democrats such as George S. McGovern (Democrat, South Dakota), assuring one of them that "the last thing we want to do is become involved in a land war in Asia."[19] On August 7 the Senate, with only two dissenting votes, and the House, by a unanimous vote, gave their support for all measures deemed necessary by the commander-in-chief to repel future attacks on the armed forces of the United States and endorsed whatever measures the president believed necessary to assist any member of SEATO that asked for help to defend its freedom.

Johnson was pleased. The Gulf of Tonkin Resolution, he remarked, was "like grandma's nightshirt—it covered everything."[20] But the president did not, in fact, view the resolution as a way in which to take the nation into a major undeclared war. Thinking in short-range terms, he saw it as a way to ensure the cooperation of Congress, deprive his Republican opponent in the upcoming election, Senator Barry M. Goldwater (Republican, Arizona), of the Vietnam War as a campaign issue, and show American resolve to leaders in Hanoi. So long as Vietnam remained an advisory war with few American casualties, the Congress and the American people gave the president great freedom of action.

The Campaign of 1964

In September and October Johnson concentrated on the presidential campaign. He portrayed himself as a prudent defender of national security, while painting Goldwater as a reckless war hawk. For his part, Goldwater, a conservative in domestic affairs and a hard-line anti-Communist in foreign affairs, made no attempt to move toward the center of the political spectrum. He made it clear that he wanted to bomb North Vietnam heavily and give the American military a free hand in prosecuting the war.

In contrast, Johnson told the voters that he was not "ready for American boys to do the fighting for Asian boys" and included the phrase "We seek no wider war" in many of his campaign speeches.[21] But the United States would also, he declared, not withdraw. His goal was to preserve South Vietnam's freedom and independence through limited American involvement. Come November LBJ won a landslide victory, as did Democrats in both houses of the Congress.

Although preoccupied with domestic politics, Johnson remained concerned about instability in South Vietnam—and uncertain what to do. In August Khanh's efforts to seize more power had provoked violent protests that revealed a widespread longing for peace. Now Johnson's choices seemed unappealing. No diplomatic solution seemed possible without strengthening the South Vietnamese government, but Johnson was wary of any escalation of the conflict. He rejected the advice of Senate majority leader Mike Mansfield and of the prominent journalist Walter Lippmann to pursue a negotiated settlement, but he also resisted pressure from hawks in the Congress and the military to bomb North Vietnam. In December Johnson admitted to Turner Catledge of the *New York Times* that "We are in bad shape in Vietnam. . . . Yet we can't afford to, and we will not, pull out."[22]

Despite his uncertainties, by the end of 1964 Johnson realized that the 23,000 military advisers in South Vietnam might not be enough. Indicating the direction of his thought, he cabled Ambassador Taylor that "I myself am ready to substantially increase the number of Americans in Vietnam if it is necessary to provide this kind of fighting force against the Viet Cong."[23]

America Steps Forward

In December 1964 the Viet Cong began an offensive throughout South Vietnam. Determined to expose the vulnerability of the Americans and their installations, it launched a series of terrorist attacks, ranging from the bombing of the Brinks Hotel in Saigon, which housed American officers, to an assault on the American air base at Pleiku that killed eight Americans and destroyed ten planes. After these dramatic initial successes, the Viet Cong regrouped, then in May 1965 resumed the attack, overrunning a provincial capital and raiding a government military headquarters. By June the Viet Cong had destroyed many of ARVN's elite battalions. South Vietnamese troops, fearful and demoralized, deserted in increased numbers, while ARVN officers became rattled, moving their mechanized forces up and down roads without troops on the point or the flanks: these units were ambushed and slaughtered with monotonous regularity. The Saigon government, close to panic, prepared to evacuate its five northern provinces. Without massive American intervention in 1965, the Republic of Vietnam would never have lived to see 1966.

In late January 1965, two of Johnson's most influential advisers, Bundy and McNamara, warned him that "our current policy can lead only to disastrous defeat. . . . The time has come for harder choices."[24] The president was finally ready to make them. In early February he sent Bundy to South Vietnam; during his stay there, the Viet Cong attack on the American airbase at Pleiku led the national security adviser to urge the bombing of North Vietnam. "Without new U.S. action," he warned, "defeat appears inevitable."[25] Johnson agreed, first authorizing retaliatory attacks against North Vietnam, then approving operation Rolling Thunder, the sustained bombing of that nation. Some of the president's advisers reasoned that Rolling Thunder would improve morale in Saigon; others believed it would slow the flow of men and supplies down the Ho Chi Minh trail; still others saw it as a way to force North Vietnam to the conference table on American terms. A bombing campaign in which targets were carefully selected, they argued, would allow the American government to dangle the prospect of stopping the bombing in return for political concessions. Whatever their rationale, most agreed that the time had come to attack the North Vietnamese directly from the air.

But not everyone in the administration supported the escalation, especially Vice President Hubert H. Humphrey, who sought to move policy in a different direction. In mid-February he gave the president a long memorandum, arguing against an escalation of the conflict. "The Public," Humphrey observed, "is worried and confused. . . . People can't understand why we would run grave risks to support a country which is totally unable to put its own house in order." Warning that an expanded war would bring steadily mounting domestic opposition, the vice president urged a settlement in 1965, "the year of

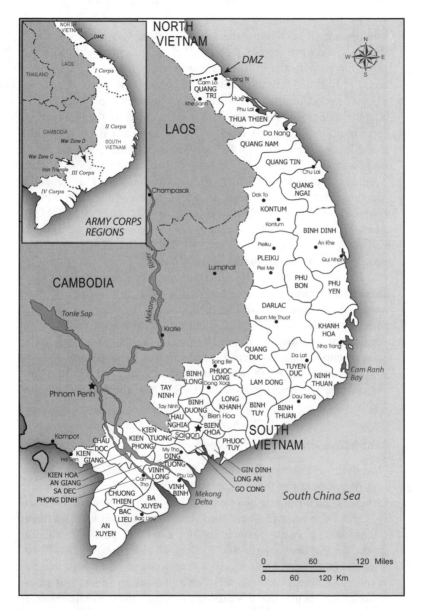

Provinces and Provincial Capitals

minimum political risk for the Johnson Administration. Indeed it is the first year when we can face the Vietnam problem without being preoccupied with the political repercussions from the Republican right."[26] Johnson, furious over what he perceived as a challenge from his vice president, banished Humphrey for several months from all Vietnam policy discussions and limited his access to the inner circle.

Humphrey's dissent hardly slowed the rush to war. Almost immediately, the bombing of North Vietnam caused General Westmoreland to worry about the security of American airfields in South Vietnam. At the end of February the president accepted the general's recommendation to use American troops to defend the airbase at Da Nang, a large city on the south-central coast. On March 8, 3,500 U.S. Marines landed at a nearby beach, where they were greeted by Vietnamese girls handing out garlands of flowers and holding a poster proclaiming "Welcome to the Gallant Marines."

Prime Minister Phan Huy Quat, who had been appointed by Khanh in a swirl of factional chaos, had hardly been consulted. Two days earlier, Ambassador Taylor had mentioned to the prime minister the imminent arrival of the Marines, but it was not until the day of the landing that an American diplomat arrived at his house to help draft a joint communiqué in Vietnamese and English. What became known, for better or worse, as the "Americanization" of the war left little time for consultation with the leaders of the nation the Americans were trying to save.

War Moves and Peace Moves

Despite these dramatic initiatives, the president still searched for a policy that held out the prospect for victory while convincing the Congress and the public that he knew what he was doing in Vietnam. He confided to his wife "Lady Bird" that "I can't get out. I can't finish it with what I have got. So what the Hell can I do?" In a more hopeful mood, he told one adviser that Rolling Thunder would push North Vietnam into a settlement within a year or a year and a half, that the bombing of North Vietnam was like a "filibuster—enormous resistance at first, then a steady whittling away, then Ho [Chi Minh] hurrying to get it over with."[27]

In early March the president expressed his frustrations in a conversation with Army Chief of Staff Harold K. Johnson, just before dispatching him on a special mission to Saigon. "Bomb, bomb, bomb," Johnson complained. "That's all you know. Well, I want to know why there's nothing else. You generals have all been educated at the taxpayers expense, and you're not giving me any ideas and any solutions for this damn little piss-ant country. Now, I don't need ten generals to come in here ten times and tell me to bomb. I want some solutions. I want some answers." As the general departed, the president, poking a finger at his chest, told him to "Get things bubbling, General."[28]

In retrospect, the president moved toward committing the United States to fight a limited war against an enemy that was totally dedicated to revolutionary war. The reasoning behind his escalation was the same as that of Kennedy and his advisers. Johnson viewed the war in South Vietnam as a test of American credibility and resoluteness, as a symbolic struggle of the Cold War. The loss of South Vietnam to communism would, he believed, have repercussions around the world. He also feared the domestic reaction to a defeat there, arguing that it would provoke a bitter debate over who was responsible for the triumph of communism. Johnson worried about attacks from the right, never anticipating that he would eventually be ambushed by those on the left of the political spectrum. Or as he told Undersecretary of State George W. Ball: "George, don't pay attention to what those little shits on the campuses do. The great beast is the reactionary elements in this country. Those are the people we have to fear."[29]

After leaving office LBJ revealed the intensity of these fears to his biographer Doris Kearns. Always envious of John and Robert Kennedy, Johnson remembered a dream in which Robert Kennedy would be "out in front leading the fight against me, telling everyone that I had betrayed John Kennedy's commitment to South Vietnam. That I had let a democracy fall into the hands of the Communists. That I was a coward. An unmanly man. A man without a spine. . . . Every night when I fell asleep I would see myself tied to the ground in the middle of a long, open space. In the distance, I could hear the voices of thousands of people. They were all shouting at me and running toward me: 'Coward! Traitor! Weakling!' They kept coming closer. They began throwing stones. At exactly that moment I would generally wake up . . . terribly shaken."[30]

Johnson also sincerely believed that the United States could do good in South Vietnam. It comforted him to view American involvement there as a way to help the Vietnamese people achieve a better life and help atone for the destruction of the war. The president spoke of a Mekong River project, similar to the Tennessee Valley Authority, part of an ambitious plan for the betterment of both Vietnams. He wanted to modernize Vietnamese society, to break down enclosures of mind and of spirit and to free the Vietnamese peasantry from the narrow confines of village life. The promise of America would become the promise of Vietnam, or, as Johnson phrased it, "I want to leave the footprints of America in Vietnam."[31]

As the first American ground troops moved into South Vietnam, the president decided to give a major speech at the Johns Hopkins University, one designed to answer critics of his policy, display the willingness of the American government to enter negotiations, and, finally, should his offer of "unconditional discussions" be turned down, lay the groundwork for public acceptance of further escalation of the war. Insisting that the United States had "a promise to keep" in South Vietnam, on April 7 Johnson declared: "We will not be defeated. We will not grow tired. We will not withdraw, either openly or under the cloak of a meaningless agreement."[32] Warning of the devastation war would bring, Johnson promised a billion-dollar plan to develop all of Vietnam, if only Hanoi would guarantee the independence of the south.

Johnson's domestic critics—though still few in number by this point—were not appeased by this speech; their criticism of the administration's foreign policy had been sharpened by his dispatch of Marines on April 28 to put down what he characterized as a Communist-led rebellion in the Dominican Republic. Most Americans, however, found the president's line of reasoning persuasive. The public's confidence in his leadership, and support for his policies in Vietnam, remained high.

The day after Johnson's Johns Hopkins speech, North Vietnamese premier Pham Van Dong responded, insisting that Hanoi would agree to peace talks only after the United States ended the bombing, unconditionally withdrew from Vietnam, and a coalition government—

one that included the NLF—had been formed in Saigon. By asking, in effect, for capitulation by the United States and its ally in Saigon, North Vietnamese leaders indicated they were not interested in engaging in serious peace negotiations. In fact, they preferred to wait for the outcome of their next offensive in the south and then reassess the balance of forces. In early May, when Washington decreed a brief bombing pause in order to explore Pham Van Dong's response, Ho Chi Minh denounced the pause as a "warn-out trick of deceit and threat."[33]

Nor was Washington prepared to engage in serious negotiations. Behind the vague proposals in Johnson's recent speech, American leaders had given little thought to the form or substance of possible negotiations or to the motivations of their enemy. Secretary of State Rusk, rather than explore differences between the leaders in Hanoi and those of the NLF, dismissed the southern organization as a puppet on a string and claimed that the war in the south was solely the result of aggression from the north. As the big American war grew near, the gap between the two sides remained enormous.

The Forty-Four Battalion Request

In early March, after the Marines had landed in Da Nang, the American war effort expanded inexorably. The Marines were soon allowed to leave their defensive positions and go on the offensive, while more American troops arrived to defend other bases. On June 7, with 82,000 American troops in South Vietnam, Westmoreland warned of the disintegration of ARVN and the collapse of the government in Saigon. He asked for an increase in American strength to 175,000 troops— 41,000 immediately and another 52,000 over the remainder of the year—for a total of forty-four battalions. He was eager for his forces to abandon their "defensive posture" and "take the war to the enemy." But he warned that "we must be prepared for a long war which will probably involve increasing numbers of U.S. troops."[34]

Westmoreland's request forced the president and his inner circle of advisers to concentrate intensively on the war in Vietnam. Confronted with a crucial decision—whether to plunge into a major war or accept a defeat—Johnson hesitated, determined to hear all points of view within the U.S. government. Throughout the remainder of June and into July, he consulted such a wide range of people that even his White House secretaries could not keep track of all the interviews and phone calls.

Two groups of skeptics questioned his policy of gradual escalation. Hard-liners within the administration, led by the Joint Chiefs of Staff and Secretary of Defense McNamara, wanted to go beyond Westmoreland's troop request. They proposed calling up the reserves and launching a massive offensive against North Vietnam, mining its harbors, bombing every installation of any military value, and cutting its rail and road links to China. Such a strategy, McNamara concluded, "stands a good chance of achieving an acceptable outcome within a reasonable time."[35]

Despite Johnson's admiration for McNamara, he was not about to go this far. Extreme measures against North Vietnam would arouse the public and the Congress and, worse still, might provoke China, Hanoi's close ally. China had aided the Viet Minh in its struggle against the French and by the summer of 1965 had a large advisory mission in North Vietnam comprising air defense, engineering, railroad, and other kinds of support troops. Mao, who viewed the United States as "the most ferocious enemy of the people of the world,"[36] sent warnings to Washington through a variety of channels that if the United States sought to destroy North Vietnam or to invade North Vietnam and China, Chinese forces would enter the conflict. Thus Johnson knew that it was essential to keep the war against North Vietnam below a well-defined threshold that would not provoke full-scale Chinese intervention.

The second group of skeptics opposed even moderate escalation of the war. Vice President Humphrey and three influential senators close to Johnson—Mike Mansfield, Richard B. Russell, and J. William Fulbright—all argued against the dispatch of ground combat troops and advocated a negotiated settlement. Their case was spelled out most forcefully by Undersecretary of State Ball, who saw the costs of a big American war clearly and urged Johnson to cut the nation's losses and pull out. Ball wrote that "politically, South Vietnam is a lost cause. . . . In a very real sense, South Vietnam is a country with an army and no government." He further argued that both the Viet Cong and the North Vietnamese were deeply committed, and that *"a deep commitment of United States forces in a land war in South Vietnam would be a catastrophic error. If ever there was an occasion for a tactical withdrawal, this is it."* "No one," he concluded, "has yet shown that American troops can win a jungle war against an invisible enemy." Ball concluded, "Every great captain in history was not afraid to make a tactical withdrawal if conditions were unfavorable to him."[37]

Johnson patiently listened to all his advisers, but he put the burden of proof on those who sought a way out of the war, not on those who wanted to move more deeply into it. The real question in his mind was not whether to put in more troops, but how many more and at what pace.

In the course of these deliberations, senior military leaders also sent the president a mixed message, one that even now is hard to read. Sometimes they offered pessimistic projections about the cost and length of the war. Marine Commandant Wallace M. Green and Army Chief of Staff Johnson estimated that the war would require half a million American troops and last five years. It is unlikely, however, that Johnson took their pessimistic views at face value. When he pressed military leaders, he got different answers; they responded with a firm, can-do attitude. When the president asked what North Vietnam would do if the United States escalated the war, General Green replied, "Nothing." General Earle G. Wheeler, chair of the JCS, believed the North Vietnamese would also escalate, but he insisted that logistical difficulties would prevent them from putting more than 25 percent of their 250,000-man army in South Vietnam and concluded that they "can't match us on a buildup." Wheeler even posited that a large-scale North Vietnamese intervention in South Vietnam would be a good thing because it would "allow us to cream them."[38]

The President's Decision

In July 1965 the president chose a middle course that did not require any rethinking of old assumptions and that was far easier to justify than a withdrawal or a massive attack on North Vietnam. As he summed up: "Withdrawal would be a disaster, a harsh bombing program would not win and could easily bring a wider war, and standing pat with

existing forces was only slow defeat."[39] While Johnson wavered between confidence in victory and fear of the unknown, he and most of
his advisers found it hard to believe that the United States was entering a long and protracted war. Throughout all the memoranda and
meetings of July, there runs a clear sense among most of the participants that American intervention would be decisive, if not in defeating the enemy outright then in quickly turning the tide of battle in
Saigon's favor. To most it seemed inconceivable that Vietnamese revolutionaries could withstand American power and technology.

Ultimately, neither pressure from the public, nor the media, nor
the Congress, nor the nation's allies forced Johnson to expand the
war: the American people remained apathetic about the conflict in
Vietnam, willing to follow the president's lead; some prominent col-
umnists and newspaper editors had already come out in print against
deeper involvement; in the Congress, many Democrats doubted the
wisdom of escalation but only a few of them were willing to break
publicly with the administration; and the nation's allies, while regret-
ting America's obsession with Vietnam, were all caught in an intricate web of relations with the United States, and their leaders, with
the exception of President Charles de Gaulle of France, were unwilling to take on Johnson over his policies in Vietnam.

Despite the lack of any clamor for war, the president did not seriously consider moving in a different direction. He felt the weight of
American history—the nation had never lost a war—as well as the
momentum of America's commitment to Vietnam, stretching back
through Kennedy, Eisenhower, and Truman. At the same time, he did
not understand the magnitude of the challenge in Vietnam, that
America's Vietnamese allies lacked staying power while its Vietnamese enemies would prove to be relentless, merciless foes. It would
have required an extraordinary leader to have foreseen the future and
taken the nation into the uncharted terrain of a negotiated settlement.

On July 28 Johnson held a press conference (at noon, when the
television audience was smallest) to announce that troop strength in
Vietnam would increase to 125,000 men, with more to be sent later.
While he noted that draft calls would have to increase, he refused to
mobilize reservists or to put the economy on a war footing. In effect,
Johnson told the public and the Congress as little as possible, hoping

that the war in Vietnam would be a brief one that would not require serious sacrifices.

The Generals Take Over

General Westmoreland, who set the ground strategy in South Vietnam, viewed the struggle in conventional terms: a war that required large-scale, big-unit operations and the use of tanks, helicopters, and heavy artillery. He planned to engage in search-and-destroy missions in the remote provinces of South Vietnam and inflict unacceptable casualties on Viet Cong and North Vietnamese forces, using American soldiers and technology to grind the enemy down. First he would deploy American troops to protect air and supply bases, thus halting the losing trend. Then he would gain the initiative and seek out major Viet Cong and NVA units. Finally, in the victory phase, he would destroy all such units and their base areas. He estimated that his plan would take about three and a half years to execute. Given the fact that the United States and its allies had defeated both Germany and Japan in World War II in three and a half years, this seemed to him, and others, a reasonable estimate.

Yet one American diplomat, Howard Simpson, perhaps jaded by his observation of the French war, could not believe his own ears as he sat through the press briefings of American officials. "I could have shut my eyes," he remembered, "and imagined myself sitting through a briefing at the French High Command in 1953. . . . I sensed a great, possibly dangerous gap between what was going on in the air-conditioned conference room and what I had known as the on-the-ground reality of Vietnam." General Westmoreland, he suspected, with his "Eagle Scout demeanor, his firm-jawed handsomeness, his by-the-book replies . . . had no real understanding of Vietnam."[40]

Initially Westmoreland's strategy carried the day. While Army Chief of Staff Johnson had doubts about his approach, Westmoreland was the commander in the field and had the confidence of General Wheeler. Like many of America's military leaders, the JCS chair viewed this war like all wars, as one of movement and attack, and he determined to meet the enemy head on. "No one," General Wheeler remarked, "ever won anything by remaining on the defensive."[41]

All of these American projections and calculations, however, continued to exclude the South Vietnamese. In mid-July, when McNamara and Wheeler traveled to South Vietnam, they met the new prime minister, Nguyen Cao Ky, the former head of the air force. Ky represented a faction within the military that had—with the support of American officials—overthrown Quat in June and assumed power. At a dinner the night of McNamara's and Wheeler's arrival, Ky made a striking impression. "He walked in," one American official remembered, "wearing a tight, white dinner jacket, tapered, formal trousers, pointed, patent leather shoes, and brilliant red socks. A Hollywood central casting bureau would have grabbed him for a role as a sax player in a second-rate Manila night club."[42] While amused by Ky's appearance, McNamara displayed little interest in assessing his abilities or in informing him about American policy. In a formal meeting the next day, the secretary of defense pursued his own agenda. "Precise but affable," Ky's special assistant recalled, "scribbling notes on a yellow pad as he went, he fired his questions about numbers, organization, management, and logistics as if he were bent on assembling all the factors and components for the solution of some grand mathematical equation." South Vietnamese officials learned little about American plans and objectives from the meeting. They could only assume that the Americans, who "came in like bulldozers," knew exactly what they were doing.[43]

The army that the United States deployed in Vietnam in 1965 and after was an impressive force. During the 1960s the U.S. armed services had been rebuilt and reequipped so that they could play a major role in the Kennedy administration's doctrine of flexible response. Much care and expense had been lavished on this task. Officers at all levels had faith in their anti-Communist mission and confidence in their weapons and combat skills. Philip Caputo, a young Marine lieutenant at the time, recalled that when he and his buddies splashed ashore at Da Nang in March 1965, "we carried, along with our packs and rifles, the implicit conviction that the Viet Cong would be quickly beaten and that we were doing something altogether noble and good."[44]

One example of this new American army was the First Cavalry Division, the "Air Cav.," which arrived in South Vietnam in mid-September 1965. It was the first military organization in history to take full advantage of the helicopter—both as a vehicle to transport troops and weapons to and from almost any battle site and to bring firepower to bear on the enemy. The First Cavalry brought with it to Vietnam 435 helicopters—transports, gunships, and large cargo carriers—and the ability to penetrate even remote enemy sanctuaries. But the First Cavalry Division, like all units in the American army, had been organized on the assumption that, in the event of a major war, reserve units would be called up. Therefore, it went to Vietnam under-strength; in a long war, Chief of Staff Johnson worried, the quality of the American army might quickly erode.

In late August 1965 the first phase of the big American war began in earnest with a drive on the central coast near Quang Ngai. There the Marines assaulted a Viet Cong regiment that occupied a series of fortified hamlets, bringing enormous firepower to bear on the enemy. On the second day of the battle, the enemy forces slipped away. Nevertheless, the Marines were amazed at the stamina of their new enemy. As one Marine general, a veteran of Saipan and Iwo Jima, remarked: "I thought that once they ran up against our first team they wouldn't stand and fight. I made a miscalculation."[45]

Battle of the Ia Drang Valley

The next major encounter extended from October 19 to November 26, when elements of the Air Cav engaged NVA troops in and around the Ia Drang Valley, a rugged, remote area in the Central Highlands near the Cambodian border: it was the first clash between American and North Vietnamese troops. Like the battle of Ap Bac, it was an illuminating event that foreshadowed the future.

The Ia Drang Valley was a sanctuary for Communist forces, one that had never been penetrated by the French or ARVN. In November 1965 about 1,700 NVA troops were resting and regrouping on the Chu Pong massif at the southern end of the valley. Their commanders knew that the lessons they had learned fighting the French were dated, and they expected an American assault. But they welcomed the coming battle, for they knew that they needed to learn how to fight the Americans—to search for flaws in their thinking and their fancy machines—if they were to teach their men how to kill them.

U.S. Army intelligence located an enemy base camp somewhere in the Ia Drang Valley, and the leaders of the First Cavalry Division were determined to find it and engage the enemy. On the morning of November 14 Colonel Harold G. Moore's First Battalion, Seventh Cavalry, consisting of 450 men, landed a few hundred yards from the main enemy force at landing zone X-Ray. Only a few hours after the first helicopter had landed, the NVA attacked the small perimeter surrounding X-Ray. Expecting a quick assault, Moore had lined up his fire support and sent out patrols to disrupt advancing enemy units. Troops were quickly engaged at close quarters, and during the first day of fighting the situation of Moore's battalion grew precarious. At dawn on the second day of the battle, the NVA launched a human-wave assault; on the morning of the third day, it launched another. By the late morning of November 16 the battlefield was littered with enemy dead and the struggle for landing zone X-Ray was over. In this case, North Vietnamese soldiers had died in large numbers because they had attacked an exceptionally well-led American unit without the assistance of heavy weapons. Even so, Colonel Moore's battalion had survived a close call.

The battle of the Ia Drang Valley, however, had not yet ended. When Moore's battalion pulled out, two fresh battalions replaced it. On November 17 these men left X-Ray on foot, then split up, each marching to a different landing zone where helicopters were to pick them up. One of the two battalions, that led by Colonel Robert McDade, moved toward landing zone Albany. McDade, who had far less combat experience than Moore, allowed his officers and men to relax, and they gradually became strung out in a long column, without any security on the flanks, as they moved through terrain covered with brush, thick scrub trees, and chest-high elephant grass. Worse still, mid-day on November 17, after having captured several NVA soldiers, McDade halted the column for half an hour while his company commanders joined him in a conference. It was the last of a series of fatal mistakes.

McDade's battalion had walked right into a classic U-shaped ambush; while his troops were relaxing, strung out in elephant grass and trees, the NVA struck. For the next sixteen hours the most savage one-day battle of the Vietnam War was fought. As the NVA cut through the battalion's column, American troops formed small perimeters at the front and rear while the center collapsed and degenerated into hand-to-hand fighting. During the night, troops in the two perimeters could hear wounded American soldiers crying out for help as North Vietnamese moved through the elephant grass, methodically killing them. When dawn came and reinforcements arrived, the NVA had withdrawn and the carnage on the battlefield made it clear that both sides had paid dearly. The Second Battalion of the Seventh Cavalry had been decimated: of its 450 men, 155 had been killed and 124 wounded.

The reactions to the battle on both sides were revealing. McNamara, visiting South Vietnam shortly after it had ended, was briefed on Ia Drang by Colonel Moore, who conveyed a vivid picture of North Vietnamese soldiers boiling down off the Chu Pong massif in the kind of human-wave assault American officers had not seen since the Korean War. McNamara was shaken by what he heard of the Battle of the Ia Drang Valley, which dashed his illusions of a quick American victory. He now knew that the Vietnam War had exploded into an open-ended conflict with no end in sight. "It will be," McNamara told reporters, "a long war."[46]

In contrast, General Westmoreland believed that the battle confirmed his strategy of attrition. American forces had engaged the enemy and had won, with a favorable kill ratio of twelve to one. A general with more imagination than Westmoreland, however, might have realized that sending American units into remote areas of South Vietnam to run down the NVA was a questionable strategy. Even if American forces prevailed, the American people, once they became aware of the scale of the fighting, might not equate the lives of their boys with those of the enemy. In short, a strategy of attrition was sure to become controversial if the big American war also became a big long war.

North Vietnamese leaders—while pleased with the performance of their troops—were amazed at the mobility and firepower of the American army. As one officer recalled years later, "When the Americans entered the war, we spent all our time trying to figure out how to fight you. . . . [We] talked about it constantly. It was a matter of life and death. The incredible density of your shelling and your mobility were our biggest concerns. . . . Our losses were huge. We had to admit you had a terrible strength. So how could we preserve our forces, but still engage you?"[47] The heavy loses at the Ia Drang Valley deepened divisions over the appropriate strategy in the South. Some commanders favored more set-piece battles, others protracted guerrilla warfare. But all were confident that in time they could wear down the American army and exhaust the patience of the American people.

At the end of 1965, leaders on both sides underestimated the determination and staying power of the other. Rather than admit that the war was becoming a stalemate, they persisted in the belief that, if only they put more pressure on their foe, somehow victory would be achieved.

Notes

1 Quoted in Deborah Shapley, *Promise and Power: The Life and Times of Robert McNamara* (Boston, 1993), 293.

2 Quoted in Stanley Karnow, *Vietnam: A History* (New York, 1991), 341.

3 Quoted in Robert Dallek, *Flawed Giant: Lyndon Johnson and His Times, 1961–1973* (New York, 1998), 99.

4 Quoted in Waldo Heinrichs, "Lyndon B. Johnson: Change and Continuity," in Warren I. Cohen and Nancy Bernkopf Tucker, eds., *Lyndon Johnson Confronts the World: American Foreign Policy, 1963–1968* (New York., 1994), 26.

5 Quoted in Fredrik Logevall, *Choosing War: The Lost Chance for Peace and the Escalation of War in Vietnam* (Berkeley, Calif., 1999), 79; Heinrichs, "Lyndon B. Johnson," in Cohen and Tucker, eds., *Lyndon Johnson Confronts the World,* 26.

6 Quoted in Michael R. Beschloss, ed., *Taking Charge: The White House Tapes, 1963–1964* (New York, 1997), 370.

7 Karnow, *Vietnam,* 339.

8 Quoted in George McT. Kahin, *Intervention: How America Became Involved in Vietnam* (New York, 1986), 205.

9 Bui Diem with David Chanoff, *In the Jaws of History* (Boston, 1987), 115.

10 Quoted in Karnow, *Vietnam,* 357.

11 Quoted in William Conrad Gibbons, *The U.S. Government and the Vietnam War: Executive and Legislative Roles and Relationships, Part II., 1961–1964* (Princeton, N.J., 1986), 253–54.

12 Quoted in Cecil B. Currey, *Victory at Any Cost: The Genius of Viet Nam's Gen. Vo Nguyen Giap* (Washington, D.C., 1997), 245.

13 Quoted in William J. Duiker, *Ho Chi Minh* (New York., 2000), 541; quoted in Qiang Zhai, *China and the Vietnam Wars, 1950–1975* (Chapel Hill, N.C., 2000), 131.

14 Quoted in Bechloss, *Taking Charge,* 338.

15 Quoted in Dallek, *Flawed Giant,* 104; Shapley, *Promise and Power,* 303.

16 Quoted in Samuel Zaffiri, *Westmoreland: A Biography of General William C. Westmoreland* (New York, 1994), 114.

17 Quoted in Karnow, *Vietnam,* 363.

18 Ibid., 387–88.

19 Ibid., 392.

20 Quoted in Dallek, *Flawed Giant,* 154.

21 Ibid., 154.

22 Ibid., 245–46.

23 Quoted in Gibbons, *The U.S. Government and the Vietnam War, II.,* 383.

24 Quoted in Gibbons, *The U.S. Government and the Vietnam War: Executive and Legislative Roles and Relationships, Part III., January–July 1965* (Princeton, N.J., 1989), 47–48.

25 Quoted in Kai Bird, *The Color of Truth: McGeorge Bundy and William Bundy: Brothers in Arms, A Biography* (New York, 1998), 307.

26 Quoted in Gibbons, *The U.S. Government and the Vietnam War, III.,* 94–95.

27 Quoted in Dallek, *Flawed Giant,* 255, 257.

28 Quoted in David Halberstam, *The Best and the Brightest* (New York, 1972), 564; quoted in Gibbons, *The U.S. Government and the Vietnam War, III.,* 149.

29 Quoted in Clark Clifford, *Counsel to the President: A Memoir* (New York, 1991), 417.

30 Quoted in Doris Kearns, *Lyndon Johnson and the American Dream* (New York, 1976), 253.

31 Ibid., 267.

32 Quoted in Dallek, *Flawed Giant,* 260–61.

33 Quoted in Robert K. Brigham, *Guerrilla Diplomacy: The NLF's Foreign Relations and the Viet Nam War* (Ithaca, N.Y., 1999), 45.

34 William C. Westmoreland, *A Soldier Reports* (New York, 1976), 181.

35 Robert S. McNamara, *In Retrospect: The Tragedy and Lessons of Vietnam* (New York, 1995), 204.

36 Quoted in Zhai, *China and the Vietnam Wars,* 140.

37 Quoted in Larry Berman, *Planning a Tragedy: The Americanization of the War in Vietnam* (New York, 1982), 86–87, 109.

38 Quoted in George C. Herring, *LBJ and Vietnam: A Different Kind of War* (Austin, Tex., 1994), 35.

39 Quoted in Dallek, *Flawed Giant,* 275.

40 Howard R. Simpson, *Tiger in the Barbed Wire, An American in Vietnam, 1952–1991* (New York, 1992), 186, 228.

41 Quoted in Herring, *LBJ and Vietnam,* 42.

42 Chester L. Cooper, *The Lost Crusade: America in Vietnam* (New Yorks, 1970), 281.

43 Bui Diem, *In the Jaws of History,* 152–53.

44 Philip Caputo, *A Rumor of War* (New York, 1977), xii.

45 Quoted in Neil Sheehan, *A Bright Shining Lie: John Paul Vann and America in Vietnam* (New York, 1988), 537.

46 Quoted in Harold G. Moore and Joseph L. Galloway, *We Were Soldiers Once . . . and Young: Ia Drang, The Battle that Changed the War in Vietnam* (New York, 1992), 339.

47 Quoted in Currey, *Victory at Any Cost,* 256–57.

CHAPTER FIVE

The Stalemated War, 1965–1967

On November 2, 1965, in a garden near the Pentagon, within sight of Secretary of Defense McNamara's office, a thirty-one-year old pacifist Quaker from Baltimore, Norman Morrison, soaked himself with gasoline, set his infant daughter aside, and burned himself to death. Earlier he had asked his wife: "What will it take to stop this war?"[1] As he prayed to God the answer came to him. His self-immolation was a principled act of protest against the war, a sign of the way in which the conflict would touch Americans in mysterious and unforeseen ways.

Early on President Johnson sensed that he would have trouble explaining this war to the American people. In mid-1965 the government produced a film entitled *Why Viet-Nam,* which opened with Johnson reading a letter from a midwestern woman asking why her son was in Vietnam. He responded by asking questions of his own. "Why must young Americans, born into a land exultant with hope and with golden promise, toil and suffer and sometimes die in such a remote and distant place?" "The answer," the president concluded, "like the war itself, is not an easy one."[2] As the film progressed the narrator attempted to answer this question, explaining the war as an effort to honor America's commitment to the government of South Vietnam and prevent communism from spreading into all of Southeast Asia. But these explanations failed to satisfy many Americans, and questions about the purpose of the war would not go away.

Preparing for a Long War

As 1965 drew to a close it seemed as if the war in Vietnam was going well. In South Vietnam the influx of American troops had saved the government from collapse; in the United States both the media and the public supported the Johnson administration's escalation of the conflict. At the end of the year, two-thirds of the public approved the president's handling of the war, while his personal approval rating soared at 64 percent. For the third year in a row Americans chose LBJ as the most admired man in the world.

The assessments of the president's advisers, however, were sobering. The Joint Chiefs of Staff wanted an additional 113,000 troops sent to South Vietnam, so that General Westmoreland could shift more rapidly to the offensive, and also urged an intensified bombing of North Vietnam and the blockading and mining of its principal ports. As JCS chair General Wheeler warned, unless the United States began "using our principal strengths—air and naval power— . . . we would risk becoming involved in another protracted Asian ground war with no definitive solution."[3] McNamara was even gloomier. A few months earlier the secretary of defense had been a zealous manager, gearing up the machinery of war with pride and boasting that "we moved 100,000 men 10,000 miles in 100 days."[4] But his visit to Saigon at the end of November, during which he had been briefed on the nightmare at Ia Drang, impressed him with the savageness of the fighting. Even with substantial increases in troop strength, McNamara predicted that the war would remain stalemated at a higher level of violence into 1967. Convinced that a military solution was unlikely, he now pondered a diplomatic or political one and urged an extended bombing pause, reasoning that Hanoi might respond positively to such a signal, thus breaking the cycle of military escalation. "Then, no matter what we do in the military field," the president asked his secretary of defense, "there is no sure victory?" "That's right," McNamara replied, "We have been too optimistic."[5]

Despite the objections of most of his advisers, on December 27 Johnson accepted a bombing pause. He had little hope, however, that it would bring a negotiated end to the conflict. Peace would come, Johnson believed, only after a sustained military effort; he viewed a bombing pause as a way to appease domestic critics of the war and prepare the public for a longer conflict. "We don't have much confidence," he told one adviser, "that much will come out of this but that is no reason not to try." The day after he made the decision, Johnson launched a "peace offensive," sending personal envoys abroad to explain the U.S. position on the war to 115 governments. While the administration did not, in fact, have a plausible plan for a negotiated end to the fighting, Johnson was determined to seize the high ground in his contest with leaders in Hanoi. The president, Secretary of State Rusk explained to Ambassador Lodge, "is now gathering his political forces at home and abroad. Indeed, if I were a leader in Hanoi and not prepared for peace, I would be a very worried man."[6]

Signs of Discontent

By early 1966 most Americans still supported the war, but as casualties mounted (1,639 U.S. soldiers had been killed in action, 4,091 wounded) signs of discontent were beginning to appear. On college campuses in the United States some young people, frightened by the draft and angry over Johnson's policies in Vietnam, had joined the Students for a Democratic Society (SDS)—the leading campus-based antiwar organization—and had begun protesting against the war. Even in Congress, where the administration still enjoyed overwhelming support, doubts about the wisdom of American policies were growing. On January 31 when Johnson announced the resumption of the bombing of North Vietnam, Senator Robert F. Kennedy (Democrat, New York) denounced the decision, while a few days later Senator J. William Fulbright's Foreign Relations Committee began nationally televised hearings on the conflict in Vietnam. The gavel-to-gavel coverage allowed the public for the first time to hear national leaders debate the war. Rusk and Taylor defended the administration's record in

Vietnam, while General James M. Gavin presented the case for an enclave strategy and George F. Kennan, the father of the containment policy, warned that America's intervention in Vietnam should be liquidated "as soon as this could be done without inordinate damage to our prestige or stability in the area." While the hearings did not have a decisive impact on public opinion, they gave a new respectability to efforts to question the war.[7]

Johnson realized, as he told his staff, that "the weakest link in our armor is American public opinion. Our people won't stand firm in the face of heavy losses, and they can bring down the government."[8] Initially he was tolerant of opponents of the war, but by the time of the Fulbright hearings he viewed critics with disdain—as dupes of Communist propaganda—and combated their attacks by any means at his command. In order to distract the nation from the Fulbright hearings, he scheduled a conference in Honolulu between American and South Vietnamese leaders. At this meeting Prime Minister Ky, aware of Johnson's desire for social reform and democracy in South Vietnam, called for sweeping changes in his nation. The final communiqué of the conference, "The Declaration of Honolulu," echoed the president's insistence on "building a society" in South Vietnam. The United States and South Vietnam were not only waging a war against Communist aggression, but they stood united in the mission to establish a "free self-government, the attack on hunger, ignorance, and disease, and the unending quest for peace."[9]

Now Johnson and his senior advisers had committed their personal prestige and that of their nation to the war in Vietnam. Whatever private doubts they harbored, they felt that they must see the war through to a successful conclusion. As Johnson's biographer writes, "They had come too far to turn back."[10]

Westmoreland's War

When General Westmoreland first arrived in Saigon in late January 1964, the charm of the city impressed him: the wide, tree-shaded boulevards, the bougainvillea climbing the walls of pastel-colored villas, the slender, black-haired Vietnamese women dressed in their traditional *ao dais* (a close-fitting tunic with long panels at the front and back which is worn over loose black or white trousers) riding on bicycles, all of it suggesting a curious mingling of French and Vietnamese cultures. Evidence of the war was, to be sure, revealed everywhere, whether in the coils of barbed wire on the walls of important villas, the chicken-wire fencing protecting sidewalk cafes against the shrapnel of grenade blasts, the presence of armed soldiers guarding bridges and the entrances of government buildings, or the prostitutes walking the streets in skin-tight jeans and see-through blouses. Still, for the capital of a nation at war, Saigon had a lethargic quality. South Vietnamese officials took long lunch breaks and seemingly ignored the war on weekends and holidays. Despite a Viet Cong campaign of terror against Americans in the capital, Westmoreland took up temporary residence in a downtown hotel. Soon his wife and two children would join him (in February 1965 the dependents of U.S. servicemen were ordered home).

As Westmoreland traveled throughout South Vietnam, he was struck by the nation's social fragmentation and lack of development. It had only one major north-south road and few major roads that ran the width of the country, while its principal railroad was a narrow-gauge, single-track line. Its communication grid was dated. Its only major port, Saigon, was connected to the ocean by the Saigon River, and it had only one reasonably modern airport. The entire infrastructure was in poor condition.

American troops and supplies poured into South Vietnam so fast that Westmoreland's command struggled to provide the essential logistical infrastructure. In 1965, 1966, and 1967 army engineers and private contractors constructed four new jet air bases, four central supply and maintenance depots, six new deep-water ports, twenty-six permanent base camps, twenty-six hospitals, seventy-five new tactical airfields, a modern telephone and teletype network, and a new, two story, air-conditioned headquarters near Tan Son Nhut Airport for the four thousand people working in MACV. Many of the base camps were like small cities, filled with amenities seldom seen in earlier wars—solidly build barracks, hot-water showers and flush toilets, and air-conditioned trailers for more senior officers. Given the nature of the American military machine, much of this was essential, but never before had the nation fought such an affluent war.

The so-called Americanization of the war transformed South Vietnam. An American diplomat found that Saigon had changed rapidly

from a "sleepy colonial capital . . . [to] a crowded, dirty wartime me-
tropolis," surrounded by slums (as peasants migrated from the countryside) and filled with beggars. Hundreds of thousands of South Vietnamese served the rich foreigners, as prostitutes, domestic help, or
construction workers. Well-connected South Vietnamese profited in
other ways, managing businesses that catered to Americans, controlling the burgeoning narcotics trade, taking bribes for construction
permits, or siphoning into the black market some of the American-
financed commodities that flooded the nation. "The Vietnamese of
the South," one historian notes, "found themselves in a world turned
upside down,"[11] one in which old traditions were challenged by the
new American war.

Westmoreland knew that, if he was to prevent the collapse of
South Vietnam, he had no choice but to deploy American troops rapidly and to press ahead full steam with his operations. By early 1966
what he called the fire-brigade phase of the war had ended and he
shifted American forces into phase two of his campaign—an attempt
to gain control of certain high-priority areas through large-scale search-
and-destroy operations. In 1966 Westmoreland focused on the area
around Saigon, where the enemy had constructed massive base areas
(including elaborate networks of tunnels), on the coastal lowlands
running north from Binh Dinh Province—a rich rice-growing area
that fed many hostile troops—and on northern I Corps, where Westmoreland worried that the NVA and VC might try to capture Hué, the
old imperial capital.

Strategy of Attrition

At the Honolulu Conference in early February the president and his
key advisers formally approved Westmoreland's strategy of attrition.
In a memorandum outlining his mission for 1966, McNamara and
Rusk gave the general ambitious goals—to "Attrit [sic], by years end,
Viet Cong and North Vietnamese forces at a rate as high as their capability to put men into the field [and to] increase the percentage of VC
and NVA base areas denied the VC from 10–20% to 40–50%."[12] But,
for his part, the president seemed tense and uncertain how to proceed.
"General," he told his commander in the field, "I have a lot riding on
you." And he pressed Westmoreland without success to predict how

long the war would last. At his Honolulu press conference, Westmoreland warned that "the nature of the enemy is such, that we cannot expect him to be defeated by a single battle or series of battles. He will have to be ferreted out over a period of time, which will involve many campaigns, many operations."[13]

Given the restrictions placed on his forces, Westmoreland felt that he had no alternative but to pursue a strategy of attrition. He could not attack North Vietnam, invade sanctuaries in Laos or Cambodia, or position American troops all along the lengthy borders of South Vietnam. His only choice, he believed, was to seek out enemy units and to inflict heavy casualties on them, "until Hanoi wakes up to the fact that they have bled their country to the point of national disaster for generations."[14]

Westmoreland did not believe that his war of attrition would bring a clear-cut American victory in the field. Rather, it would damage NVA and VC forces so badly that ARVN would gain time to become an effective fighting force and pacify much of the South Vietnamese countryside. Or, as General Wheeler defined his vision of victory, the United States would prove to "the Communists that they cannot win."[15]

Whatever the rationale for Westmoreland's strategy, it soon collided with the peculiar nature of the Vietnam War. The only measure of progress, the body count, was difficult to apply, since enemy troops generally removed their dead from the battlefield. Nor did Westmoreland's command have any sure way to measure the combat strength or determine the location of enemy forces. They were a blend of main force NVA and VC units and of an elaborate guerrilla organization in South Vietnam, one that included women and children. In short, American military power fit poorly with the war being waged in Vietnam. The American army, designed for conventional warfare, had powerful battalions supported by air and artillery and an elaborate logistical apparatus. As military experts phrased it, these battalions had a "big tail, sharp teeth." If American forces were to prevail, they had to "find, fix, fight, and finish" their opponents.[16] But finding enemy forces was extremely difficult; and it was not much easier, once having found the enemy, to pin them in place long enough to destroy them with superior American firepower. Many large enemy units operated near the Demilitarized Zone (DMZ) between North and South Vietnam, or near Laos or Cambodia so that, when attacked, they could slip across these borders to safety. Given the elaborate preparations required for American search-and-destroy operations, Communist commanders usually knew when their base areas within South Vietnam would be assaulted. They often chose not to defend such places, or to initiate combat on terms that seemed more favorable to their style of warfare.

Westmoreland's war of attrition did, however, bring certain positive results. It gave the American army the tactical initiative, disrupted base areas, drove enemy troops away from population centers, and, for all of its imprecision, inflicted heavy casualties on main force units. Nevertheless, Westmoreland's forces could not drive the NVA and VC from the field.

America's Enemy

As leaders in Hanoi escalated the war in South Vietnam, they sent more and more troops down the Ho Chi Minh Trail. North Vietnamese soldiers, in their pith helmets and green uniforms, became a familiar sight to American troops, who quickly learned to distinguish them from local guerrillas. The NVA was a formidable enemy, well led and well trained. Moving largely at night, it excelled at defense, at masking its true position, and at executing a wide variety of carefully concealed ambushes. The NVA sought to draw American troops into camouflaged bunker complexes with interlocking fields of fire. Fighting at such close quarters, American firepower could be neutralized and American units cut apart while seeking to extract themselves from the situation. "You'll never hear Marines say the North Vietnamese aren't tough," one American soldier remembered. "They're probably the toughest fighters in the world as far as I'm concerned. They knew what they were fighting for. They understood why they were there and they were there for the duration."[17]

But like any military organization, the NVA had both strengths and weaknesses. It was far better at defense than offense; its offensive actions were often ineffective and until near the end of the war their commanders lacked the ability to coordinate large attacks. Hanoi's primitive logistical system forced its planners to preposition food and supplies, "feathering the nest in advance,"[18] which made forces in the

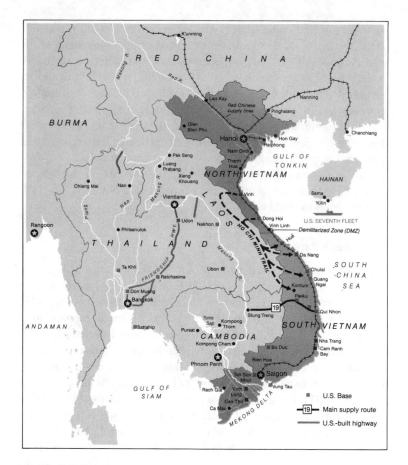

The Ho Chi Minh Trail

field vulnerable to American spoiling operations. And since the NVA lacked the power to soften up an objective—with heavy artillery—its assaults on fortified American positions were often disastrous, bringing heavy casualties. American troops could range throughout South Vietnam, confident of air and of artillery support. In contrast, enemy soldiers had to be more cautious, relying on careful preparations, surprise attacks, and defense in depth to give them an edge against superior American firepower.

Basic training in North Vietnam had not prepared that nation's soldiers for the trip south or for life in the jungles there. Most North Vietnamese soldiers had grown up in the lowland or coastal areas of North Vietnam. Moving down the Ho Chi Minh Trail, many NVA troops suffered from shortages of food, malaria, intestinal disorders, as well as from frequent American air attacks. Once in South Vietnam, they faced the hazards of combat in what seemed in many ways a foreign land. Political cadres in the north had told them that they would receive a warm welcome in the south, where people were allegedly eager to be liberated from their American oppressors. "Move fast," some troops were told, "or there will be nothing left for them to liberate and they will lose the honors reserved [for the liberators] by the people." Once there, however, the NVA regulars received a mixed reception from the South Vietnamese people and sometimes found themselves fighting the ARVN. While American soldiers typically served a one-year tour of duty, North Vietnamese soldiers were in it for the duration of the conflict. Thus their motto: "Born in the North, to die in the South."[19]

Despite the hardships of war in the south, a system of strict indoctrination and supervision bound soldiers together and helped maintain morale. As General Giap wrote, "political work in its ranks is of first importance. *It is the soul of the army.*"[20] Recruits were encouraged to transfer their loyalties from their families to the army and the revolution, and they were carefully watched by their officers and political cadre for signs of homesickness and malingering. All soldiers had to engage in frequent self-criticism sessions designed to eliminate sources of fear and of discontent. These three-man cells were the primary group and tactical unit of the NVA, functioning as an instrument of party discipline as well as a fire team in combat. Members of each cell watched each other, part of a pervasive system of surveillance and thought control.

The NVA also provided positive inducements to encourage soldiers to perform at the highest level. In contrast to the ARVN, where most officers hailed from an urban, educated elite, the NVA served as a path of upward mobility, offering even the peasant soldier the prospect of achieving more status and power by becoming an officer and even a member of the Communist party.

This elaborate system of control and rewards, however, might not have maintained morale had not NVA commanders been able to control the tempo of the fighting. Given their knowledge of the terrain and excellent intelligence, they initiated most combat and could ease the pressure on their troops by withdrawing to sanctuaries once conditions turned unfavorable. While North Vietnamese soldiers moved frequently and trained incessantly, in the course of a year the typcial unit fought only a few engagements.

In motivating its soldiers, the government in Hanoi also drew on the long Vietnamese tradition of sacrifice and endurance in war. For two thousand years the Vietnamese had fought against invading foreigners and had come to think of themselves as giant killers. Accustomed to winning against great odds, they believed they were more resolute and more intelligent than their opponents. Martial tales and legends celebrated this tradition, forming the subject matter of songs and plays that were performed by minstrels and actors throughout the country. Vietnamese revolutionaries were fighting a war for survival in which all their basic values—loyalty to ancestors, love of country, and resistance to foreigners—were at stake.

A War without a Front

The war in Vietnam differed from the wars most Americans remembered. Enemy forces were largely invisible, blending in with the peasantry or hiding in remote jungle or mountain sanctuaries, and generally able to control the pace of the conflict, striking American units when it was advantageous to do so. North Vietnamese soldiers displayed a fanatical devotion to their cause and great ingenuity and persistence in exploiting the land and people. By American standards NVA units took staggering casualties, but time after time they were able to withdraw and rebuild their strength. Worse still, enemy soldiers acquired an almost heroic stature. William Broyles Jr., a Marine officer, remembered: "In our minds the enemy wasn't another soldier, a man like us. He was mysterious and elusive—a vision from the unknown, a bogeyman with terrible powers rising up out of the earth. . . . The primitive methods that the enemy adopted in the face of our technology made him that much more formidable."[21]

While the enemy in Vietnam was mysterious and formidable, American troops who dealt with their South Vietnamese counterparts were initially shocked, then angered, by the unwillingness of many ARVN units to fight aggressively. Occasionally American officers were impressed by the dedication and skills of South Vietnamese commanders, but more often relations between American and South Vietnamese troops were tense. Robert Mason, an American helicopter pilot, had heard stories from other pilots about problems in transporting ARVN troops to and from battle sites. Even so, he was unprepared for ARVN Rangers who, when he carried them into a landing zone, refused to get off board until his crew chief threatened them with a pistol. "Whose war," he wondered, "was this, anyway?"[22]

Initially the expectations of American officers and men were high. Most American commanders believed that their forces would inflict unacceptable casualties on enemy troops and break their will to resist. Both generals and soldiers soon realized, however, that the war in Vietnam did not fit their preconceived notions. By the autumn of 1965 Lieutenant Philip Caputo, who had landed with the Marines at Da Nang in March, remembered, "What had begun as an adventurous expedition had turned into an exhausting, indecisive war of attrition in which we fought for no other cause than our own survival."[23] The enemy was elusive, the climate and terrain were treacherous, and peasants in the countryside were often unfriendly. The pattern of warfare that emerged was formless yet lethal, consisting of haphazard episodic contacts with the NVA and VC and daily encounters with ingenious, deadly booby traps. Rarely did the enemy engage in set-piece battles.

In contrast to World War II or the Korean War, Vietnam was a war without a front, one with no clear direction or momentum and in which progress was measured by the number of enemy troops killed rather than by the amount of territory gained. Combat there had a circular quality; American units would often patrol the same territory, engaging in fleeting contacts with the enemy, or take an objective only to abandon it. For Harold G. Moore, who arrived in South Vietnam in September 1965 and led a battalion at the battle of the Ia Drang

Valley, doubts began to emerge in early 1966, when he led his brigade in a campaign against NVA troops in a densely populated rice-farming region along the coast of Central Vietnam. After heavy fighting American units prevailed, but soon thereafter enemy troops reappeared. Two separate times in the spring Moore's brigade had to return to drive them out. How, he wondered, could the United States ever win if the South Vietnamese government could not reestablish control in such newly cleared areas?

Confusion and Disillusionment

For American combat soldiers the war bred confusion. Most were young (their average age was nineteen) and came from working-class backgrounds; they were unfamiliar with the history of Vietnam and knew little about the history of the French or the first phase of the American war there. As the war lengthened, the confusion only deepened, and the old and comforting myths dissolved. Young soldiers arrived in Vietnam with images of war derived from John Wayne movies; as they gained experience, Wayne's name was used to identify acts that might look good on the big screen but would bring certain death in combat. As one historian notes, "It's a sign of how completely the old values had faded that Wayne, hero of the Westerns and war movies that the Vietnam War generation had grown up on, and the embodiment of what seemed a particularly American kind of independent courage, had become a soldier's joke, an anti-hero, everybody's example of how *not* to fight a war."[24]

For some American officers and soldiers the war retained a clarity and sense of moral purpose; for others it brought disillusionment and a loss of faith. The acclaimed fiction writer Tobias Wolff, who served as an adviser to an ARVN battalion in the Mekong Delta, noticed that a nearby American unit seemed in a state of hopelessness. "At Dong Tam," he recalled, "I saw something that wasn't allowed for in the national myth—our capacity for collective despair. . . . The resolute imperial will was all played out here at the empire's fringe, lost in rancor and mud. Here were pharaoh's chariots engulfed; his horsemen confused; and all his magnificence dismayed."[25]

In Vietnam a troubling reversal of images occurred. In World War II, especially in Europe, American solders had generally been hailed as liberators, often aided by resistance groups and surrounded by cheering crowds as they occupied cities and towns. In Vietnam, American units that moved through the countryside encountered a wary, if not dangerous, peasantry, especially in those areas controlled by the NLF. Villages were often emptied of young men and surrounded by land mines and booby traps, hidden pits with stakes in them, or hand grenades or other explosives attached to trip wires. Confronted with an often hostile population and what seemed, at first glance, a primitive, repugnant way of life, many American units retaliated, sometimes far out of proportion to the threat. David Donovan, an officer who had received training in Vietnamese history, culture, and language, was appalled by the "contempt and disrespect" of most American soldiers toward the Vietnamese and by "the generally abysmal relations between Americans and Vietnamese villagers."[26] General Creighton Abrams, who became Westmoreland's deputy commander in May 1967, remembered that "Americans as a whole had trouble with the whole idea of the Vietnamese. Their color was a little different, their eyes were a little different, they were kind of small—those kinds of differences tend to bother Americans."[27]

John Del Vecchio's novel *The 13th Valley* sums up the futility felt by many American soldiers about ground combat in Vietnam. His novel tells the story of a campaign against an NVA base camp in a remote valley of South Vietnam. As American troops move lower into the valley from the heights above it, they encounter trails, roads, and bunker complexes, and engage in firefights with the enemy. Alpha Company, led by Lieutenant Rufus Brooks, is experienced and well disciplined and intent on what some think is a "suicide mission," penetrating to the floor of the valley and attacking an enemy headquarters complex on a knoll at its center. Unlike most American ground-combat units, Alpha Company has learned how to fight from the NVA, slipping quietly through the jungle, observing strict light and noise discipline, and, as it nears its objective, confusing its opponents by foregoing helicopter resupply—which would give away its position—and by moving at night, resting during the day, hiding and hitting the enemy. Alpha Company reaches the floor of the valley, then the top of the knoll, only to discover a field of bunkers and a supply cache beyond anything its troops had ever seen. As it explores the complex, pandemonium breaks out, as if Alpha "has ripped the top off an ant hill."[28] The NVA attacks the company's perimeters as it attempts a helicopter extraction, killing Lieutenant Brooks and inflicting heavy casualties. Despite heroic sacrifice and inspired leadership, Alpha Company's mission seemed doomed from the start, unlikely to change the course of the war.

Seeking a Steady Course

In the late winter and spring of 1966 it looked as if South Vietnam might fall apart. In early March Prime Minister Ky, ignoring the autonomy enjoyed by ARVN commanders, fired General Nguyen Chanh Thi, who ruled over Central Vietnam. It was a dangerous move, for the politically ambitious Thi had allied himself with militant Buddhist leaders and soon demonstrations and riots broke out in Hué and Da Nang. Drawing on widespread war weariness and anti-American sentiment, Buddhists called for democracy, negotiations, and an end to the war. As the influential monk Thich Tri Quang observed, "Today, the Vietnamese and the Americans are like a couple who do not love each other anymore, but who cannot obtain a divorce because they have a child—their common fight against the communists. So they continue to live with each other, but without love."[29] Soon thousands of ARVN troops loyal to General Thi joined the rebellion. After several months of political maneuvering and occasional clashes between government and dissident forces, Ky crushed the revolt. But Americans both in South Vietnam and at home were shocked by the spectacle of the South Vietnamese fighting among themselves even as American troops sought to win the war against the North Vietnamese.

Turmoil in South Vietnam, along with the inability of American forces to break the will of the enemy, frustrated the American public, which tended to blame the apparent stalemate in South Vietnam on the president and his administration. Democratic senator Richard Russell caught the popular mood when he remarked that it was time to "get it over or get out." Johnson knew, however, that the available options were more varied and complex. In the spring of 1966 he sought to rally public support for a policy of patience and moderation, urging national unity and warning that the nation's adversaries counted on "a weakening of the fiber and determination of the people of America."[30] He had become scornful of critics of the war, belittling them in public and harassing them in private. His adviser Eric Goldman recalled that "the ebullient leader given to moments of testiness and rage was now, day after day, bitter, truculent, peevish—and suspicious of the fundamental good sense and integrity of anyone who did not endorse the Vietnam War."[31]

Despite the deepening divisions at home, Johnson pressed on, ignoring the doubts of some of his closest advisers and instead choosing to listen to those who evinced more optimism. In April 1966 Walt W. Rostow (who had replaced Bundy as national security adviser in late March) told the president that the time would soon come "*to pour it on* and see if we can't force, in the months ahead, a resolution of the conflict." Johnson agreed. He promised Westmoreland 65,000 more troops, for a total of 325,000 by late summer, and in June he decided to intensify the bombing of North Vietnam, targeting petroleum, oil, and lubrication (POL) targets near Hanoi and Haiphong. He hoped that mounting pressure on the enemy might bring an end to the war by the middle of 1967. He had, after all, the assurance of his commander in the field, who told him that "we're going to win this war for you without mobilization."[32]

Search and Destroy

As Westmoreland received more troops and improved his logistical infrastructure, he intensified his search-and-destroy operations, taking a heavy toll on NVA and VC forces. Most enemy units still sought to avoid open combat, but in February 1966 two NVA divisions slipped across the DMZ into Quang Tri Province, while other units moved from Laos into the next province to the south. Westmoreland, worried about the isolation and vulnerability of South Vietnam's two northern provinces, ordered the Marines in I Corps to attack into the DMZ. Soon the fighting there took a different form than elsewhere in South

Vietnam, as both sides, supported by artillery, built a series of strong-points and engaged in entrenched battles reminiscent of World War I.

Westmoreland's dispatch of the Marines to the DMZ exacerbated a long-standing difference between him and Marine commanders. The Marines' tactical zone of operations was I Corps, consisting of the five northern provinces of South Vietnam. It was a difficult place to fight, one in which the rural population had long been controlled by the NLF. Furthermore, the terrain impeded military operations. The flat, sandy coastal areas gave way to rice paddies, dikes, narrow village roads, and eventually sloped up to mountains covered with thick rain forests. As the Marines settled in around three coastal zones, their officers studied the enemy carefully, concluding that a rural pacification strategy would be more successful than search-and-destroy operations. Convinced that the key to success lay in the control of the villages, they sent small units into the countryside, where they combined with local Popular Forces—part-time, local soldiers—to offer the peasantry more permanent protection.

In these Combined Action Platoons (CAPS), the Marines and Popular Forces sought to protect villagers from NLF coercion and, as they did so, win their support and collect from them intelligence on enemy troop movements. In short, they worked to avoid supporting the negative stereotypes that most American soldiers had of the Vietnamese peasantry and learned about the peasants' perspective on the war. Together the CAPS engaged in a bitter, deadly local war fought at close quarters.

Marines commanders also questioned Westmoreland's strategy of attrition, contending that the enemy's manpower pool was so large that, even with a favorable kill ratio, it could not be exhausted. Leaders in Hanoi, they argued, wanted violent, close-quarter combat that would diminish the effectiveness of American artillery and air power and inflict heavy casualties on American forces. A strategy of attrition was playing the enemy's game; or as General Victor H. Krulak put it, pacification and social and economic reform were "a design for victory"; attrition was "the route to defeat."[33]

Westmoreland's most perceptive critic in Washington was Army Chief of Staff Johnson, who also had become convinced by the end of 1965 that the big-unit war would not work. "In the last analysis,"

Johnson argued, "it is this fellow that's guarding the peasant night after night and keeping his throat from being slit that is going to be the important security factor out there [in South Vietnam]." Johnson commissioned an elaborate study of the ground war, Program for the Pacification and Long-Term Development of Vietnam (PROVN). Completed in March 1966, PROVN laid out the rationale for a strategy of pacification. But Johnson's views did not prevail. Westmoreland rejected a pacification approach, as did the JCS. "The essence of the problem in Vietnam," General Wheeler remarked, "is military."[34] Most of the members of the JCS focused on ways to expand the war beyond South Vietnam; they preferred to let Westmoreland manage the war within that nation.

Hopes for Victory

In the summer and fall of 1966 LBJ continued to receive optimistic reports about the war. His ambassador in Saigon, Henry Cabot Lodge Jr. (who replaced Taylor for a second tour in July 1985), reported "a progressive decline in [enemy] morale and fighting capacity," adding he sensed "a smell of victory" in the air. "We are not losing," he claimed, "we cannot lose in the normal sense of the word; never have things been going so well."[35] Developments in South Vietnam also encouraged some American officials. In early September large numbers of voters turned out for an election to chose delegates for a constituent assembly, which was to draft a new constitution for the nation. Now that their military government was stable enough to allow them to respond to American pressure to institute democratic reforms, Prime Minister Ky and Chief of State Nguyen Van Thieu had taken the first step toward the creation of a representative government in South Vietnam. Two months later a new Independence Palace was opened, a striking modern building that embodied South Vietnam's national aspirations. The night of its dedication, Westmoreland felt "for the first time a genuine optimism over political developments [in South Vietnam]."[36]

While the president held out hope for victory, he also searched for signs that leaders in Hanoi might be interested in a negotiated settlement. Throughout 1966 one abortive peace initiative followed another;

lacking any direct communication, the United States and North Vietnam probed each other's intentions through a variety of third parties. But neither side was willing to make the concessions necessary for the beginning of serious talks. Hanoi continued to insist that the United States stop the bombing of North Vietnam unconditionally, withdraw its forces from South Vietnam, and include the NLF in the peace process. Washington continued to insist that in return for a bombing halt North Vietnam must end its infiltration of troops into the South. Nor did the United States have any intention of abandoning its commitment to South Vietnam or of recognizing the NLF as a legitimate political force in the government of that nation. The gap between the two sides remained wide.

The lack of any prospect for peace deepened the pessimism of Secretary of Defense McNamara. In mid-October, after another visit to South Vietnam, he reported to the president that "I see no reasonable way to bring the war to an end soon."[37] He had not seen any signs of a break in enemy morale and he no longer believed that Westmoreland's large-unit operations would succeed. Searching for a way out, McNamara urged that the American military effort be sustained—within limits—with the modified objective of improving the chances for a reasonable political settlement. Such a settlement, he argued, must involve a bombing pause, the inclusion of the NLF in peace talks, and the withdrawal of American forces from South Vietnam at the end of the fighting.

McNamara's personal encounters with the antiwar movement further eroded his confidence. On November 7, during a visit to Harvard University, he left one of the undergraduate houses to travel by car to a classroom where he was scheduled to speak. As the secretary's car proceeded down a narrow street, students pressed in around it and began to rock it. Unable to drive off, McNamara climbed onto the roof of the car, from which he engaged in a tense question-and-answer session with the students surrounding him. Eager to show them that he could not be intimidated, he shouted, "I was tougher than you then [at the University of California, Berkeley] and I'm tougher today. I was more courteous then and I hope I am more courteous today."[38] Failing to make any headway, McNamara jumped off the top of the car and with the aid of a friendly student made his way to a series of underground tunnels and eventually to the classroom. The war had become so controversial at home that senior members of the administration, including the president, could no longer move freely around the nation.

Most of the president's senior advisers rejected McNamara's new position. If anything, they wanted more troops in South Vietnam, more bombing of North Vietnam, and more emphasis on pacification programs. Most remained optimistic about the year ahead. Rostow wanted the United States "to lean more heavily on the North," while McGeorge Bundy reassured Johnson that "you are still dead right on all the big issues & you still know more about how to make them come out right than any man in America."[39]

So Johnson pressed on, worried about urban riots, the economy, the fate of his Great Society programs, and Democratic prospects in the 1968 presidential elections, but determined to fulfill his obligations in South Vietnam. In late October the president traveled to Manila, where he attended a three-day conference with America's allies in South Vietnam—Australia, New Zealand, the Philippines, South Korea, and Thailand. These nations had all contributed troops—ranging from South Korea's 50,000 to New Zealand's 552—and all shared, to one extent or another, the American government's fear of Chinese expansion into Southeast Asia. Designed to bolster Johnson's morale and sell the war to the American public, the conference confirmed the allies determination to resist aggression in South Vietnam and advance democracy and social development there. From Manila Johnson made a hurried visit to Vietnam, landing at the huge U.S. base at Cam Ranh Bay, where he promised the assembled American troops that "we shall never let you down" and urged them, as only LBJ could have phrased it, "to nail that coonskin to the wall."[40]

In 1965 the United States had escalated the war without the support of its European allies, who remained skeptical of American involvement in Vietnam. With the exception of France, allied governments did not publicly oppose the war; neither did they provide troops or money and, in private, British Prime Minister Harold Wilson promoted a negotiated settlement. As the war lengthened, allied leaders were caught between their ties to the United States and growing domestic opposition to the conflict. A frustrated Johnson asked, "Are we the sole defenders of freedom in the world?" while Secretary of State Rusk told a British journalist that "When the Russians invade Sussex, don't expect us to come and help you."[41]

While America's European allies offered little support, Hanoi won massive amounts of aid from the Soviet Union and China. Despite differences over negotiations—Moscow favored peace talks while Beijing opposed them—each North Vietnamese ally sought to win the upper hand in Hanoi. Undoubtedly, Soviet and Chinese assistance limited American options and enabled North Vietnam to resist American pressure and continue the conflict. In the international arena, the United States had been outmaneuvered and, by the end of 1967, stood largely alone.

Despite the lack of substantial foreign assistance, President Johnson was eager to get on with the war in Vietnam, but now he worried deeply about the erosion of his domestic support. In November Senator Stuart Symington (Democrat, Missouri), a long-time hawk on the war, revealed that he had lost confidence in the adminis-tration's policies. "We are," he remarked, "getting in deeper and deeper with no end in sight. In 1968 Nixon will murder us."[42] By the end of the year Johnson's approval rating had fallen to 48 percent, while only 43 percent of the public supported the way in which he was handling the war.

Prospects for 1967

At the beginning of 1967, Westmoreland reported to Washington that in 1966 the enemy, while badly hurt, was still far from defeated. He outlined a campaign plan for 1967 remarkably similar to that of the previous year. American forces, along with elite ARVN units, would fight the big-unit war, while the rest of ARVN would focus on pacification. In the new year he also planned to launch a series of sustained assaults on enemy base areas, aimed at destroying the NVA's and VC's logistical capability. As 1967 unfolded these massive operations—Cedar Falls, Junction City, and others—penetrated previously untouched enemy sanctuaries. They did not, however, have a decisive impact on the course of the war.

Even Westmoreland's command found progress difficult to measure. In early 1967 it reported that the rate of enemy-initiated actions was 2.5 times higher than it had been a year ago. The implications of these figures—that the war was stalemated at a higher level of violence—upset General Wheeler back in Washington. "I cannot go to the president," Wheeler told his commander in the field, "and tell him that, contrary to my reports and those of the other chiefs as to the progress of the war in which we have laid great stress upon the thesis that you have seized the initiative from the enemy, the situation is such that we are not sure who has the initiative in Vietnam."[43] In fact, Westmoreland's adjustment of these numbers suggested that all attempts to measure the progress of the war—whether enemy initiated actions, enemy casualties, or its rate of infiltration down the Ho Chi Minh trail—teemed with uncertainty.

Now even Westmoreland could offer only a glimmer of hope. At a conference on Guam from March 20 to 22, the president asked him: "Are they [the North Vietnamese] bringing in as many [troops] as they're losing?" The general responded cautiously: "Up until now, no, sir. Their gains have exceeded their losses. However, if the present trend continues I think we might arrive at the crossover point perhaps this month, or next month. And by the crossover point, I mean when their losses are greater than their gains."[44]

Returning to the United States in late April, Westmoreland offered more bad news, both in public and in private. He told the National Press Club in Washington, D.C., that "I foresee in the months ahead some of the bitterest fighting of the war. . . . I see no end of the war in sight." And he told the president that without substantial reinforcements "we will not be in danger of being defeated, but it will be nip and tuck to oppose the reinforcements the enemy is capable of providing." Johnson responded with anguish, asking: "Where does it all end? When we add divisions, can't the enemy add divisions? If so where does it all end?" Westmoreland replied that with a "minimum essential force" of 550,500 American troops in South Vietnam (80,500 troops beyond the force level of 470,000 already approved for 1967), the war could go on for five years; with an "optimum force" of 670,000, it could last for three years.[45]

Doubts and Divisions

The endless ambiguity of the situation in Vietnam, combined with mounting opposition at home, weighed heavily on the president and led to explosive behavior. In a meeting with Robert Kennedy in February, Johnson predicted that the war would be over by the summer and warned Kennedy that "I'll destroy you and every one of your dove friends. . . . You'll be dead politically in six months." When Kennedy urged an end to the bombing and a negotiated settlement, the president erupted: "There just isn't a chance in hell I will do that. Not the slightest chance."[46] He then accused Kennedy and his friends of prolonging the war and of having American blood on their hands. Kennedy left the encounter shaken at the president's intemperate conduct.

In the spring of 1967 Johnson continued to receive a mixture of good and bad news. The CIA reported food shortages and poor army morale in North Vietnam; at home the antiwar movement gathered momentum. In April Martin Luther King Jr. publicly joined the antiwar protest, denouncing the United States as "the greatest purveyor of violence in the world today."[47] In mid-May a long memorandum from McNamara created a storm of controversy within the administration. McNamara began by admitting that "no attractive course of action" existed. The big-unit war was going well, the pacification effort poorly, but Hanoi remained uninterested in a political settlement. Given this impasse, McNamara worried that the war might spin out of control. "The picture," he wrote, "of the world's greatest superpower killing or seriously injuring 1,000 noncombatants a week, while trying to pound a tiny backward nation into submission on an issue whose merits are hotly disputed, is not a pretty one."[48] McNamara recommended strict limits on the bombing, additional deployments of only 30,000 men, and the adoption of a flexible bargaining position. His doubts about American policy were growing.

McNamara's memorandum intensified a nagging debate over military strategy in South Vietnam within the administration. Hardliners who wanted a more aggressive campaign against the enemy included the JCS and General Westmoreland, along with key civilian officials such as Rusk and Rostow. Skeptics of the current policies clustered around McNamara and his civilian aides in the Pentagon. But McNamara lacked support among senior officials, few of whom wished to ponder the process of disengaging American forces from South Vietnam.

The president had no intention of giving up the war. Convinced that sooner or later North Vietnam would agree to talks on American terms, he searched for ways to apply American power in South Vietnam more effectively. In the spring of 1967, responding to criticism of Westmoreland's approach to the war, Johnson decided to place more emphasis on programs designed to strengthen the ARVN and win the support of the peasantry. He dispatched General Creighton Abrams to South Vietnam to serve as Westmoreland's deputy in charge of relations with the ARVN, while the new ambassador to South Vietnam, Ellsworth Bunker, and the special ambassador in charge of pacification, Robert W. Komer, were to reorganize and revitalize this alternative approach to the war.

Questions about the scale and direction of the American war effort, however, remained unresolved, and in early July Johnson sent McNamara and General Wheeler to Saigon to assess the war and reach an agreement with Westmoreland on the appropriate number of additional troops. In Saigon these two emissaries received upbeat briefings. Ambassador Bunker asserted that the war was not stalemated, while Westmoreland, who had always been guarded in his estimates, had turned genuinely optimistic. Increased enemy battlefield deaths had convinced him that the crossover point had been reached, or, as he told the secretary of defense: "The war is not a stalemate. We are winning slowly but steadily. North Vietnam is paying a tremendous price with nothing to show for it." Now was the time, he posited, to reinforce American success and go for a knockout blow against the enemy.[49]

These authoritative assessments caused McNamara to waiver in his skepticism of the war. As he recalled, these briefings "had momentarily eased my long-standing doubts about the war's progress in the South." Back in Washington, when Johnson asked him, "Are we going to be able to win this goddamned war?" McNamara answered that the war was not stalemated. And he stated in one White House meeting that "if we follow the same program we will win the war and end the fighting." Other senior advisers agreed. Rostow argued that "we are moving uphill—slowly but steadily," while Wheeler noted that "there has been an unbroken series of military successes"; he saw "no great military problems in sight."[50] But McNamara continued to insist on limiting ground combat strength, convincing the president to give Westmoreland only 47,000 more troops, for a new ceiling of 525,000.

Despite his own cautious optimism, the president knew that the administration had not convinced most Americans that the war was going well. Many shared Senator Fulbright's belief that it was "a hopeless venture." One poll revealed that 66 percent of the American people had lost confidence in Johnson's leadership, that 50 percent had no idea what the war was about, and that only 25 percent believed South Vietnam could survive a withdrawal of American troops. On August 7, a long, authoritative article in the *New York Times* reported that victory was not close at hand and that most Americans in South Vietnam—aside from the senior civilian and military leaders—believed that the war was stalemated. Understandably, the president complained to his advisers that "We have got to do something to win. We aren't doing much now."[51]

The Order of Battle Controversy

Early in the war Westmoreland's command had compiled a list of enemy units operating in South Vietnam, the so-called enemy order-of-battle. Preoccupied with enemy main-force units (NVA and VC), MACV concluded that the United States faced a force of around 270,000 soldiers. The CIA, however, was skeptical of Westmoreland's approach to the war, and in August 1965 it gave one of its young analysts, Sam Adams, the task of studying enemy morale. Pouring over captured documents, POW interrogations, and interviews with defectors, Adams estimated enemy strength, including administrative units, political cadre, and local guerrillas, at around 600,000 men. One captured document from Binh Dinh province listed 50,244 soldiers, while MACV's figure was only 4,668. Gradually Adams realized that the NLF consisted of a vast, intricate organization, most of which was hidden from view. The well-armed main-force units on which Westmoreland's command focused were only the tip of a large funnel that ran all the way down to the village level, part of a resilient organization that could replace its losses quickly. If Adams was right, the calculations of the American military about the number of troops needed and the time it would take to win the war were grossly inaccurate. His figures suggested that the war was stalemated at a high level of violence.

By the time Adams reached these conclusions, Westmoreland had declared that the crossover point had been reached. His staff offered elaborate mathematical proof to show that enemy strength had peaked in late 1966 at around 300,000 troops, and that by November 1967 it had declined to 242,000. Convinced that NVA and VC numbers were in decline, Westmoreland and his staff engaged in an intense argument with the CIA over who to count and who to exclude from the enemy order-of-battle. In September 1967 Westmoreland prevailed; in the end, given the mood of the president and his senior advisers, CIA director Richard Helms had to give ground. As he explained to a frustrated Adams: "You don't know what it's like in this town. I could have told the White House there were a million more Vietcong out there, and it wouldn't have made the slightest difference in our policy."[52]

The president's handling of this dispute revealed that, as the war progressed, Johnson did not evolve into an effective commander-in-chief. Despite the fact that by the summer of 1967 his senior advisers had made major miscalculations about the war, he would not hold them accountable for earlier poor advice. Johnson sought consensus, not confrontation; he was not comfortable trying to resolve differences over military strategy. As a result, the president allowed his administration to drift, without any concrete plan for a military victory or any concrete plan for a political settlement of the conflict. McNamara and his civilian advisers moved toward restraint, even as Westmoreland and the JCS pushed for an expansion of the war. The president wavered, fearful that too much restraint would provoke a revolt by the Joint Chiefs and that a wider war would provoke China. Filled with anguish over growing American casualties and blind rage toward domestic opponents of the war, his impulses were conflicting. On the one hand, he wanted to pound the enemy into submission; on the other, he feared the domestic and international consequences of trying to do so.

Illusions of Victory

In the late summer and early fall of 1967 Johnson searched for a way out of his dilemma. With 67 percent of the public disapproving of his handling of the war, he was eager to probe Hanoi's willingness to negotiate. Once again, third-party contacts revealed the intransigence of North Vietnam's leaders; they rejected any talks until all acts of war against North Vietnam were unconditionally ended. "The problem," Johnson observed, "is not one of communication. The problem is that Ho wants South Vietnam."[53] Frustrated in his dealings with North Vietnam, Johnson hoped that developments in South Vietnam might strengthen his hand in future negotiations. Earlier in the year a constituent assembly had met in Saigon and drafted a new constitution along American lines. Ky and Thieu, recognizing the importance their American supporters placed on political reform and confident that they and their allies in the military would retain control, accepted the new document. After tense wrangling, they agreed to a combined ticket with Thieu as the presidential candidate and Ky as the vice-presidential one. In an early September election, in which 80 percent of the registered voters turned out, they won with a disappointing 35 percent of the vote. Johnson and his advisers chose to view the election as one more sign of South Vietnam's progress toward political stability.

Despite his desire for peace, the president was not prepared to question the assumptions on which U.S. policy rested. In August, when McNamara told a Senate subcommittee that continued bombing would not bring North Vietnam to the peace table, Johnson was furious at his open dissent from administration policy. On September 12 he received a secret memorandum from CIA director Helms, arguing that the United States could withdraw from South Vietnam without any lasting injury to its national security. The director had concluded that the domino theory was not valid in Southeast Asia. The president did not respond to Helms's memorandum or show it to his other senior advisers.

Instead, Johnson authorized more intensive bombing of North Vietnam, escalating Rolling Thunder in an effort to impede rail and road traffic from China, isolate Hanoi from its port city of Haiphong, and separate the Hanoi-Haiphong area from logistical bases in the southern part of North Vietnam. Now U.S. warplanes hit many targets near Hanoi and Haiphong. Within a month the JCS were convinced that the bombing had finally fragmented North Vietnam's logistical system.

In the fall bitter fighting erupted along the borders of South Vietnam. At Con Thieu, one of six American strongpoints on the DMZ, Marines endured a long siege that was finally broken by massive strikes from long-range, four-engine bombers (B-52s). At Dak To, a special-forces camp located in a valley in the Central Highlands near the Cambodian and Laotian borders, the NVA had constructed fortified positions on many of the jungle-covered peaks and ridges surrounding it, forcing American units to attack its concealed bunker complexes. Bitter fighting at close quarters was costly to both sides. In the end American forces prevailed, inflicting a defeat on the NVA, but the twelve American rifle companies involved in the battle suffered 51 percent losses in just one month. Few Americans could take much comfort in Westmoreland's assessment: "I think it's the beginning of a great defeat for the enemy."[54]

As the war went on and American deaths in combat mounted— 1,369 in 1965, 5,008 in 1966, and 9,377 in 1967—an increasing number of Americans felt a sense of futility about the fighting and some antiwar protestors turned to more active forms of resistance. In early October the Reverend Philip Berrigan and his followers poured blood on draft records in Baltimore. On October 21 nearly 100,000 demonstrators marched on the Pentagon, encircling the complex and taunting the thousands of troops who protected the nation's military command center. And polls showed that only 28 percent of the public approved of the administration's Vietnam policies, while 57 percent disapproved. Johnson was puzzled by the scale of the discontent and repelled by the young protestors, with their strange lifestyles and images of alienation and aloneness. After viewing Dustin Hoffman in *The Graduate,* he asked his biographer Doris Kearns: "How in the hell can that creepy guy be a hero to you? All I needed was to see ten minutes of that guy, floating like a big lump in a pool, moving like an elephant in that women's bed, riding up and down the California coast polluting the atmosphere, to know that I wouldn't trust him for one minute with anything that really mattered to me."[55]

In the Congress, too, no matter what position representatives took on the war, they were increasingly dissatisfied with the administration's policies. The defection of moderate, previously prowar Democrats particularly upset Johnson. In September Representative Tip O'Neill of Massachusetts, a prominent House Democrat, concluded that the war could not be won "and that our involvement there was wrong." An anxious president told his advisers that "We've got to do something about public opinion."[56]

On November 1 the president received a pessimistic memorandum from his secretary of defense. If current policies continued, McNamara warned, casualties would double and public support would further erode. He urged "a policy of stabilization," including a cap on ground forces, a halt to the bombing of North Vietnam, and a transfer of more responsibility to the South Vietnamese government. In effect, McNamara remembers telling Johnson "that we could not achieve our objective in Vietnam through any reasonable military means, and we therefore should seek a lesser political objective through negotiations."[57] Angry over the defection of one of his closest advisers, at the end of November Johnson announced that McNamara would leave office early in the new year to become president of the World Bank.

Despite the assurances of his hard-line advisers, the president felt a growing sense of urgency about the war. He wanted more reliable data on the progress of the conflict and wanted the South Vietnamese to take over more of the fighting. But he remained determined to continue the war and force the enemy to yield. "I'm not," he remarked, "going to be the first American President to lose a war."[58]

In November Johnson orchestrated a campaign to sell the war more effectively to the Congress and the American people. Its centerpiece was the return of Westmoreland and Bunker to Washington on November 16. In his most optimistic remarks on the war to date, Westmoreland told the National Press Club that it had entered a new phase "when the end begins to come into view." A few days later, during an appearance on the Sunday-morning talkshow *Meet The Press,* the general was more precise, stating that it was "conceivable that within two years or less the enemy will be so weakened that the Vietnamese will be able to cope with a greater share of the war burden."[59] Phase four—the withdrawal of American ground combat forces—was coming into view.

While the president's credibility had fallen, most Americans still admired Westmoreland, the embattled commander in the field. But his authoritative pronouncements, should they turn out to be false, ran the risk of bringing a further backlash against the administration's conduct of the war.

Notes

1 Quoted in Paul Hendrickson, *The Living and the Dead: Robert McNamara and Five Lives of a Lost War* (New York, 1996), 196.

2 Quoted in Tom Engelhardt, *The End of Victory Culture: Cold War America and the Disillusioning of a Generation* (New York, 1995,) 12.

3 Quoted in Robert Dallek, *Flawed Giant: Lyndon Johnson and His Times, 1961–1973* (New York, 1998), 341.

4 Quoted in Deborah Shapley, *Promise and Power: The Life and Times of Robert McNamara* (Boston, 1993), 350.

5 Quoted in Robert McNamara, *In Retrospect: The Tragedy and Lessons of Vietnam* (New York, 1995), 224–25.

6 Quoted in Dallek, *Flawed Giant,* 346–47.

7 Quoted in Randall Bennett Woods, *Fulbright: A Biography* (New York, 1995), 405.

8 Quoted in Stanley Karnow, *Vietnam: A History* (New York, 1991), 495.

9 Quoted in Dallek, *Flawed Giant,* 354.

10 Ibid., 356.

11 Howard R. Simpson, *Tiger in the Barbed Wire: An American in Vietnam, 1952–1991* (New York, 1992), 187; Neil Sheehan, *A Bright Shining Lie: John Paul Vann and America in Vietnam* (New York, 1988), 624.

12 Quoted in Phillip B. Davidson, *Vietnam at War: The History, 1946–1975* (New York, 1988), 400.

13 Quoted in William C. Westmoreland, *A Soldier Reports* (New York, 1976), 207.

14 Quoted in Samuel Zaffiri, *Westmoreland: A Biography of General William C. Westmoreland* (New York, 1994), 161.

15 Ibid., 161.

16 Quoted in Eric M. Bergerud, *The Dynamics of Defeat: The Vietnam War in Hau Nghia Province* (Boulder, Colo., 1991), 88; quoted in Davidson, *Vietnam at War,* 404.

17 Quoted in Ronald H. Spector, *After Tet: The Bloodiest Year in Vietnam* (New York, 1993), 71.

18 Quoted in Bergerud, *The Dynamics of Defeat,* 96.

19 Quoted in Spector, *After Tet,* 82–83.

20 Quoted in Davidson, *Vietnam at War,* 60.

21 William Broyles, Jr., *Brothers in Arms: A Journey from War to Peace* (New York, 1986), 3.

22 Robert Mason, *Chickenhawk* (New York, 1983), 226.

23 Philip Caputo, *A Rumor of War* (New York, 1977), xii.

24 Samuel Hynes, *The Soldiers' Tale: Bearing Witness to Modern War* (New York, 1997), 215.

25 Tobias Wolff, *In Pharaoh's Army: Memories of the Lost War* (New York, 1994), 23.

26 David Donovan, *Once A Warrior King: Memories of an Officer in Vietnam* (New York, 1985), 28, 33.

27 Quoted in Lewis Sorley, *Thunderbolt: General Creighton Abrams and the Army of His Time* (Dulles, Va., 1998), 353.

28 John M. Del Vecchio, *The 13th Valley* (New York, 1982), 589–90, 616.

29 Quoted in Robert J. Topmiller, *The Lotus Unleashed: The Buddhist Peace Movement in South Vietnam* (Lexington, Ky., 2002), 113.

30 Quoted in Dallek, *Flawed Giant*, 364, 66.

31 Eric F. Goldman, *The Tragedy of Lyndon Johnson* (New York, 1969), 590–93.

32 Quoted in Dallek, *Flawed Giant*, 361, 379.

33 Quoted in Sheehan, *A Bright Shining Lie*, 631.

34 Quoted in Lewis Sorley, *Honorable Warrior: General Harold K. Johnson and the Ethics of Command* (Lawrence, Kans., 1998), 236, 238.

35 Quoted in Dallek, *Flawed Giant*, 379–80.

36 Westmoreland, *A Soldier Reports*, 246.

37 Quoted in William Conrad Gibbons, *The U.S. Government and the Vietnam War, Executive and Legislative Roles and Relationships, Part IV: July 1965–January 1968* (Princeton, N.J., 1995), 458.

38 McNamara, *In Retrospect*, 255.

39 Quoted in Dallek, *Flawed Giant*, 387–88.

40 Ibid., 385.

41 Quoted in George C. Herring, "Fighting Without Allies," in Marc Jason Gilbert, ed., *Why The North Won the Vietnam War* (New York, 2002), 80; quoted in Fredrik Logevall, *Choosing War: The Lost Chance For Peace and the Escalation of War in Vietnam* (Berkeley, Calif., 1999), 133.

42 Quoted in Dallek, *Flawed Giant*, 386.

43 Quoted in Zaffiri, *Westmoreland*, 189.

44 Ibid., 191.

45 Ibid., 195, 198–99; *Westmoreland, A Soldier Reports*, 298–99.

46 Quoted in Jeff Shesol, *Mutual Contempt: Lyndon Johnson, Robert Kennedy, and the Feud that Defined a Decade* (New York, 1997), 366.

47 Quoted in James T. Patterson, *Grand Expectations: The United States, 1945–1974* (New York, 1996), 661.

48 Quoted in McNamara, *In Retrospect*, 266, 269.

49 Quoted in Zaffiri, *Westmoreland*, 215.

50 Quoted in McNamara, *In Retrospect*, 283; quoted in Shapley, *Promise and Power*, 424; quoted in Dallek, *Flawed Giant*, 471.

51 Ibid., 474, 477.

52 Quoted in Sam Adams, *War of Numbers: An Intelligence Memoir* (South Royalton, Vt., 1994), 168.

53 Quoted in Dallek, *Flawed Giant*, 481.

54 Quoted in Edward F. Murphy, *DAK TO: America's Sky Soldiers In South Vietnam's Central Highlands* (Novato, Calif., 1993), 328.

55 Quoted in Doris Kearns, *Lyndon Johnson and the American Dream* (New York, 1976), 332.

56 Quoted in Dallek, *Flawed Giant*, 485.

57 McNamara, *In Retrospect*, 308, 313.

58 Quoted in Dallek, *Flawed Giant*, 500.

59 Quoted in Larry Berman, *Lyndon Johnson's War: The Road to Stalemate in Vietnam* (New York, 1989), 116.

*Top: The first major battle of the American Vietnam War, the Battle of Ia Drang,
October–November 1965. U.S. Army Photo.*
*Bottom: A search-and-destroy mission yields Viet Cong prisoners, 1965.
Courtesy of the National Archives. ARC 541868.*

Top: Injured American soldier with a leg burned by a VC white phosphorus booby trap, 1966. Courtesy of the National Archives. ARC 541863
Bottom: Youthful hardcore Viet Cong awaits interrogation. Captured after Tet Offensive, 1968. Courtesy of the National Archives. ARC 541867.

*Top: Viet Cong soldier in bunker with
SKS rifle, 1968. Courtesy of the National
Archives. ARC 530624.*
*Bottom: A Viet Cong base camp under
attack by the Ninth Infantry Division,
1968. Courtesy of the National Archives.
ARC 530621.*

Top: Marine rifleman in rice paddy during a search-and-destroy mission, 1966. Courtesy of the National Archives. ARC 532474.
Bottom: First Air Cavalry Division searching house for Viet Cong northeast of Saigon, 1966. Courtesy of the National Archives. ARC 530612.

Top: Tank from First Battalion moves through Saigon, 1966. Courtesy of the National Archives. ARC 541873.
Bottom: Company C Huey Helicopter. U.S. Army Military History Institute.

*Top: Terrified villagers
being evacuated after a
Viet Cong attack on their
village, 1966. Courtesy of
the National Archives.
ARC 541871.
Bottom: Girl holds baby
amid ruins of their home
after a VC attack on
Saigon, 1968. Courtesy of
the National Archives.
ARC 541980.*

Top: Weeping over the dead, after civilians happened on a Viet Cong land mine near Tuy Hoa, ca. 1966. Courtesy of the National Archives. ARC 541978. Bottom: A woman weeps over the body of her husband, a South Vietnamese Army casualty, 1965. Courtesy of the National Archives. ARC 542295.

Opposite top: A U.S. Soldier directs traffic after a firefight with Viet Cong, 1968. Courtesy of the National Archives. ARC 541844.
Opposite bottom: Three women search for meager belongings amid the rubble after a VC attack, 1968. Courtesy of the National Archives. ARC 541849.
Top: Remains of a Saigon suburb burned by the South Vietnamese army after the Tet Offensive, 1968. Courtesy of the National Archives. ARC 558530.

Below: Porters on the Ho Chi Minh Trail, 1964. Library of Congress. DS557.A62.S6, General Collections.

CHAPTER SIX

Tet and Beyond, 1968

In the predawn hours of January 31, as the people of Saigon were preparing to celebrate Tet, Vietnam's most important holiday, a squad of Viet Cong commandos approached the American Embassy in the center of the city. This impressive six-story structure, completed the year before, was shielded by a honeycombed concrete screen and sat in the middle of a compound surrounded by a protective wall. With storming the main entrance out of the question, the commandos blasted a hole in the perimeter wall and ran into the compound; they did not get far before a handful of American military police opened fire. After six and a half hours of fighting, the guerrillas, who never gained access to the embassy building itself, were wiped out. But the audacity of their attack was extraordinary, as was the general offensive of which it was a small part. As the day unfolded, elsewhere in the capital and across the nation 80,000 enemy troops, mostly Viet Cong units, surged into thirty-six of the sixty-four provincial capitals, five of the six major cities, the sixty-four district capitals, and fifty hamlets. The 4,000 insurgents who entered Saigon mostly attacked major South Vietnamese facilities—Independence Palace, Navy headquarters, the Joint General Staff compound, and the state-run radio station. For the first time the war had shifted into South Vietnam's cities, where enemy troops stayed put, determined to defend their positions. What soon became known as the Tet Offensive signaled a new phase of the Vietnam War.

Origins of the Tet Offensive

By the summer of 1967 leaders in Hanoi worried about the course of the war. The aggressive strategy pursued by General Nguyen Chi Thanh, the director of the insurgency's Central Office for South Vietnam (COSVN), had resulted in heavy casualties and raised the bitter criticism of General Giap and his allies in the North Vietnamese government. The mounting intensity of the war had strained the resources of the Viet Cong and the North Vietnamese and precipitated a decline in the morale and combat capabilities of forces fighting in the south. As one Hanoi official predicted, "If we keep fighting five more years, all that will be left of Viet Nam will be a desert."[1] With Thanh's death in July 1967, the balance of forces in Hanoi shifted toward a strategy in the south designed to bring a rapid end to the war.

The result was the decision to launch a "General Offensive, General Uprising" that, if successful, would crush the South Vietnamese government and army and force the withdrawal of the United States from the conflict. The first phase of the operation, which began in the fall of 1967, consisted of NVA attacks along the borders of South Vietnam intended to draw American forces away from the urban areas. The second phase, which began on January 31, 1968, was the assault on the cities and especially key South Vietnamese facilities within them. The third and final phase, which did not begin until May 5, included further attacks on the cities intended to complete the destruction of the South Vietnamese government and army. Even if they failed to achieve the maximum objective, leaders in Hanoi reasoned that the Tet Offensive would weaken the position of the United States and push the Johnson administration into a new, more vulnerable phase of the war.

North Vietnamese and NLF officials believed their own propaganda—that ARVN lacked motivation and would collapse, that the government of South Vietnam had little support among its own people, and that most of the people of South Vietnam despised the Americans and would, if given a chance, turn on them. Or, as one document put it, "the majority of the people [of South Vietnam] have sympathy for and confidence in the Revolution. They are ready to stand up and liberate themselves, but this is still impossible since they are living in enemy controlled areas and are being misled by the psywar and propaganda machinery."[2]

In fact, Communist revolutionaries in Hanoi were an inbred group who had worked together for many years and held a mystical faith in the possibility of a great uprising. Thus they accepted exaggerated reports from cadres and commanders fighting in the south that conditions there were ripe for a popular revolt and prepared an ambitious offensive designed to break their enemy's will to resist.

The Siege of Khe Sanh

Ten days before the opening of the Tet Offensive, on January 21, the NVA opened artillery fire on the American garrison at Khe Sanh— this the final phase of the border attacks designed to conceal the impending assault on the cities. Located in the northwest corner of South Vietnam, six miles from the Laotian border, the base at Khe Sanh sat on a plateau surrounded by high hills. Initially the base served as a touchpoint to monitor the flow of North Vietnamese troops and supplies down nearby branches of the Ho Chi Minh Trail, but in September 1966 Westmoreland ordered a Marine battalion to Khe Sanh and the upgrading of the airstrip there. In the spring of 1967 Marine and NVA units engaged in bloody clashes in the nearby hills, and in August enemy forces cut Route 9, the only road to the coast. Khe Sanh could now only be resupplied by air. Late in 1967 Westmoreland, informed that between 32,000 and 40,000 NVA troops were converging on the base, increased troop strength there to 6,000 and laid plans for a massive bombing campaign (Operation NIAGARA) to punish besieging troops. He believed the battle was a "vain attempt" by the North Vietnamese to "restage Dienbienphu."[3] Convinced American firepower would prevail, Westmoreland eventually planned to use Khe Sanh to support a large-scale operation into Laos aimed at cutting off the Ho Chi Minh Trail.

The motives of Westmoreland's counterpart, General Giap, in laying siege to Khe Sanh remain difficult to determine. He may have viewed the siege as a feint, designed to draw American troops and the attention of American commanders away from the populated areas of South Vietnam. Or he may actually have hoped to overrun the base, beating the Americans as he had once beaten the French at Dien Bien Phu and ushering in the final phase of the American War.

The Shock of Tet

Communist leaders had made serious miscalculations in launching the Tet Offensive. Unable to coordinate successfully such a far-flung operation, they failed to prevent the premature assaults on four provincial capitals in the Central Highlands, thus prompting U.S. and ARVN commanders in other areas to put their forces on alert (although many of the South Vietnamese troops who were on leave to observe the new year holiday did not return to their units in time to be of any help). Underestimating the firepower and mobility of U.S. forces, the North Vietnamese decision makers had put elite VC units in urban areas, instructing them to hold their positions. And blinded by their own ideology, they had misjudged the morale of ARVN, which, with its back against the wall, fought bravely. Finally, and perhaps most embarassingly, they had misjudged the mood of the urban masses, who by no means rose up in revolt. Of the roughly 80,000 NVA and VC troops involved in the Tet Offensive, 30,000 were killed, wounded, or captured. As a military operation, the great general offensive and uprising had failed. As one Viet Cong soldier complained, "Hanoi was guilty of grievous miscalculation, which squandered the strength of the Southern forces."[4]

Even so, the fighting was intense. In most cities and towns it only lasted a few days, but in Saigon street skirmishes continued sporadically for two weeks. In Hué (the former imperial capital), which was occupied by largely NVA forces, U.S. Marine and ARVN units slugged it out with the enemy in bitter street fighting for twenty-five days before the NLF flag was finally pulled down from the Imperial Citadel. And during the occupation of Hué, enemy cadres rounded up three thousand government officials and anyone else connected to the

Saigon regime and summarily killed them, dumping their corpses in mass graves.

The fighting in the cities revealed more vividly than ever before the brutality of the war. For many Americans, both in Vietnam and at home, the war's savagery was captured in a striking image taken by an Associated Press photographer. In it General Nguyen Ngoc Loan, chief of the national police, having just taken a prisoner from an ARVN patrol, holds his revolver against the terrified man's head and seconds later, without so much as a word, pulls the trigger. The whole world watched as the dead man's body collapsed to the pavement, blood pouring from the head wound. Few who saw the photograph knew that Loan had been moving through Saigon looking for revenge against Communist invaders who had killed some of his men.

Westmoreland and his staff had not anticipated the scope and intensity of the Tet Offensive. They believed that the war was going well and that the enemy, crippled by high casualties and logistical difficulties, had lost the initiative and now had no choice but to fight on the borders of South Vietnam. Despite mounting evidence that Communist forces were gathering for an assault on the cities, they reasoned that any attack on urban areas was far less of a threat than the siege of Khe Sanh, which they were convinced the enemy sought to overrun. Given American estimates of the capabilities of Allied forces, it seemed inconceivable to American commanders that the enemy would launch an offensive doomed to fail. Or, as one MACV intelligence officer remarked, "If we'd gotten the whole battle plan, it wouldn't have been believed. It just wouldn't have been credible to us."[5]

One American commander, General Frederick C. Weyand, who led American troops stationed near Saigon, had viewed enemy activities differently. Worried about increased Communist radio traffic around the capital, he convinced Westmoreland to let him pull more U.S. combat units back toward Saigon. As a result, American forces defended this vital city far more effectively than would otherwise have been the case.

Americans at home had been even less prepared for the Tet Offensive. Having been lulled by Westmoreland's optimistic assessments of the war, they expressed shock over the fact that this allegedly defeated enemy had attacked seemingly anywhere in South Vietnam it wished to and even penetrated the American Embassy compound. Their impressions of Tet were shaped by press and television coverage, which focused on the drama of the fighting in the cities, on strafing jets, devastated neighborhoods, and crying women and children. Minor street actions looked like full-scale battles on the small screen, and television commentators, misunderstanding military aspects of the war, portrayed Tet as a disaster for the United States and its South Vietnamese allies. They also ignored facts that did not fit their image, such as the bravery of the ARVN soldiers or the confused and frightened enemy units that lost their way or retreated under fire. Few in the media accepted Westmoreland's assertion that the Tet assaults were a diversion for the main enemy thrust against Khe Sanh. The syndicated columnist Art Buchwald portrayed a confident General George Armstrong Custer boasting that "the battle of Little Big Horn had just turned the corner" and that the Sioux were "on the run."[6]

In the Congress, the Tet Offensive reinforced the views of those who were already disillusioned with the war. Senator Edward M. Kennedy (Democrat, Massachusetts) declared that the success of the attacks was a result of the "deadly apathy" of the South Vietnamese people, while the new Senate Majority Whip, Robert Byrd (Democrat, West Virginia)—a man who had supported Johnson's Vietnam policy—told the president that "we had poor intelligence . . . were not prepared for these attacks, we underestimated the morale and vitality of the Viet Cong [and] we overestimated the support of the South Vietnamese government in its people. . . . Something is wrong over there."[7]

Outside the Congress, public opinion elites who had been reluctant to express their doubts about the war became much more skeptical. Walter Cronkite, CBS's influential newscaster, after reading the early wire reports describing the Viet Cong's attack on the American Embassy, remarked to an associate: "What the hell is going on? I thought we were winning the war!" After a quick trip to South Vietnam to gain a first-hand impression, Cronkite told nearly 20 million American television viewers that it seemed "more certain than ever that the bloody experience of Vietnam is to end in a stalemate."[8]

The Tet Offensive
First Wave of Attacks—Jan. 30, 1968
Second Wave of Attacks—Jan. 31, 1968

The president and his advisers also had been unprepared for the scale and boldness of the attacks. They had believed Westmoreland's reports from the field and had never imagined that enemy forces could carry out such an ambitious operation. Even Secretary of State Rusk, a long-time hawk, now realized that time was running out for the administration's policies, while Harry McPherson, a White House speechwriter and presidential confidant, recalled the power of the television images that he saw: "I watched the invasion of the American embassy compound, and the terrible sight of General Loan killing the Vietcong captive. You got a sense of the awfulness, the endlessness, of the war—and, though it sounds naïve, the unethical quality of a war in which a prisoner is shot at point-blank range. I put aside the confidential cables. I was more persuaded by the tube and by the newspapers. I was fed up with the optimism that seemed to flow without stopping from Saigon."[9]

At a press conference on February 2, President Johnson announced that the Tet Offensive had come as no surprise and that as a military campaign it had been "a complete failure."[10] He instructed senior officials in Washington and General Westmoreland and Ambassador Bunker in Saigon to reassure the American people about progress in Vietnam. Johnson did not, however, make a sustained effort to rally the public or explain to the American people that Tet had pushed the United States into a new phase of the war. Confronted with disillusionment at home and growing divisions even among his closest advisers, LBJ, alone and confused, was again uncertain how to respond to the shifting contours of the war.

The U.S. Military's Response

The Tet Offensive also seriously damaged Westmoreland's reputation. Senator Richard B. Russell (Democrat, Georgia) claimed that Westmoreland had been "outgeneralled and outwitted by North Vietnam's Minister of Defense Giap," while Senator Robert F. Kennedy (Democrat, New York) decried the fact that a huge American and South Vietnamese military force was "unable to secure even a single city from the attacks of an enemy whose total strength is about 250,000."[11]

Critics questioned Westmoreland's strategy and generalship, and some even called for his removal.

From Westmoreland's perspective, however, the military situation in South Vietnam was hopeful. As the assault on the cities wound down, his attention focused on the siege of Khe Sanh, where throughout February and early March North Vietnamese artillery shelled the base, while some limited assaults were made on its perimeter and fierce battles were fought on the hills surrounding it. The U.S. Marines, reinforced by a battalion of South Vietnamese Rangers, frantically hardened their positions, while American air power, including the use of fighters and B-52 bombers, saturated the surrounding countryside with bullets and bombs. Westmoreland still looked forward to a set-piece battle, confident that the enemy could not overrun the base. The president, however, haunted by memories of Dien Bien Phu, warned the chairman of the Joint Chiefs of Staff, "I don't want no damned Dinbinfoo[sic]."[12] And the American press, portraying the Marines in the garrison as imperiled, fed public fears of an impending catastrophe.

In fact, as Westmoreland pointed out, the analogy between Khe Sanh and Dien Bien Phu was a poor one. The French had been trapped in an inaccessible valley far from the coast, with weak artillery and air support, and with the enemy holding the high ground. American forces at Khe Sanh held most of the hills surrounding the base, were only thirty miles from the coast—where reinforcements had gathered—and had a huge armada of aircraft available to attack enemy supply lines and troop concentrations. In short, Westmoreland had assembled too much raw military power for enemy forces to prevail at Khe Sanh.

And by early March Giap began to pull back his forces. On April 1, American troops on the coast started their advance up Route 9, reaching Khe Sanh on April 15 and formally lifting the siege. But as the Army's First Cavalry Division approached the base, its commander was shocked at the devastation surrounding it. "The place was absolutely denuded," he wrote later. "The trees were gone . . . everything was gone. Pockmarked and ruined and burnt . . . like the surface of the moon. Scattered around the apocalyptic landscape, 1st Cavalry troopers found hundreds of enemy corpses. Some lay where they had fallen. Others were buried in shallow, hastily-dug graves."[13] Approximately 10,000 North Vietnamese soldiers died during the battle, while American deaths numbered 650. Whatever Giap's motives in encircling the base, his troops had died in unprecedented numbers.

As the fog of battle in the cities and at Khe Sanh lifted, Westmoreland began to appreciate the full extent of the enemy's catastrophe. Convinced that the military situation was now more favorable than ever, he hoped to seize the initiative and launch a series of offensive operations into Cambodia, Laos, and North Vietnam. "Exploiting this opportunity," he argued, "could materially shorten the war."[14] Badly misreading the mood in Washington, the commanding general now believed that he might receive the full level of troop increases necessary for these ambitious undertakings.

Westmoreland's optimistic assessment was not shared by Joint Chiefs of Staff chair General Wheeler, who worried about new attacks on the cities of South Vietnam and the perilous state of U.S. forces worldwide. Johnson's earlier refusal to call up the reserves had forced the JCS to strip men and equipment from units in Asia and Europe and draw down the strategic reserve in the United States. By March 1968, with only one combat-ready division uncommitted, the Joint Chiefs feared that the American military would be unable to respond to an emergency in Berlin or Korea.

At long last, Wheeler was determined to break through the domestic constraints on the prosecution of the war and manipulate both the president and his commander in the field in order to achieve his objectives. First he encouraged Westmoreland to ask for reinforcements; both generals agreed that 206,000 more troops were needed, but Westmoreland understood that only 108,000 of this total would be deployed in South Vietnam, and then only if Johnson decided to expand the war. The rest would help reconstitute the strategic reserve. In reporting back to the president, however, Wheeler said nothing of the contingent nature of Westmoreland's request. Instead, he sought to frighten the president, painting a pessimistic picture of the situation in South Vietnam and claiming that the Tet Offensive was "a very near thing." Portraying Westmoreland as an embattled field commander, Wheeler warned that "if we did not send troops in the number requested [206,000] that we might have to give up . . . the two northern provinces of South Vietnam."[15]

Reassessment in Washington

The president and his senior advisers were stunned. They did not want a military disaster in South Vietnam; neither did they want a reserve call-up in a politically explosive domestic atmosphere. Faced with such unattractive choices, Johnson temporized, directing his new secretary of defense, Clark M. Clifford, to assemble a task force to "Give me the lesser of evils. Give me your recommendations."[16]

A long-time Washington insider and adviser to Democratic presidents, Clifford had consistently defended Johnson's policies in Vietnam. He found, however, that the members of his task force were deeply divided: some wished to approve the troop request, others wanted to shift to a less costly strategy. After consulting with members of the Congress and querying the JCS, Clifford developed doubts about the war. His meeting with the JCS turned into a tense question-and-answer session. Clifford asked, "What is the plan for victory?" The JCS responded that "There is no plan" because of the restrictions imposed on American forces.[17] Nor would they speculate on how long it might take to defeat the enemy.

Clifford's task force agreed on a compromise, recommending that the president dispatch 22,000 more troops to South Vietnam and issue a limited reserve call-up. In fact, however, the new secretary of defense already had concluded that the war was stalemated and that the time had come to begin scaling down the American presence in South Vietnam. As he told Johnson, "As we build up our forces, they build up theirs. . . . We seem to have gotten caught in a sinkhole."[18]

On March 10, shortly after Clifford's recommendation, the *New York Times* reported that Westmoreland had made an emergency request for 206,000 more troops. With no mention of Westmoreland's contingency plan for offensive operations, the front-page article portrayed him as near desperation. The story further startled those already shaken by Tet, suggesting that the war was a bottomless pit, and emboldened Westmoreland's critics, who now wondered how in the world he could proclaim Tet as an American victory and in the same breath urgently request a massive troop increase. They had no way of knowing that Westmoreland was as puzzled as they by the article.

In mid-March the Johnson administration also faced a serious economic crisis. In previous years the president had avoided giving the public and the Congress honest figures on the cost of the war, which may have amounted to as much as $3.6 billion a year. Expenditures on the war, added to heavy spending on Great Society programs, spurred inflation, increased the balance-of-payments deficit, and weakened the dollar in international money markets. In March pressure on the dollar mounted, as many currency speculators sold their dollars and caused a run on the gold markets. Emergency measures stemmed the gold crisis, but Secretary of the Treasury Henry Fowler warned the president that the adoption of the military's proposal for 206,000 additional troops would cost $2.5 billion in 1968 and $10 billion in 1969, adding to the balance-of-payments deficit and forcing a major tax increase as well as cuts in domestic spending. Now many business leaders were alarmed about the cost of the war and its impact on the American and world economy.

Faced with a divided administration, an economic crisis, and a disillusioned public, Johnson continued to vacillate in his approach to the war. He was attracted to Rusk's proposal to stop the bombing of most of North Vietnam in order to give the enemy an incentive to come to the bargaining table. But he also wished to convince Hanoi that the United States was prepared for the long haul, declaring in mid-March that "We shall and we are going to win."[19] Beset by conflicting impulses, the president searched in vain for a way to lead the nation out of the Vietnam quagmire.

Johnson was also troubled by his current political situation. The public approval of his handling of the war had fallen to an all-time low, while even his dominance of his beloved Democratic party had been challenged by insurgents. By the fall of 1967, a "Dump Johnson" movement had emerged within the party. In November Senator Eugene J. McCarthy (Democrat, Minnesota), encouraged by the vocal antiwar Democrats, had announced his candidacy for the nomination. Initially McCarthy did not seem a serious threat to Johnson's renomination, but the Tet Offensive changed the mood of the nation and that of the Democratic party. On March 12 Johnson's new vulnerability was revealed in the New Hampshire primary, where McCarthy only narrowly lost to the president, 49 to 42 percent. Worse still, four days later the president's nemesis, Robert Kennedy, finally entered the race for the Democratic nomination. As Johnson recalled, "The thing I feared from the first day of my Presidency was actually coming true. Robert Kennedy had openly announced his intention to reclaim the throne in the memory of his brother. And the American people, swayed by the magic of the name, were dancing in the streets. The whole situation was unbearable for me. After thirty-seven years of public service, I deserved something more than being left alone in the middle of the plain, chased by stampedes on every side."[20]

Toward the end of March, Johnson convened a meeting of the so-called Wise Men, the senior members of the foreign-policy establishment. As late as November 1967 this group had supported the war; now many of its members had turned against it. After a day of briefings on the impact of the Tet Offensive, McGeorge Bundy, Johnson's former national security adviser, summed up the conclusions of the majority of the group: "There is a very significant shift in our position. When we last met we saw reason for hope. We hoped then there would be slow but steady progress. Last night and today the picture is not so hopeful particularly in the countryside. Dean Acheson summed up the majority feeling when he said that we can no longer do the job we set out to do in the time we have left and we must begin to take steps to disengage."[21]

The shift of the Wise Men confirmed the president's conviction that his policies in Vietnam had to change. Lamenting the panic and demoralization in the nation and his own overwhelming disapproval in the polls, Johnson knew that to follow the advice of his hard-line advisers would further disrupt his administration and risk an even more severe domestic crisis. The Tet Offensive and the reaction to it had finally forced him to rethink his policies.

Well before Tet, Johnson had thought of retiring from the presidency. Emotionally exhausted, fearful of suffering another heart attack (he had suffered a severe one in the summer of 1955), and realizing that he would face a bitter fight for renomination and reelection, on March 31 LBJ spoke to the nation. In an address devoted to "Steps to Limit the War in Vietnam," the president announced a unilateral halt to the bombing of North Vietnam, except in the area directly north of the DMZ. Hoping that an end to the bombing would induce the

North Vietnamese to begin negotiations, he named W. Averell Harriman as his personal representative in any peace talks. Then, at the conclusion of his address, Johnson announced "I shall not seek, and I will not accept, the nomination of my party for another term as your President."[22]

Johnson had made up his mind, but he was bitter over the vilification that he had suffered and puzzled by the degree of opposition to his policies. "How is it possible," he asked in retrospect, "that all these people could be so ungrateful to me after I had given them so much?"[23] Less than four years after his great landslide victory, he had become one of the most unpopular presidents in American history.

The War at Home

In the spring of 1968 it seemed as if the nation's social fabric was unraveling. Martin Luther King Jr.'s assassination on April 4 sparked a new wave of urban riots, while later in the month student radicals occupied five buildings at Columbia University, including the office of the president. After a six-day occupation, in which red flags were raised above several university buildings, police responded, injuring some students and arresting nearly seven hundred. Even the nation's most prestigious institutions no longer seemed immune to the spreading unrest.

Johnson's announcement on March 31 that he would not run for reelection stunned the American people and threw both the McCarthy and Kennedy campaigns into disarray. The president's leadership had suddenly been removed as the major issue for both candidates; now they had to redefine their campaigns and face off in a series of primary contests. Meanwhile, Vice President Humphrey, Johnson's heir apparent, who announced his candidacy in mid-April, rapidly gathered delegates in nonprimary-holding states.

In the spring and early summer McCarthy and Kennedy confronted each other in a series of intense primary campaigns. McCarthy—an urbane, intelligent, and articulate candidate—appealed to many on the left wing of the Democratic party, what he called "a constituency of conscience."[24] Kennedy, the heir to "Camelot," the mythology surrounding his brother, appealed to minorities and the underprivileged and received a frenzied reception as he traveled across the nation. The reaction of the crowds, one team of British reporters noted, "had some of the yearning that was once poured out before the great queens of Hollywood. . . . It was real, that yearning for the young prince of the House of Kennedy; but it was also close to hysteria."[25]

Both McCarthy and Kennedy denounced the war in Vietnam, assailing the hawks, advocating a total bombing halt over North Vietnam, and urging that the NLF be given a role in any peace talks and in South Vietnam's postwar political life. But McCarthy went further, attacking the Cold War mentality of those—including John and Robert Kennedy—who had helped draw the nation into the war. "Involvement in Vietnam," he declared, "was no accident," but had been inspired by "the idea that somehow we had a great moral mission to control the entire world."[26] McCarthy was prepared in advance to endorse a coalition government in South Vietnam that included the NLF; Kennedy would not go this far, nor was he prepared to abandon the American commitment to South Vietnam. If the negotiations failed, he remarked, "then I think that we can take retaliatory action." In contrast, McCarthy moved close to urging American disengagement from South Vietnam whatever the cost. "I think," he said in mid-June, "the time has come when we must say we shall take our steel out of the land of thatched huts."[27]

While Kennedy won more primaries than McCarthy did, neither candidate was able to gain a clear edge over the other. In early June, Kennedy prevailed by a narrow margin in California, but at the time of his assassination in Los Angeles on June 4 he had no assurance of winning the nomination. McCarthy planned a strong challenge in the final primary in New York, and Kennedy, despite the emotionalism of his appeal, had been unable to construct a broad coalition of minorities and working-class whites. While he and McCarthy fought for delegates, big-city bosses, southern governors, and labor leaders rallied around Humphrey as the candidate who would defend their interests against party insurgents and perhaps put together a winning coalition in November. At the time of Robert Kennedy's death, the vice president was far ahead in the delegate count and likely to prevail at the Democratic convention to be held that August in Chicago.

The Bloodiest Year

Both Westmoreland, and his Communist adversaries in Hanoi, believed that the Tet Offensive had seriously weakened the other side. Westmoreland ordered his commanders to "maintain maximum pressure on the enemy in the south. . . . Maximum pressure at this point could demoralize the enemy in the south and bring about an unprecedented defection rate"; the Communist high command in South Vietnam explained that "the U.S. ground forces are now short of personnel, the negroes have risen up to oppose the government. . . . Our position is still strong. Our personnel strength has doubled."[28]

On April 1 Westmoreland began a counteroffensive designed to sweep away enemy units near the heavily populated coastal lowlands and penetrate large enemy sanctuaries on the borders. On May 5 Communist forces shelled hundreds of cities and towns and once again attacked Saigon, where more street fighting erupted. The major battles in May, however, were in I Corps, where U.S. Marines and NVA units met in a series of confused and costly encounters. In most cases the Marines prevailed, but only after taking heavy casualties.

Sometimes, however, the enemy's advantage was too decisive and American forces had to give way. At the Special Forces base at Kham Duc, ten miles from the Laotian border and ninety miles southwest of Da Nang, news of large NVA units in the area brought a reinforcing of the base. But American commanders soon began to have second thoughts. Aware of the weaknesses of the position and unwilling to undertake another long and wearing siege as at Khe Sanh, Westmoreland ordered an evacuation of the 1,500 defenders that was marked by panic and confusion. As one American officer wrote, "This was an ugly one and I expect some repercussions."[29]

Despite occasional reverses, Westmoreland denied that the war was stalemated, claiming that "The quality of the enemy's battlefield performance is—well, it approached the pathetic in some cases," and announcing that the United States was "on top again in Vietnam."[30] Westmoreland failed to understand, however, that time had run out for his approach to the war; his intransigence was out of favor in Washington. On March 23 the president announced that Westmoreland would step down as commander of U.S. forces in South Vietnam and become Army Chief of Staff. On June 9 Westmoreland left Saigon. There was no triumphal return home for the discredited commander. He flew from Tan Son Nhut to the Philippines, where he picked up his wife and daughter, boarded a U.S. warship for a leisurely journey to Hawaii, and in late June flew from Honolulu to Washington. On July 3 he was quietly sworn in as Army Chief of Staff.

Westmoreland's successor, General Creighton Abrams, had arrived in South Vietnam in May 1967 as deputy commander. One of the best tank commanders in World War II, Abrams had served in Korea and had risen rapidly through the ranks of the post–World War II army. Abrams combined an innovative approach to warfare—many thought he was the "smartest officer in the army"—with a blunt, volatile personality and little tolerance for mediocre staff work. His assignment was to work with the ARVN and increase its role in the war. Westmoreland had all but pushed ARVN out of the way; Abrams traveled widely throughout South Vietnam, trying to understand the problems involved in bringing Vietnamese forces up to their potential. As he worked with Vietnamese commanders and observed their troops in the field, he noted that ARVN officers were "trapped by their own training. They remember how the French did it. In their culture some of them are more French than Vietnamese."[31] He concluded that it would take many years for South Vietnamese forces to overcome their inadequacies.

The new commanding general viewed the war as both a conventional and guerrilla conflict and took a different approach than had Westmoreland. De-emphasizing the body count and big-unit operations, Abrams instead sought to protect the population, capture enemy supplies, and interdict infiltration along the Ho Chi Minh Trail. "The mission," he remarked, "is not to seek out and destroy the enemy. The mission is to provide protection for the people of Vietnam."[32]

As part of this shift toward a more innovative strategy, Abrams encouraged commanders to adapt their methods to the peculiar conditions of warfare in Vietnam. With Abrams's approval, Major Raymond G. Davis, commander of the Third Marine Division then spread along the DMZ, transformed his division, removing complacent officers and shifting his troops away from defensive positions toward high-mobility warfare. Acquiring better intelligence through the use of long-range reconnaissance patrols, Davis moved his forces around rapidly, targeting the Communist network of roads, supply trails, way stations, and storage areas. These leapfrog operations and systematic searches often proved to be dangerous and bloody, but they enabled Davis's Marines to find and uproot the massive quantities of prepositioned supplies essential to NVA operations.

Abrams also worked closely with civilian officials to disrupt the NLF's shadow government and secure as much of the countryside as possible, both through the commitment of U.S. and South Vietnamese troops and the development of a variety of new programs. Territorial Forces, made up of local, part-time soldiers, were expanded and re-equipped, the Chieu Hoi Program, which sought to encourage enemy defectors, was intensified, and the Phoenix Program, a combined CIA–South Vietnamese effort, was devised to identify and destroy the NLF's organization. At the end of 1968 John Paul Vann—now a senior official in the pacification program—reported that "the situation in Vietnam today gives cause for more optimism than at any time since 1961."[33]

Despite these shifts in the American war effort, the NVA was still a formidable opponent, the NLF infrastructure remained intact in many areas of South Vietnam, and weaknesses within the South Vietnamese government could not be quickly or easily overcome. ARVN became larger and better equipped, but it continued to suffer from poor leadership and a high rate of desertion. At the end of 1968 one American adviser rated two ARVN divisions "outright poor," eight no better than "improving," and only one "excellent."[34] After Tet, Thieu's regime gained more popular support and finally passed a draft and mobilization law—allowing for increases in the size of the ARVN—but it remained corrupt and inefficient, divided by rivalries between Ky and Thieu and confronted by militant Buddhists who wanted peace above all else. As the American journalist Robert Shaplen noted, "Divisiveness is still endemic, and rivalries exist across the board, in politics, in the Army, among religious groups, and so on." He concluded that the South Vietnamese seemed "more and more like men who know they are suffering from an incurable malady."[35]

For leaders in Hanoi, the failure of the Tet Offensive had far-reaching results. Many of the Viet Cong's most experienced cadres and soldiers had died in the offensive, and morale in the ranks of the southern revolutionaries had reached an all-time low. NVA troops flowed south to replace the losses, but the savage fighting of the spring and summer of 1968 brought new casualties and strengthened the hands of party members who concluded that the "correlation of forces" temporarily favored the United States and its allies. "At times," one prominent Communist argued, "under certain circumstances, we must shift to the defensive to gain time, dishearten the enemy, and build up our forces to prepare for a new offensive."[36]

When the Communists launched another offensive in mid-August, it sputtered from the start. This time American forces anticipated the attacks and, as a result of American spoiling operations, many NVA units found themselves short of supplies and unable to mass for the assault. "The final and decisive phase" of the general offensive had ended in a dismal failure.[37]

That fall many NVA and VC units withdrew to remote bases where they could reorganize and replace their losses. Abrams and his commanders knew that the Communists had suffered badly and that their logistical system was in disarray. They wanted to press the American advantage, exploit the edge their troops had acquired on the battlefield, and pursue the enemy into their strongholds in Cambodia. Militarily, Abrams reported to Washington, the United States faced "a moment of supreme opportunity."[38]

Washington's Calculations

Johnson's announcement on March 31 that he would suspend the bombing of most of North Vietnam led the government in Hanoi to express an interest in contact with U.S. representatives. Not until May 3, however, did the two sides agree on Paris as the site where they would meet to begin their discussions. These talks, which began in mid-May, quickly became deadlocked. The North Vietnamese were unyielding, demanding a complete end to the bombing and a withdrawal from Vietnam of U.S. forces. The president linked cessation of the bombing with the demand that Hanoi not improve its military position in the south, and he was unwilling to compromise his goal of an independent South Vietnam. Clifford and Harriman urged Johnson to be more flexible, suggesting that he stop the bombing and see how the North Vietnamese responded. But Johnson listened to hard-line advisers such as Rusk, telling Clifford that "I don't think being soft will get us peace," and expressing a wish to "knock the hell" out of North Vietnam.[39]

In early July, Johnson asked Clifford to travel to South Vietnam to assess the situation there, especially to determine if more of the burden of the war could be shifted to the ARVN, a policy that generally became known as the "Vietnamization" of the war. Once in Saigon, Clifford warned Ky and Thieu that "the American public would simply not support the war effort much longer. If we could not achieve a settlement in Paris, we expected the South Vietnamese gradually to take over the war." Between July 18 and 20, at a meeting with Johnson and his key advisers in Honolulu, Clifford gave a pessimistic report on conditions in South Vietnam. He doubted that the South Vietnamese Army—poorly led, inadequately trained, and underequipped—could take over the fighting in the near future, and he concluded that while "we could not win the war," that South Vietnamese leaders "did not want the war to end—not while they were protected by over 500,000 American troops and a 'golden flow of money.'"[40] He urged the president to make a strong effort to settle the conflict within the next six months.

Back in Washington, a frustrated and angry Johnson chafed over his inability to find a way out of the war. He had bought time at home by reducing the bombing and beginning negotiations, but the governments in Saigon and Hanoi dug in their heels and his own advisers could not agree over how to proceed. LBJ was unwilling to make major concessions to the North Vietnamese, but neither was he in a mood for heroic measures in South Vietnam, where American casualties remained high and the prospects for victory seemed bleak. The president simply could not find a way out of his dilemma. As he told his cabinet on August 22, "We want peace now worse than anyone in the world—but with honor, without retreat."[41]

The Fall Campaign

Amid all of the upheaval in 1968, it was easy to focus on the forces of change in American life and forget that the ground underneath the various protest movements was shifting. By the spring the youth rebellion had largely self-destructed, the civil rights movement had fragmented, and a conservative backlash had set in against many of the programs of the Great Society. Many white middle-class Americans—shocked to see young people burning their draft cards and even the American flag in the streets—had lost whatever sympathy they once had with the protest movements of the decade; many had even come to associate the Democratic party with lawlessness and disorder.

After Robert Kennedy's murder in June, the contest for the Democratic nomination lost much of its excitement. McCarthy withdrew from his campaign, realizing that party bosses would never turn to him for the nomination. Humphrey emerged as the clear front runner, but he already seemed a dated figure, tied too closely to the Johnson administration and its policies in Vietnam. And Johnson, who was now reconsidering his decision not to run, gave Humphrey only lukewarm support, doubting his qualifications for the presidency and privately describing him as weak and disloyal.

In late August the Democratic convention in Chicago was a disaster for Humphrey and his campaign. "Chicago," Humphrey remembered, "was a catastrophe. My wife and I went home heartbroken, battered, and beaten."[42] Mayor Richard J. Daley's oppressive security measures led to clashes with antiwar protestors. Chicago police, in full riot gear, made little attempt to distinguish between peaceful protestors and innocent bystanders as they swept the street in front of the convention hotel and nearby Grant Park, where youthful antiwar demonstrators had gathered, liberally using mace, tear gas, and nightsticks. Within the convention hall, the party's establishment refused to accept a compromise plank on the Vietnam War, prompting McCarthy delegates to put on black armbands and chant "Stop the war" and peace delegates from New York to sing chorus after chorus of "We Shall Overcome." Humphrey emerged from the convention without having articulated a different policy on the war and trailing badly in the polls.

While the Democratic party tore itself apart in Chicago, the Republicans united behind their recently chosen candidate, Richard M. Nixon. After losing his bid for the presidency in 1960 and his race for the governorship of California in 1962, Nixon, whom many pundits declared politically dead, staged a remarkable comeback, rebuilding his position within the party and in 1968 rolling through the Republican primaries, winning the nomination on the first ballot.

Nixon was an old hawk on the Vietnam War, one who had consistently criticized the Johnson administration for not doing enough to win it. After Tet, Nixon had moderated his position, suggesting vaguely that "the war can be ended if we mobilize our economic and political and diplomatic leadership."[43] But Nixon refused to be more specific, and after Johnson withdrew from the race and peace talks began, he declared a moratorium on the debate over the war as long as there was any hope for successful negotiations. At their convention in Miami in early August the Republicans backed a platform that called for "a progressive de-Americanization of the war" and offered "a program for peace" that would be "neither peace at any price nor a camouflaged surrender of legitimate United States or allied interests."[44] In fact, Nixon's position on the war differed little from that of the president.

As the campaign progressed, the most exciting figure was the candidate of the American Independent party, former governor George Wallace of Alabama. Appealing to those who were alienated by rapid racial and cultural change, Wallace, who supported the war, had no idea how to end it. He promised, if elected, to give the Joint Chiefs of Staff whatever resources they needed to win the conflict. But Wallace, realizing that the war was not popular among his followers, concentrated on running against the antiwar protestors, the long-haired "silver-spooned brats." "I tell you when November comes, the first time they lie down in front of my limousine," he declared "it'll be the last one they'll ever lay down in front of; Their day is *over*."[45]

Nixon ran a smoothly organized campaign, exploiting voter unease about the direction of the nation, promising to "end the war on an honorable basis," and eventually to "move toward an all-volunteer armed force."[46] In contrast, Humphrey's campaign was a shambles, disorganized, underfunded, and the target of angry antiwar protestors. Humphrey realized that his only chance was to separate himself from the position of the Johnson administration on the war.

On September 30 Humphrey went on evening television to talk about Vietnam. Rejecting unilateral withdrawal or further escalation, he promised that "As President, I would stop the bombing of the North as an acceptable risk for peace because I believe it could lead to success in the negotiations and thereby shorten the war."[47] Humphrey did not suggest what the terms of a settlement might be, and he added qualifications to his promise to end the bombing. But the speech marked the turning point of his campaign. It was conciliatory enough to neutralize the war issue within the Democratic party and to induce many antiwar liberals to drift back to support of his candidacy.

By mid-October, as the old Democratic coalition began to come together again, the presidential race had narrowed. Moreover, in Paris American and North Vietnamese representatives had achieved a break-through, agreeing that, in return for a total bombing halt, the North Vietnamese would exercise military restraint in the south and that peace talks would begin two days after the bombing had been stopped. While the North Vietnamese refused to negotiate directly with the "puppet" government in Saigon,[48] and while Thieu refused to join in any negotiations in which the NLF participated, a formula was agreed upon allowing each side to work out the composition of its own del-egation to the talks. On October 27 both Vietnamese governments agreed that Johnson would announce a bombing halt on October 31 and that talks would start on November 2.

Throughout the fall, Nixon had been fearful that an agreement in Paris would tip the election to Humphrey. In public Nixon supported Johnson's negotiating position; in private his campaign used an inter-mediary, Anna Chennault, a prominent Republican and widow of the founder of the World War II Flying Tigers, to encourage Thieu to boycott the peace talks. Fearful of an American "sellout," South Vietnam's president refused to participate, calculating that his nation would receive a better deal if Nixon won the election. Now American pressure mounted, with Johnson warning Thieu that if the American people held him responsible for delaying peace, "God help South Viet-nam, because no President could maintain the support of the Ameri-can people." A defiant Thieu replied: "You are powerful. You can say to small nations what you want . . . but you cannot force us to do anything against our interests. This negotiation is not a life and death matter for the US, but it is for Vietnam."[49] On October 31 Johnson announced a bombing halt, but was unwilling to open formal talks without the presence of South Vietnamese representatives. Not until after the elections did Thieu agree to send emissaries to Paris.

In the end, Nixon won a narrow victory by less than one percentage point, in part because the voters were looking for a candidate who seemed likely to end the war in Vietnam. In fact, none of the candidates knew how to do so, and all of them blurred their positions on the war, promising to resolve the conflict without compromising the honor of the nation. But Humphrey was tied to the policies of the past, while Nixon encouraged the impression that his foreign policy experience and contacts with world leaders would allow him to disentangle the nation from the conflict.

Since its transformation in 1965, the Vietnam War had acquired a deadly momentum of its own. Despite the bloody fighting in 1968, both sides continued to underestimate the determination and staying power of the other. Leaders in Hanoi remained confident of victory, realizing that, whatever the military costs of the Tet Offensive, it had convinced most Americans that the war could not be won at an acceptable price or in an acceptable time frame. President Johnson, aware of the loss of public support for the war, still clung to his original goal of a non-Communist South Vietnam and encouraged Abrams to "keep the enemy on the run. . . . Keep pouring it on. Let the enemy feel the weight of everything you've got."[50] By the end of 1968 neither side had gained a clear advantage; but neither side was willing to take decisive measures to break the military and political stalemate.

Notes

1 Quoted in Cecil B. Currey, *Victory at Any Cost: The Genius of Viet Nam's Gen. Vo Nguyen Giap* (Washington, D.C., and London, 1997), 263.

2 Quoted in James J. Wirtz, *The Tet Offensive: Intelligence Failure in War* (Ithaca, N.Y., and London, 1991), 74.

3 Quoted in Stanley Karnow, *Vietnam: A History* (New York, 1991), 554.

4 Quoted in Peter Macdonald, *Giap: The Victor in Vietnam* (New York and London, 1993), 268.

5 Quoted in Samuel Zaffiri, *Westmoreland: A Biography of General William C. Westmoreland* (New York, 1994), 259.

6 Quoted in Karnow, *Vietnam*, 560.

7 Quoted in Zaffiri, *Westmoreland*, 290; quoted in Robert Mann, *A Grand Delusion: America's Descent into Vietnam* (New York, 2002), 573–74.

8 Ibid., 290.

9 Quoted in Karnow, *Vietnam*, 562.

10 Quoted in Robert Dallek, *Flawed Giant: Lyndon Johnson and His Times, 1961–1973* (New York, 1998), 504.

11 Quoted in Zaffiri, *Westmoreland*, 298–99.

12 Ibid., 275.

13 Ibid., 319.

14 William C. Westmoreland, *A Soldier Reports* (New York, 1976), 463.

15 Quoted in Phillip B. Davidson, *Vietnam at War: The History, 1946–1975* (New York, 1991), 504–506.

16 Quoted in Dallek, *Flawed Giant*, 508.

17 Quoted in Davidson, *Vietam at War,* 514.

18 Quoted in Dallek, *Flawed Giant,* 509.

19 Ibid., 510.

20 Quoted in Doris Kearns, *Lyndon Johnson and the American Dream* (New York, 1976), 343.

21 Quoted in Larry Berman, *Lyndon Johnson's War: The Road to Stalemate in Vietnam* (New York, 1989), 196.

22 Quoted in Lyndon Baines Johnson, *The Vantage Point: Perspectives of the Presidency, 1963–1967* (New York, 1971), 435.

23 Quoted in Kearns, *Lyndon Johnson and the American Dream,* 340.

24 Quoted in Lewis L. Gould, *1968: The Election That Changed America* (Chicago, 1993), 22.

25 Quoted in Ronald Steel, *In Love with Night: The American Romance with Robert Kennedy* (New York, 2000), 148.

26 Ibid., 178.

27 Quoted in Allen J. Matusow, *The Unravelling of America: A History of Liberalism in the 1960s* (New York, 1984).

28 Quoted in Ronald H. Spector, *After Tet: The Bloodiest Year in Vietnam* (New York, 1993), 24.

29 Ibid., 175.

30 Quoted in Zaffiri, *Westmoreland,* 321.

31 Quoted in Lewis Sorley, *Thunderbolt: General Creighton Abrams and the Army of His Times* (Washington, D.C., 1998), 206.

32 Ibid., 237.

33 Quoted in Davidson, *Vietnam at War,* 577; Quoted in Lewis Sorley, *A Better War: The Unexamined Victories and Final Tragedy of America's Last Years in Vietnam* (New York, 1999), 94.

34 Quoted in George C. Herring, *America's Longest War: The United States and Vietnam, 1950–1975* (New York, 2002), 258.

35 Ibid., 235.

36 Quoted in Davidson, *Vietnam at War,* 543–44.

37 Quoted in Spector, *After Vietnam,* 240.

38 Ibid., 296.

39 Quoted in Dallek, *Flawed Giant,* 542; quoted in Herring, *America's Longest War,* 565–66.

40 Quoted in Clark Clifford, *Counsel to the President: A Memoir* (New York, 1991), 550–52.

41 Ibid., p. 569.

42 Quoted in Matusow, *Unravelling of America,* 422.

43 Quoted in Gould, *1968,* 39.

44 Ibid., 101–02.

45 Quoted in Dan T. Carter, *The Politics of Rage: George Wallace, The Origins of the New Conservatism, and the Transformation of American Politics* (New York, 1995), 345, 366.

46 Quoted in Gould, *1968,* 139.

47 Quoted in Matusow, *Unravelling,* 431.

48 Quoted in Herring, *America's Longest War,* 263.

49 Ibid., 238–39.

50 Quoted in Sorley, *Thunderbolt,* 253.

CHAPTER SEVEN

Nixon's War, 1969–1970

January 20, 1969, the day on which Richard M. Nixon took the oath of office, was a gray and windy one. As the new president prepared to drive from the Capitol back to the White House for the inaugural parade, the Secret Service insisted on closing the top of the presidential limousine, for antiwar demonstrators had gathered along portions of Pennsylvania Avenue. After proceeding a few blocks through friendly crowds, Nixon spotted the hundreds of protestors pressing against police lines: some lifted a NLF flag; others chanted, "Ho, Ho, Ho Chi Minh, the NLF is going to win," or "Four more years of death"; a few even hurled sticks, stones, beer cans, and bottles at the president's car.[1] As soon as the demonstrators had been left behind, Nixon ordered his sunroof opened, but he was angry that a group of protestors, if only briefly, had held him captive within his own limousine. This was the first disruption of an inaugural parade in American history, and a reminder to the new president that the fierce passions aroused by the war in Vietnam had not subsided.

The New Administration Takes Hold

Nixon entered office under a cloud of doubt and mistrust. A minority president (the Democrats had retained control of the Congress) and a controversial political figure, his ability to lead the nation in either foreign or domestic policy seemed uncertain. He was, Henry Kissinger remarked, a "withdrawn and elusive man," angry, moody, and tightly controlled, a leader who spent an unusual amount of time by himself and interacted with only a few advisers.[2] For all his personal idiosyncrasies, however, Nixon was a shrewd, intelligent, and experienced politician. Over the course of a long career he had studied with care the shifting currents of American and world politics and developed a keen instinct for his own survival.

Foreign policy fascinated Nixon, and it was in the foreign arena that he hoped to leave a great legacy. He intended to dominate his administration's foreign policy but knew that, given his need for solitude, he must have a powerful national security adviser to help carry out his ideas. Nixon chose Henry Kissinger, a Harvard University professor and a young, ambitious member of the foreign-policy establishment. Kissinger shared many of Nixon's beliefs about American foreign policy and also shared his views about how it should be implemented. Thus he was willing to collaborate with the president in circumventing Secretary of State William P. Rogers and the Department of State and to make the White House the center for foreign-policy decisions and the execution thereof. Both the president and his national security adviser—suspicious of the people and institutions of the permanent government—had a penchant for secrecy, intrigue, and making the unexpected move.

Nixon and Kissinger believed that the United States must take a more pragmatic approach to the Cold War and accept the fact that since the late 1940s American power had suffered a relative decline. The Soviet Union had nearly achieved nuclear parity, and the geopolitical position of the United States had also weakened with the rise of competing centers of power in China, Europe, Japan, and the U.S.S.R. Through a policy of "linkage," Nixon and Kissinger hoped to shape relations with Communist powers by cooperating with them in economic and strategic matters only if they worked with the United States in various areas of the globe to avoid dangerous crises and maintain the status quo. As Nixon remarked early in his presidency, "The great issues are fundamentally interrelated. . . . Crisis or confrontation in one place and real cooperation in another cannot be sustained simultaneously."[3]

Nixon also concluded that the American people, weary of the burdens of the seemingly endless war in Vietnam, were turning inward. On July 25, 1969, he announced the Nixon Doctrine, which emphasized the intention of the United States to rely more on its allies in combating Communist aggression. Or, as Nixon explained in early 1970, "America cannot—and will not—conceive *all* the plans, design *all* the programs, execute *all* the decisions, and undertake *all* the defense of the free nations of the world."[4] Only nine years after the exalted rhetoric of John F. Kennedy's inaugural address, Nixon offered the American people a far more subdued vision of the nation's role in world affairs.

The Vietnam Dilemma

During the presidential campaign, Nixon had promised to bring "peace with honor" in Vietnam; in fact, he entered the White House with no plan to end the conflict. While Nixon realized that the United States could no longer win a decisive military victory there, he was an old hawk who, before winning the presidency, had warned that "If the credibility of the United States is destroyed in Vietnam, it will be destroyed in Europe as well."[5] Nixon did not intend to be the first American president to lose a war. Like most of the senior figures in the American establishment, he misunderstood the war—viewing it as the result of Communist aggression rather than an indigenous revolutionary struggle—and refused to concede that this time the United States would not have its way.

For Nixon, the war was a profound challenge—the dominant issue of his presidency—and during his early months in office he and Kissinger devised a strategy to end it quickly, but on America's terms. By gradually withdrawing American troops, they would reduce casualties and undercut the pressure at home for a more abrupt departure. As this policy of the "de-Americanization," or "Vietnamization" as it came to be known, proceeded, an expanded and re-equipped South Vietnamese Army would take over ground combat, while pacification programs would weaken the hold of the NLF in the countryside and spread the authority of the government in Saigon.

Bold diplomacy would also help to erode the will of leaders in Hanoi. Nixon hoped to convince the Soviet Union and China—allies that provided Hanoi with massive amounts of economic and military aid—to pressure North Vietnam to make major concessions at the bargaining table. He intended to isolate and threaten North Vietnam's leaders, to convince them that he would take extreme measures to end the conflict—including an irrational, unpredictable, and dispropor-tionate use of force. As Nixon explained his "Madman Theory" to an aide, "I want the North Vietnamese to believe I've reached the point where I might do *anything* to stop the war. We'll just slip the word to them that, 'For God's sake, you know Nixon is obsessed about Com-munism. We can't restrain him when he's angry—and he has his hand on the nuclear button'—and Ho Chi Minh himself will be in Paris in two days begging for peace."[6]

For two self-styled realists, Nixon and Kissinger were naïve about the prospects for a quick and honorable end to U.S. participation in the Vietnam War. Before taking office, Nixon assured an aide that "I'm not going to end up like LBJ, holed up in the White House afraid to show my face on the street. I'm going to stop that war. Fast." And in March 1969, he "flatly" told his cabinet that "the war will be over by next year." Kissinger shared Nixon's optimism. "Give us six months," he told an antiwar group, "and if we haven't ended the war by then, you can come back and tear down the White House fence."[7] Buoyed by their victory over the Democrats in November and exhila-rated by their newly acquired power, Nixon and Kissinger were con-vinced that the United States and its ally in Saigon would prevail.

No Quick Exit

Soon after taking office, Nixon ordered Kissinger to canvass U.S. of-ficials in Washington and Saigon about the prospects for success in South Vietnam. Their responses revealed disagreements over the progress of the ARVN, the effectiveness of the government in Saigon, the size of Communist forces in South Vietnam, and even over the resumption of the bombing of North Vietnam. The Joint Chiefs of Staff, General Abrams, and Ambassador Bunker argued that the en-emy was in retreat and that the government in Saigon was growing stronger. But the State Department, the CIA, and some civilians in the Pentagon were more pessimistic about the course of the war. All agreed, however, that the Thieu regime could not handle the Communist threat without substantial, continuing American military and financial support.

The disagreement within the U.S. government made it easier for Nixon and Kissinger to pursue their own policies. They made their first move in neutral Cambodia, where, Generals Wheeler and Abrams pointed out, the North Vietnamese had positioned 40,000 fresh troops; the generals wanted to decimate these troop concentrations with B-52 raids as well as destroy COSVN, the headquarters for Communist operations in South Vietnam. Nixon agreed, in mid-March ordering the secret bombing of enemy base areas in Cambodia. Aside from their important military objectives, Nixon viewed these air strikes as an oblique threat to North Vietnam, a signal that unless leaders in Hanoi made significant concessions, tougher measures would follow.

Nixon knew that he was engaged in a struggle, not only in Vietnam but also for the hearts and minds of the American people. By the spring of 1969 the antiwar movement had become so widespread that it was difficult for the president to appear on most college campuses. That year General Westmoreland, now Army Chief of Staff, undertook an extended tour of the United States, giving more than two hundred speeches about the U.S. military and the Vietnam War. At nearly half of the places where he appeared, Westmoreland encountered organized antiwar demonstrators. At the University of Nebraska, students surrounded the building in which he was speaking carrying signs that read, "Westmoreland—War Criminal" and "Westmoreland—America's Eichmann."[8] At Yale University, a crowd of angry students carrying NLF flags and hostile signs seized the hall where he was supposed to talk, forcing him to cancel his address and return to Washington.

Nevertheless, during his first year in office, Nixon maneuvered to save South Vietnam in a way that was acceptable to the American people. While he denounced student revolutionaries, he also moved to undercut their base of support, forming a commission to study the creation of an all-volunteer army and asking for major changes in the Selective Service System—especially the creation of a lottery—that would ease the burden of the draft on the nation's young men. In mid-May Nixon went on television for a major report on the war. He proposed a mutual withdrawal from South Vietnam of all foreign troops—both American and North Vietnamese—to be followed by an exchange of prisoners-of-war (POWs) and the creation of an international body to supervise free elections in South Vietnam. Then he warned America's enemy: "Let me be quite blunt. Our fighting men are not going to be worn down; our mediators are not going to be talked down; and our allies are not going to be let down."[9] Nixon's peace proposal—quickly rejected by Hanoi—won strong public support. Even so, he recognized many signs of impatience, both among the general public and in Congress, where even some prominent Republicans showed signs of serious frustration with the prolongation of the war.

In order to buy time to give his policies a chance to work, Nixon had to address this deepening disillusionment with the war. On June 8, 1969, he conferred with President Thieu on Midway Island. South Vietnam's leader, fearful of the future, only reluctantly agreed to a policy of Vietnamization—the gradual withdrawal of American troops and the turning of the war over to the ARVN. Nixon announced the redeployment of 25,000 American soldiers, and he promised that another 40,000 would be pulled out in three months. He knew that an irreversible process had begun.

Within the administration, opinions differed on the wisdom of this American pullback. Secretary of Defense Melvin R. Laird, who had served in Congress and had close ties there, believed that the South Vietnamese must take over the war and, as he told Nixon, the American electorate "would not be satisfied with less [than the] eventual disengagement of American men from combat."[10] In contrast, Kissinger thought that Thieu's regime was weak and worried that an American withdrawal would undercut efforts to negotiate with North Vietnam, whose leaders would be unwilling to make concessions while American troops were being pulled out. "The more troops are withdrawn," he noted, "the more Hanoi will be encouraged." He wanted to threaten North Vietnam with the possibility of a "savage, punishing blow" if it did not agree to end the war largely on American terms. Or, as he remarked, "I can't believe that a fourth-rate power like North Vietnam does not have a breaking point."[11]

On the surface, Nixon's policy seemed contradictory. On the one hand, he planned to pull out American troops and largely turn the war over to the South Vietnamese; on the other, he ordered Kissinger to begin direct, secret negotiations with the North Vietnamese—bypassing both his own State Department and the government in Saigon—in order to reach a political settlement. Would not North Vietnam simply wait until all American troops were removed and then overwhelm a weakened South Vietnamese Army? Nixon calculated that—through a combination of threats, international isolation, and successful Vietnamization—he could persuade leaders in Hanoi to give up their vision of a unified Vietnam and accept its permanent division at the seventeenth parallel. And he had no intention of completely retreating. While American ground combat troops would leave, he planned to keep American advisers in South Vietnam and to use American air power as a shield for that nation.

The Allure of Vietnamization

In 1969 Nixon's hopes for Vietnamization were encouraged by prominent authorities on the war. Sir Robert Thompson, a British guerrilla-warfare expert, assured the president that the government in Saigon would survive with continued American support. When Nixon asked Thompson if he thought it was important for the United States "to see it through," his response was unequivocal: "Absolutely. In my opinion the future of Western civilization is at stake in the way you handle yourselves in Vietnam."[12] A leading American expert on the war, John Paul Vann, also told the president that victory was possible. Vann argued that the Tet Offensive had decimated the Viet Cong and that the NVA units that had replaced these local guerrillas could never achieve the same rapport with the peasantry. American-sponsored pacification programs impressed Vann; given the improved balance of forces in South Vietnam, he believed that it would be sufficient to leave a residual force of American advisers, pilots, and technicians. The ARVN, with its new heavy weapons, could handle the NVA when the two armies eventually faced off to determine the fate of the nation.

The shift in Vann's position revealed the growing polarization among Americans. In 1963 Vann, as an adviser to the ARVN's Seventh Division, had been pessimistic about the outcome of the struggle. After his return to South Vietnam in 1965 and his involvement in the pacification program, he had become a believer in the war. In 1969 Vann's friend the journalist David Halberstam challenged his assessment of the conflict, urging him to consider, in the advice he gave the president, the fact that American society was being torn apart by the struggle. But Vann was "not interested in that."[13] Like some other Americans, he had found fulfillment in Vietnam, in being a warrior king among an impoverished people.

Threats and Maneuvers

In late July, Nixon set off on a round-the-world trip, including a stop in South Vietnam, where he told troops of the First Infantry Division near Saigon that they were fighting to allow the South Vietnamese "to choose their own way" and "reduce the chances of more wars in the future." While Nixon was buoyed by his visit to the war zone, he also began to worry that time was running out for his approach to the conflict. In September Congress would reconvene, students would return to their campuses, and a new antiwar tide might sweep across the nation. In a series of mid-summer conversations with Kissinger, Nixon declared that he would "end the war one way or the other—either by negotiated agreement or by an increased use of force."[14]

Nixon moved in both directions. In August Kissinger held his first secret meeting with enemy negotiators in Paris. Carrying out the president's instructions, he threatened the North Vietnamese, warning them that if they did not withdraw their troops and agree to participate in elections, Nixon would "be compelled—with great reluctance—to take measures of the greatest consequences."[15] The deadline was November 1. But the North Vietnamese were unyielding. Refusing to admit that any NVA troops were in the south, they continued to insist that Thieu give way to a coalition regime that would supervise elections. Unmoved by Kissinger's tough talk, leaders in Hanoi still were not willing to make major concessions to end the war.

Meanwhile, Nixon prepared to make good his threat against North Vietnam. During the summer he had his staff put together a new war plan, code-named Duck Hook, that called for an all-out attack against North Vietnam, including the massive bombing of Hanoi and

Haiphong, the mining of major rivers and harbors, the destruction of the dike system along the Red River, and a possible invasion of the North and use of nuclear weapons at points along the Ho Chi Minh Trail. One way or another, Nixon was still determined to prevail.

In September Nixon considered escalating the war, informing Republican congressional leaders on September 30 that "I will not be the first President of the United States to lose a war." He also sought to undercut the reviving antiwar movement, announcing another troop withdrawal of 60,000 men, canceling draft calls for November and December, and deciding to hold the first draft lottery on December 1. In a news conference Nixon insisted that "Once the enemy recognizes that it is not going to win its objectives by waiting us out, then the enemy will negotiate and we will end this war before the end of 1970."[16]

The continuing stalemate in Vietnam and the lengthening list of casualties (30,610 killed in action by the end of 1968) brought new life to the antiwar movement. Senator J. William Fulbright (Democrat, Arkansas) announced new hearings on the war and complained that the president was not making "progress in delivering on his campaign promises to give new birth to his plan to end the war,"[17] while seventy-nine college presidents signed an appeal to Nixon to speed up the U.S. withdrawal from Vietnam. College campuses overflowed with protests, and on October 15 the Vietnam moratorium took place, the largest antiwar demonstration in the nation's history. Involving more than 2 million people in more than two hundred cities, it drew a broad range of Americans to peaceful antiwar rallies: the antiwar movement had moved beyond the campuses into the mainstream of America.

The moratorium shook the president, even though one recent poll showed that 68 percent of Americans still approved of the way in which he was handling the war. Worried about his standing with the public and faced with opposition within his administration to any escalation, Nixon repressed his urge to destroy the enemy in North Vietnam and cancelled Duck Hook. But he continued to talk tough with opponents of his administration. Vice President Spiro T. Agnew labeled the leaders of the antiwar movement as an "effete corps of impudent snobs who characterize themselves as intellectuals," while Nixon told the Soviet ambassador that a relaxation of tension was tied to Soviet help in ending the Vietnam War. "We cannot," the president warned, "allow a talk-fight strategy to continue without taking action. . . . I can assure you, the humiliation of a defeat is absolutely unacceptable to my country. . . . We will not hold still for being diddled to death in Vietnam."[18]

On November 3 Nixon gave a major television address on the Vietnam War. "For the United States," he warned, "this first defeat in our Nation's history would result in a collapse of confidence in American leadership, not only in Asia but throughout the world. . . . Precipitate withdrawal would . . . be a disaster of immense magnitude." Listing all of the steps he had taken to achieve peace, he blamed Hanoi for the failure of negotiations and claimed that Vietnamization was working. While the president did not offer any clear path out of the war, he appealed to "the great silent majority of my fellow Americans" for their support. "Let us," he concluded, "be united for peace. Let us also be united against defeat. Because let us understand: North Vietnam cannot defeat or humiliate the United States. Only Americans can do that."[19]

Despite strong public support for his "silent majority" speech, Nixon understood the frustrations of the American position in Vietnam. "We simply cannot," he confided to Secretary of State Rogers, "tell the mothers of our casualties and the soldiers who have spent part of their lives in Vietnam that it was all to no purpose."[20] As he searched for a way to justify American sacrifices in Vietnam, he realized that opposition to the war was unrelenting. In mid-November large crowds gathered in Washington to protest the continuation of the fighting. Most of those who attended Mobilization Day in the nation's capital protested in a peaceful and orderly manner, but some radicals marched to the Justice Department, where they built barriers and raised an NLF flag. Worse still, opponents of the war were outraged by ten pages of photographs in *Life* magazine of the massacre of Vietnamese civilians at the village of My Lai on the south-central coast in Quang Ngai Province. For many Americans, the atrocities at My Lai only confirmed their contention that the war must end—and soon.

The My Lai massacre revealed the growing ugliness of the war. Charlie Company, part of the poorly led and trained Americal Divi-

sion, operated in an area where the Viet Cong had strong peasant support. Frustrated by search-and-destroy operations that led to heavy
American casualties from snipers, mines, and booby traps, the company' s officers and troops longed to strike out against their hidden
enemy. Briefings for their helicopter assault on My Lai had led them
to expect resistance from a VC battalion. After landing on the morning of March 16, 1968, they encountered no opposition, only women,
children, and mostly old men cooking breakfast. Encouraged by their
officers, Captain Ernest Medina and Lieutenant William Calley Jr.,
the soldiers of Charlie Company ran wild, killing between two hundred and five hundred civilians, many of whom were left lying in a
ditch near the village. More than a year and a half later, in November
1969, journalists exposed the Army's attempted cover-up of the incident. A subsequent Army investigation revealed that thirty persons—
mostly officers—had known of the atrocities; only the most junior
officer involved, Lieutenant Calley, was convicted of murder (and the
secretary of the army later reduced his sentence).

Over the course of 1969, Nixon had withdrawn 115,500 troops
from Vietnam—a significant achievement—but by the end of the year
he knew that his plan to end the war quickly had failed. He remained,
however, optimistic, calculating that in 1970 his policies would lead
to a diplomatic breakthrough. But Nixon was grasping for straws; he
had no sure way out of the impasse in Vietnam. Like Johnson before
him, he had misjudged the leaders of the Vietnamese revolution. They
had spent most of their adult lives fighting against the Japanese, the
French, and then the Americans, and they regarded the unification of
Vietnam as a sacred duty, one worth almost any sacrifice. Nixon, like
his predecessors, lacked the power to compel these men to forsake
their cherished goals.

One War

In 1969 the American military's priorities in Vietnam continued to
shift, away from ground-combat operations toward what the American commander in Vietnam, General Creighton Abrams, termed a "one
war" strategy. Abrams viewed the war as both a conventional and
guerrilla conflict, de-emphasized the body count and the war of attri-

tion, and used more of his forces for the protection of the population in the countryside. But old habits of fighting died hard. In May, American troops searching near the Laotian border—part of an operation to clear out enemy staging areas—encountered entrenched NVA troops on Ap Bia Mountain. Over the course of the fierce ten-day battle that ensued, repeated American ground assaults, combined with air and artillery strikes, finally dislodged the enemy and inflicted heavy losses. Fifty-six Americans died in the fighting, but soon after taking Hamburger Hill, as it became known, U.S. forces simply abandoned it. The battle ignited a firestorm of protests in the United States over what seemed, to many observers, a senseless loss of life; it also led Nixon to order Abrams to hold down American casualties.

In June, after Nixon and Thieu formally approved the policy of Vietnamization at Midway, Abrams received a new mission statement for the U.S. Army in South Vietnam. His first priority was no longer the destruction of enemy forces but preparing ARVN to take over the main responsibility for ground combat. Abrams and other senior American commanders knew that they had a race on their hands: to get the South Vietnamese Army up to speed before American troops departed.

When Abrams had arrived in South Vietnam in May 1967 as Westmoreland's deputy commander, his assignment had been to work with ARVN to help it increase its role in the war. Westmoreland had avoided dealing with ARVN and maintained a perfunctory relationship with its top command. In contrast, Abrams was curious about Vietnamese culture and patient with South Vietnamese officers; he was determined to understand the difficulties of their army and how to make it a more effective force.

But as Abrams undertook this expansion and reorganization, he gradually realized the magnitude of the task. South Vietnamese senior officers were, in his judgment, more French than Vietnamese, drawn from the Vietnamese elite and trained by the French. "People must realize," Abrams remarked, "that the South Vietnamese armed forces still bear the legacy of French training and the French policy of stifling emerging leadership. It is no good to get angry and order the Vietnamese to do something; one has to persuade them or else the job will not get done. Patience is vital."[21] Worse still, the upper ranks of the ARVN had been heavily politicized by first Diem and then Thieu; the latter had developed a network of alliances with senior commanders that formed the basis of his regime. Thieu ruled through the South Vietnamese Army, viewing the political loyalty of his officers as more important than their competence as commanders. When pressed by Abrams and Bunker, who were appalled at the "political jockeying that just goes on *incessantly*,"[22] Thieu would make some changes, but he feared that any real housecleaning would bring political chaos and possibly the downfall of his regime. ARVN's junior officers, who led its mostly peasant soldiers, were better motivated and trained. But it would take years for this younger generation to move up the chain of command.

Other organizational problems also plagued ARVN. It had long relied on the American military for training and logistical support. Without major changes, ARVN could not manage its own war effort, maintaining equipment and distributing the huge amount of ammunition, fuel, and spare parts essential to keep its battalions in the field. Nor did many of its commanders know how to lead their troops in large-scale operations; in the opinion of one South Vietnamese general, as late as the spring of 1975 only one of the four corps commanders had mastered "the fundamentals of warfare."[23] Finally, although ARVN resembled a modern military force, it suffered from a high desertion rate and inadequate pay, food, and housing for its troops. ARVN soldiers, struggling to make ends meet and to take care of their families—who after 1971 could no longer live near base camps—could not help but notice, as one put it, that the Americans seemed "to have things so much better."[24]

Many American observers confirmed these weaknesses. Colonel David H. Hackworth, who advised several ARVN units, concluded "that the South Vietnamese Army was a terminally sick outfit still fighting as the French had taught them—and as we kept reinforcing—with World War II tactics certain to produce defeat."[25] In 1969, when he led a battalion of American troops in the Mekong Delta, he would not allow any Vietnamese—military or civilians—inside the fire bases under his control. Earlier in the war, in October 1965, John Laurence, a CBS television correspondent, learned that an ARVN column was moving toward the relief of a U.S. Special Forces camp in the Central Highlands. Too late to accompany the armored column, Laurence joined ARVN Rangers lifted by helicopter to a narrow pass from which the Viet Cong were likely to spring an ambush. When the VC began their attack, the Rangers did not move down from their hill and engage the enemy from behind. Nor would they mortar retreating enemy forces. An astonished Laurence concluded, *"These guys don't want to fight. . . . How can they hope to win if they let the enemy get away so easily?"*[26]

The Enemy Regroups

For Communist revolutionaries, the Tet Offensive had been a major miscalculation. They had misjudged the mood of South Vietnam's urban masses and exposed Viet Cong units to overwhelming Allied firepower. As a result, many of the Viet Cong's best soldiers, persons with years of experience, were now dead. General Tran Van Tra, who had led the VC attack on Saigon, described the situation after Tet: "Our cadres and men were fatigued. We had not time to make up for our losses, all units were in disarray, there was a lack of manpower, there were shortages of food and ammunition."[27] Given the depopulation of the countryside and the increasing effectiveness of pacification programs, the pool of recruits was smaller than in previous years. Despite years of warfare, guerrillas fighting in South Vietnam could see no light at the end of the tunnel.

Life for the rank and file of the Viet Cong had always been difficult, and it became more so after the Tet Offensive. Troops living in the jungle—many of them suffering from malnutrition and a variety of tropical diseases—had to endure aerial defoliation and repeated B-52 bombardments. Operation RANCH HAND, begun in 1962, grew in intensity as the war progressed; U.S. aircraft sprayed thousands of pounds of toxic chemical agents on South Vietnam's crops and forests, affecting the health of enemy soldiers who passed through these areas. And flights of giant bombers, flying so high that they could not be seen or heard by those on the ground, used carpet bombing techniques that devastated an area in a few seconds. Even if the bombs hit half a mile away, the shock waves would collapse the walls of unreinforced bunkers, burying alive those inside. Sometimes guerrillas received a warning of an attack; when they returned to their former location, one NLF official recalled, "It was as if an enormous scythe had swept through the jungle, felling the giant teak and go trees like grass in its way, shredding them into billions of scattered splinters. . . . There would simply be nothing there, just an unrecognizable landscape gouged by immense craters."[28]

The Tet Offensive also changed the balance between southern and northern soldiers fighting in South Vietnam and raised pressing questions about future revolutionary strategy. In the aftermath of Tet, northern troops poured into the south to fill out the depleted ranks in order to continue the struggle. By early 1969, NVA soldiers composed about 85,000 of the 125,000 troops in main-force Viet Cong units. In the spring and summer of that year Communist forces launched further attacks throughout South Vietnam. The results of these efforts were disappointing; it was now apparent to leaders in Hanoi that the war was stalemated. They decided to reduce the level of violence in the south and rest and regroup their battered army. As one party document stated, "Victory will come to us, not suddenly, but in a complicated and tortuous way."[29]

Because of the deadlock on the battlefield, Hanoi did not believe that conditions were ripe for a diplomatic settlement. Thus North Vietnam's strategy was to string out the negotiations that had opened in May 1968 and hope that a combination of American troop withdrawals, domestic unrest, and mounting American casualties would force the United States to conclude the war on North Vietnamese terms.

In order to prepare for the day when serious negotiations would take place, in June 1969 members of the NLF and other neutralist groups in South Vietnam formed a new "government of anti-U.S. resistance for national salvation."[30] This Provisional Revolutionary Government (PRG) claimed to represent the legitimate interests of the South Vietnamese people.

Ho Chi Minh's death on September 2, 1969, brought no changes in North Vietnam's policies. Le Duan became, in effect, the leader of the DRV, Pham Van Dong remained as premier, and they and their associates continued to prepare for the long haul. As they did so, tensions grew between northern and southern revolutionaries. The heavy losses of Tet had led to a greater North Vietnamese presence in the

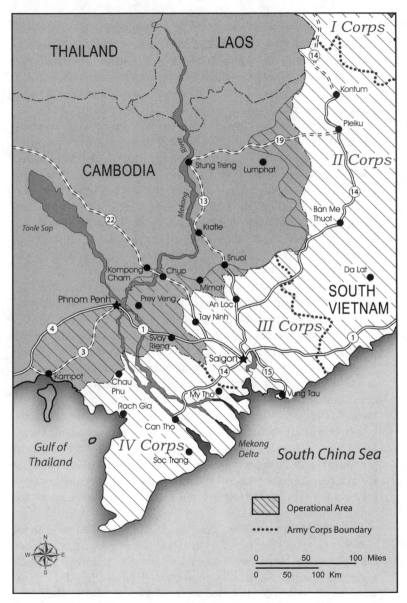

Cross-Border Operations

south, and now northern Communists sought to make their southern comrades aware of their "class deficiencies" and educate them in the finer points of Marxism-Leninism. Southern revolutionaries became anxious about the future, "trapped," as the NLF's Minister of Justice wrote, "between their loathing of the Thieu dictatorship and their fears of communism."[31] They hoped that, when victory finally came in the south, it would bring substantial autonomy rather than submergence under northern rule.

The Cambodian Incursion

In late January 1970 President Nixon sent a team led by General Alexander M. Haig Jr. to South Vietnam to assess progress in Vietnamization. Haig's report was mixed; he found some improvements in ARVN, but saw "no sign that the enemy has given up,"[32] and warned that South Vietnamese leaders were pessimistic, fearing an overly rapid American retreat. In Washington, Secretary of Defense Laird and Secretary of State Rogers continued to push for disengagement, while Kissinger worried that troop withdrawals would remove any incentive for leaders in Hanoi to bargain. Nixon was more optimistic, calculating that a combination of threats, military moves, great-power diplomacy, and Vietnamization would force Hanoi to yield. He now expected to end the war in late 1970 or early 1971.

In early 1970 Kissinger convinced Nixon to begin another round of negotiations. From February through April Kissinger met secretly in Paris with Le Duc Tho, a top party official who now became the chief North Vietnamese negotiator. But neither side was willing to yield. Kissinger still insisted on a mutual withdrawal of U.S. and NVA troops and a political settlement favoring Thieu, while the North Vietnamese rejected the formula of mutual withdrawal and insisted that the Thieu regime be replaced with a coalition government that included representation of the PRG. They seemed in no hurry to end the war. If the United States could not prevail with half a million troops in South Vietnam, Le Duc Tho asked Kissinger, "how can you succeed when you let your puppet troops do the fighting?"[33]

Frustrated in dealing with the war in Vietnam, Nixon sought refuge in heroic fantasies. Time after time, in the early months of 1970, he watched the film *Patton,* in which George C. Scott played the defiant and heroic World War II general. Patton was tough and decisive, willing to take great risks to achieve his goals. At the beginning of the film, standing in front of a large American flag addressing his troops, he proclaims that "Americans have never lost and never will lose a war because the very thought of losing is *hateful* to Americans."[34]

Longing to take bold action, Nixon maneuvered within the confines of American politics to find a solution to the war. In late April he reported to the American people on Vietnamization, stating that it was working so well that he could withdraw another 150,000 troops in 1970. But despite this dramatic announcement, it remained a fact that, according to the president's own projections, the United States in April 1971 would still have 284,000 troops in South Vietnam. Clearly his timetable for ending the war was out of kilter.

In the spring of 1970 Nixon's attention focused on Cambodia, where for years its leader, Prince Norodom Sihanouk, had maneuvered to prevent his nation from being engulfed in the war in nearby South Vietnam. He accepted the fact that 40,000 NVA troops, along with local Khmer Rouge (Communist) revolutionaries, had created a large sanctuary in eastern Cambodia, and he also accepted Nixon's secret bombing of enemy bases there in 1969. But as the war intensified and spread to Cambodia, the middle ground on which Sihanouk stood gradually disappeared. Leaders of the Cambodian military, led by General Lon Nol, were resentful of Sihanouk's tolerance of Communist forces on Cambodian territory and on March 18, while the prince was out of the country, seized control of the government. With Sihanouk stuck in exile, Lon Nol and his generals challenged the North Vietnamese presence in Cambodia. In response, the NVA pushed westward, raising fears that it might capture the capital, Phnom Penh. Without U.S. economic and military aid, Lon Nol's new pro-American regime would quickly disappear.

Nixon ordered the CIA to give all-out support to Lon Nol, but wanted what he termed "a big play" in Cambodia.[35] A joint U.S.–ARVN offensive against sanctuaries there had long been on the president's mind. Once again his advisers were divided: Laird and Rogers opposed the invasion, while Abrams, Bunker, and the JCS supported it. But Nixon, seeing himself as a beleagured commander-in-chief, was determined to act forcefully. After listening to the president, one aide wrote that "He still feels he can get it wound up this year, if we keep enough pressure on, and don't crumble at home."[36] Nixon hoped to stabilize the Lon Nol regime, destroy vital enemy supply caches and the Communist command center (COSVN) in Cambodia, and close down the port of Sihanoukville, which supplied Communist forces in parts of South Vietnam. The president was determined to show leaders in Hanoi that the United States would expand the war in order to end it.

On April 29, ARVN units moved across the border into Cambodia; two days later American troops followed, for a total Allied force of 23,700 men. The next day Nixon announced his decision to invade Cambodia to the American people. Rather than try to appease his critics—by emphasizing that the invasion was only an extension of earlier cross-border operations—Nixon delivered a pious and defiant address, claiming that the stakes in Cambodia and Vietnam were global. "If," he announced, "when the chips are down, the world's most powerful nation, the United States of America, acts like a pitiful, helpless giant, the forces of totalitarianism and anarchy will threaten free nations and free institutions throughout the world." In a dramatic conclusion, he claimed that "I would rather be a one-term President and do what I believe is right than to be a two-term President at the cost of seeing America become a second-rate power and to see this nation accept the first defeat in its proud 190-year history."[37]

Beneath the extravagant rhetoric, Nixon's decision was a modest one. American and South Vietnamese troops did not penetrate deeply into Cambodia and had departed by the end of June. While Allied forces captured huge enemy supply depots and delayed another offensive, the move into Cambodia had no long-term consequences for the war. Nevertheless, Nixon reveled in his decision. The day after his address, he drove to the Pentagon for a first-hand briefing on the Cambodian operation. Swept up in the excitement of the moment, the congratulations of military personnel and civilian workers, and the drama of the JCS briefing, Nixon expressed his great admiration for the soldiers in Vietnam, juxtaposing them to "these bums . . . blowing up the campuses."[38] Rather than moving toward healing the wounds of the nation, he managed to deepen them.

The invasion of Cambodia set off a wave of protests. In the Senate, Frank F. Church (Democrat, Idaho) complained that "the Nixon administration has devised a policy with no chance of winning the war, little chance of ending it, and every chance of perpetuating it into the indefinite future."[39] Student strikes affected 350 campuses, on some of which violence erupted. At Kent State University angry students rioted in the downtown area and then burned down the ROTC building on campus. In response, Ohio Governor James Rhodes ordered the National Guard to occupy the campus. On May 4, after hours of tense confrontation, the tired Guardsmen fired at the crowd of students, some of whom had been throwing rocks and heckling, others of whom were simply changing classes. Four students were killed and nine were wounded. Ten days later at Jackson State College in Mississippi (a predominantly African American institution), police and state highway patrolmen, after two nights of campus demonstrations, fired into a dormitory, killing two students and wounding twelve others. While one poll showed that 50 percent of the public approved of the Cambodian incursion (with 39 percent opposed), the long-term trends in public opinion—both on the continuation of the war and on Nixon's handling of it—moved downward. In general, the American people were tired of the fighting, and everywhere he looked Nixon faced an erosion of his support, whether in the bureaucracy, which was divided, or in the Congress, where Senate legislation seeking to limit Nixon's freedom of maneuver in Vietnam was gaining momentum.

On June 3, in another televised address, the president claimed that the Cambodian operation was a success, promised to have all American troops out of that nation by the end of the month, and pledged once more to pull another 150,000 troops out of Vietnam by April 1971. Reminding the American people that "only this administration can end this war and bring peace," he claimed that "the greater the support the administration receives in its efforts, the greater the opportunity to win that just peace we all desire."[40]

Nixon had ridden out the storm over Cambodia, but by the summer of 1970 he found that his dilemma in Vietnam had deepened. He had to maintain the momentum of American troop withdrawals, but he had no guarantee that ARVN would improve fast enough to take over the war. And as the size of the American expeditionary force decreased, Nixon had less and less leverage with leaders in Hanoi, who seemed unimpressed with his threats and as determined as ever to achieve the unification of Vietnam. The president could only hold on to the tired hope that, if he could strengthen South Vietnam and maintain a residual American presence there, he might keep North Vietnam at bay and force the permanent division of the nation at the seventeenth parallel.

A Changing War

At the beginning of 1970, there were still 385,000 American troops in South Vietnam, but their role in the war was changing. MACV now sought to push Vietnamization as rapidly as possible, continue the withdrawal of American forces on schedule, and lower the number of American casualties. American commanders no longer talked of military victory; their troops stayed close to fire support bases, while more ARVN units assumed offensive operations in the field. The war was entering yet another phase.

In March and April 1970 a CBS television crew, filming a program about the daily lives of American soldiers in the field, accompanied Second Company of the First Cavalry Division on operations near the Cambodian border. An experienced and well-led unit, it was under a new commander, Captain Al Rice, when the journalists rejoined the troops in early April. On patrol the next day, the soldiers arrived at a trail in the jungle, six to ten feet wide and perfectly straight, filled with dozens of fresh tracks left by North Vietnamese soldiers. The battalion commander, informed by Captain Rice of the existence of the trail, ordered the company to proceed along it, but the sergeant in charge of the squad on point refused: "That's a fuckin *road*. I ain't goin to walk down there. My whole squad ain't walkin down there." The sergeant and his squad moved away from the trail and other troops—angry and agitated—followed. Captain Rice tried to set an example, walking with his small command staff down the trail, but no one followed.[41] The captain faced a revolt of his men. Before he could decide how to handle it, battalion ordered his company to move a short distance in the other direction so that it could be extracted by helicopter. The soldiers reluctantly agreed to do so, but they had made their point—they would not allow an inexperienced officer to put their lives needlessly at risk. A new mood had settled over American soldiers in Vietnam.

The decrease in offensive combat missions, along with the obvious decision of American leaders not to seek a military victory and the effect of the antiwar movement on American soldiers, led to a decline in morale and discipline. Most American soldiers had no desire to die for what increasingly appeared to be a lost cause. As troops withdrew into enclaves or populated areas, some of them became bored and corrupt, and the rate of crime, drug use, and racial tension increased. Although the cohesion of units that stayed in ground combat remained strong, the statistics of decline were dramatic, whether measured in terms of courts-martial, desertions, fraggings (the murder of officers by their own men), or recorded acts of insubordination. And no statistics could measure the growing tendency of soldiers to engage in "search and evade" missions, that is of going on patrol in areas where they knew no enemy existed.[42]

Despite the pullback of American troops, progress continued in the countryside. The cumulative results of various programs—such as land reform, aid for the peasantry, the Phoenix program, the expansion of Regional and Popular Forces, and the restoration of village autonomy—had greatly improved security. In many areas once under NLF control, the government had established a strong presence.

These changes were especially apparent in the vital Mekong Delta, where a tranquility unknown for years prevailed. The Viet Cong—reinforced by NVA troops—remained in its strongholds, but enemy units were now on the defensive and U.S. officials could drive around the Delta on reopened roads and bridges and see firsthand the improved standard of living of the peasantry. While serious corruption remained among many government administrators, province and district chiefs sensed the change and, under the prodding of American advisers, were more willing to pursue the enemy.

Hau Nghia Province

These trends can be traced in the evolution of the war in Hau Nghia Province, an impoverished, densely populated area northwest of Saigon bordering on Cambodia. A main transit route for the NVA and VC from their sanctuaries in Cambodia into South Vietnam, Hau Nghia became a heavily contested province early in the war, and by 1965 government authority there had largely collapsed. Only the presence of ARVN troops prevented a total enemy takeoever. In December 1965, however, the tide of battle shifted with the arrival of the U.S. Twenty-fifth Infantry Division, which built a huge base camp near the town of Cu Chi. American troops now guarded installations, opened roads, and disrupted enemy operations. In August 1966 Ambassador Henry Cabot Lodge Jr. reported that "many of the things which we used to hope for—and dream about—are taking place. . . . In Hau Nghia to-day we are winning; they are losing. Our side is clearly coasting along as the Americans say."[43]

The ambassador's optimism proved to be premature; not until 1969 did the massive Allied military presence wear down Viet Cong military units. But its political apparatus—though weakened—survived. As one American civilian adviser noted, "The plan goes forward, but it is only occupation, not pacification."[44] Despite a huge Allied effort over many years, the NLF had survived, in part because various pacification programs met with mixed success. Land reform yielded limited results, aid for the peasantry did not compensate for the physical devastation of the countryside, Regional and Popular Forces performed unevenly, and prominent local people—fearful for their lives—were reluctant to stand for election. An especially bitter disappointment was the Phoenix program, which the CIA had designed to capture or kill members of the insurgents' shadow government. Government officials in Hau Nghia were well aware of the NLF's political apparatus, but they lacked the nerve to attack it, realizing that the enemy's assassination squads would quickly retaliate against any official who threatened its cadres. As a result of their apathy and caution, the NLF continued to tax, recruit, and propagandize the peasantry of the province. Phoenix remained, an American pacification adviser observed, "an American inspired, American-style program that is accepted without enthusiasm by the Vietnamese. . . . If left to the Vietnamese, [it] would soon grind to a halt."[45]

Nor had years of effort overcome the profound weaknesses of the government in Saigon. South Vietnam's ruling elite never concerned itself with the welfare of the peasantry and never pushed for fundamental changes in the political and social makeup of the countryside. Its half-hearted programs, launched in the middle of the American phase of the war, could not close the gap between the government and the peasantry. The problem facing the government, one historian writes, "was not to regain legitimacy lost but, rather, to establish legitimacy in the first place."[46] Communist revolutionaries had organized the peasants during the French war—before the government in Saigon had even existed—and over the years had offered them a powerful vision of a unified Vietnam free of foreign influence. Most Communist cadre—even during the darkest days of the revolution—were convinced of the virtue of their cause and confident of a final victory. In contrast, government officials, unwilling to spend the night outside fortified compounds, were pessimistic about the future, especially as the Twenty-fifth Division prepared to withdraw in September 1970.

The Endless War

In the fall of 1970 the war dragged on with no end in sight. The president had cut American troop strength by nearly one-half, but dissatisfaction with what seemed an endless war continued to mount. In September Nixon's popularity dropped below 50 percent for the first time in his presidency, and in the Senate thirty-nine senators voted for the McGovern-Hatfield Amendment requiring the president to bring home all American troops by the end of 1971. Nixon had to continue troop withdrawals to maintain his political base at home, but the decline of American ground combat strength weakened his bargaining position with leaders in Hanoi. In September Kissinger had resumed secret meetings with North Vietnamese negotiators in Paris, but neither side budged from its previous position. "Their demands," Kissinger complained, "are absurd. They want us to withdraw and on the way out to overthrow the Saigon Government."[47] On the real issue of who would rule in postwar Saigon, neither the United States nor North Vietnam was willing to compromise.

During the off-year congressional elections Nixon campaigned hard, promising at every stop that "As I stand before you today, I can say confidently the war in Vietnam is coming to an end, and we are going to win a just peace in Vietnam." He condemned Democrats,

taunted antiwar demonstrators—denouncing them as "violent thugs"—
and beseeched "the great silent majority of Americans to stand up and
be counted."[48] But the president's partisan campaign ended in failure; in November the Democrats easily retained control of both houses
of Congress. Midway through his first term in office, the president's
political base at home was shaky and he remained uncertain of how to
end the war in Vietnam. He now seemed to realize that the United
States was not likely to prevail in South Vietnam, and that the best he
could achieve would be some kind of face-saving formula, a "decent-
interval" solution that would give Thieu a reasonable chance to survive. He would not abandon Thieu—for that would be dishonorable—
but neither could he guarantee his continued hold on power. The fate
of his regime would largely depend on the success of Vietnamization.

Notes

1 Quoted in Stephen E. Ambrose, *Nixon: Volume Two, The Triumph of a Politician,
1962–1972* (New York, 1989), 245.

2 Henry Kissinger, *The White House Years* (Boston, 1979), 93.

3 Quoted in Melvin Small, *The Presidency of Richard Nixon* (Lawrence, Kans., 1999),
63.

4 Ibid., 63.

5 Quoted in Jeffrey Kimball, *Nixon's Vietnam War* (Lawrence, Kans., 1998), 38.

6 Ibid., 76.

7 Ibid., 101.

8 Quoted in Samuel Zaffiri, *Westmoreland: A Biography of General William C. Westmoreland* (New York, 1994), 332.

9 Quoted in Ambrose, *Nixon, Volume Two,* 276.

10 Quoted in Stanley Karnow, *Vietnam: A History* (New York, 1991), 611.

11 Quoted in Walter Isaacson, *Kissinger: A Biography* (New York, 1992), 238, 246.

12 Richard Nixon, *RN: The Memoirs of Richard Nixon* (New York, 1978), 405.

13 Quoted in Neil Sheehan, *A Bright Shining Lie: John Paul Vann and America in
Vietnam* (New York, 1988), 740.

14 Quoted in Ambrose, *Nixon, Volume Two,* 281, 287.

15 Ibid., 282.

16 Ibid., 300–01.

17 Quoted in Robert Mann, *A Grand Delusion: America's Descent into Vietnam* (New
York, 2001), 639.

18 Quoted in Ambrose, *Nixon, Volume Two,* 307; Nixon, *RN,* 407.

19 Quoted in Ambrose, *Nixon, Volume Two,* 309–10.

20 Ibid., 312.

21 Quoted in Lewis Sorley, *Thunderbolt: General Creighton Abrams and the Army of His Times* (New York, 1992), 255–56.

22 Quoted in Lewis Sorley, *A Better War: The Unexamined Victories and Final Tragedy of America's Last Years in Vietnam* (New York, 1999), 186.

23 Lam Quang Thi, *The Twenty-Five Year Century: A South Vietnamese General Remembers the Indochina War to the Fall of Saigon* (Denton, Tex., 2001), 256.

24 Quoted in Robert K. Brigham, "Dreaming Different Dreams: The United States and the Army of the Republic of Vietnam," in Marilyn B. Young and Robert Buzzanco, eds., *A Companion to the Vietnam War* (Malden, Mass., 2002), 157.

25 Colonel David H. Hackworth and Eilhys England, *Steel My Soldiers' Hearts: The Hopeless to Hardcore Transformation of 4th Battalion, 39th Infantry, United States Army, Vietnam* (New York, 2002), 406.

26 John Laurence, *The Cat from Hué: A Vietnam War Story* (New York, 2002), 247.

27 Quoted in Peter Macdonald, *Giap: The Victor in Vietnam* (New York, 1993), 323.

28 Truong Nhu Tang, *A Vietcong Memoir* (New York, 1985), 168.

29 Quoted in William J. Duiker, *The Communist Road to Power in Vietnam,* 2nd. ed. (Boulder, Colo., 1996), 304.

30 Ibid., 308.

31 Tang, *Vietcong Memoir,* 189, 192.

32 Quoted in Kimball, *Nixon's Vietnam War,* 182.

33 Quoted in Isaacson, *Kissinger,* 253.

34 Ibid., 259.

35 Quoted in Ambrose, *Nixon, Volume Two,* 342.

36 Quoted in Kimball, *Nixon's Vietnam War,* 206.

37 Quoted in Richard Reeves, *President Nixon: Alone in the White House* (New York, 2001), 208.

38 Nixon, *RN,* 454.

39 Quoted in Mann, *A Grand Delusion,* 660.

40 Quoted in Ambrose, *Nixon, Volume Two,* 360.

41 Laurence, *The Cat From Hué,* 644, 646.

42 Phillip B. Davidson, *Vietnam at War: The History, 1946–1975* (New York, 1988), 618.

43 Quoted in Eric M. Bergerud, *The Dynamics of Defeat: The Vietnam War in Hau Nghia Province* (Boulder, Colo., 1991), 162.

44 Ibid., 234.

45 Ibid., 261.

46 Ibid., 4.

47 Quoted in Ambrose, *Nixon, Volume Two,* 388.

48 Ibid., 393, 395.

CHAPTER EIGHT

From Lam Son 719 to the Paris Peace Accords, 1971–1973

On February 8, 1971, an ARVN armored column left Khe Sanh and moved across the Laotian border on Route 9. Its goal was Tchepone, a village twenty-five miles distant that was surrounded by huge enemy supply depots. As the tanks and armored personnel carriers rumbled along the narrow, twisting, single-track road, other ARVN troops were airlifted to a string of fire-support bases that paralleled the axis of advance. The armored task force and airborne elements would converge and together planned to seize Tchepone and destroy the supply caches surrounding it, depriving the NVA divisions operating in South Vietnam of logistical support. With 17,000 troops committed to this operation, it was the largest and most ambitious ARVN offensive of the war.

Lam Son 719

The American military had long wanted to attack into Laos to sever the line of communication between North Vietnam and its forces fighting in the south. After the Cambodian incursion closed the port of Sihanoukville—a major blow to North Vietnam—the Ho Chi Minh

Trail was even more important as the primary artery of support for troops in South Vietnam. Nixon and Thieu—eager to buy time for Vietnamization to work—eagerly approved Abrams's plan for a raid into Laos.

In theory, the operation made sense: it would throw the enemy off balance and destroy vital supplies and installations. In practice, however, it held great risk. ARVN was attacking a long-established enemy sanctuary where 22,000 NVA soldiers, with elaborate air defenses, were waiting. And ARVN would largely be on its own, since on December 22, 1970, the U.S. Congress had passed the Cooper-Church Amendment prohibiting U.S. troops from entering Laos or Cambodia. While South Vietnamese forces would still benefit from American air and logistical support, no U.S. advisers could accompany them.

On February 11, when the South Vietnamese armored column was about halfway to Tchepone, Thieu ordered it to halt. Cautious and indecisive, he worried that the elite units that composed the invading force—which also served as his palace guard—would take too many casualties if they moved aggressively forward. Over the furious protests of Abrams, ARVN forces held in place, giving the NVA ample time to maneuver its divisions for a counterattack. Soon fierce fighting erupted along Route 9 and the positions north and south of it, while American air strikes inflicted heavy casualties on the enemy. Nevertheless, some ARVN positions were overrun. Now Abrams urged Thieu to commit his reserve division and engage in an all-out fight, but ARVN's senior commanders had already had enough and wished to withdraw. Thieu let them do so.

As the ARVN pullout began on March 9, the NVA attacked in force, wiping out some battalions and ambushing retreating South Vietnamese troops. Some ARVN units fought bravely; others panicked and clung to the skids of helicopters in order to flee the enemy. Both sides suffered heavy casualties and equipment losses, but ARVN left Laos a beaten and demoralized force. It had fallen far short of its original mission—to seize and hold enemy base areas for ninety days.

While the South Vietnamese Army performed poorly, the performance of Abrams and his senior commanders also left much to be desired. They had hastily imposed a dated plan—an airborne, armored

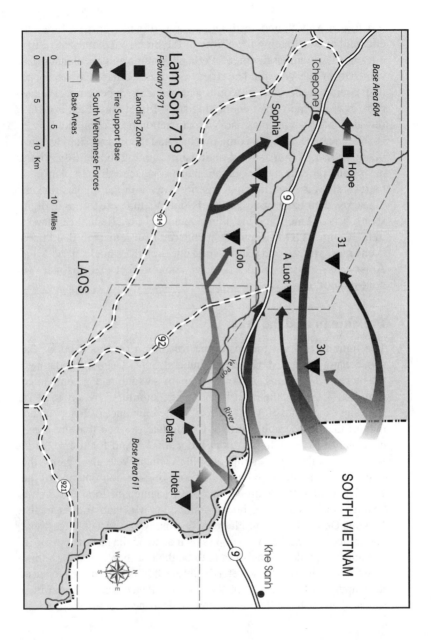

Lam Son 719
February 1971

■ Landing Zone
▲ Fire Support Base
→ South Vietnamese Forces
▢ Base Areas

0   5   10 Km
0   5   10 Miles

thrust—on ARVN, underestimating the skill and tenacity of the enemy and overestimating the ability of the South Vietnamese to carry out such a difficult assignment. Perhaps Abrams and his planners assumed that the NVA would not stand and fight; perhaps they reasoned that, even if it did, ARVN would gain valuable experience and disrupt, even if temporarily, enemy logistics. Either way, Lam Son 719 revealed that by no means had Vietnamization been completed.

Even as the invasion come to a halt and then turned into an agonizing retreat, Nixon showed optimism, claiming in a mid-February news conference that "the operation has gone according to plan" and that ARVN was "fighting in a superior way." But the images flickering across their television screens of South Vietnamese troops in flight shocked most Americans, including Democratic and Republican hawks in the Congress. One Republican congressman remarked that "Laos is one more straw—and a substantial one—on the camel's back. Most Americans—myself included—have come to feel that this war has gone on too long."[1]

Pressure to End the War

The fighting in Laos increased the frustration of opponents of the war. Senator George McGovern (Democrat, South Dakota) condemned the increased bombing of North Vietnam—which had accompanied Lam Son 719—as "the most barbaric act committed by any modern state since the death of Adolf Hitler," while Lawrence O'Brien, chairman of the Democratic National Committee, warned that the president planned "an endless war in Indochina."[2] And for four days in April several thousand members of the Vietnam Veterans Against the War camped on the National Mall, protesting the continuation of the war. The leader of this group was Navy Lieutenant John F. Kerry, a heavily decorated patrol boat commander who had fought in the Mekong Delta. Kerry gave eloquent testimony before a congressional committee, asking "How do you ask a man to be the last man to die in Vietnam? How do you ask a man to be the last man to die for a mistake?"[3] As a final act these veterans threw their medals over a fence at the Capitol. A few days later, the National Peace Action Committee staged the last large demonstration against the war in Washington, while some of the more radical antiwar demonstrators tried, without success, to close down the city.

Nixon realized that opposition to the war was becoming irresistible. Between April and July seventeen votes took place in the House or Senate to restrict the president's authority to conduct the war or to set a final date for unilateral American withdrawal. In early April, in a televised report to the nation, Nixon sought to hold off critics of the war, announcing that "Vietnamization has succeeded" and that he was withdrawing another 100,000 troops, leaving 180,000 at the end of 1971. "The American involvement in Vietnam," the president assured the public, "is coming to an end," although he would not set a date for total withdrawal. To do so, he reasoned, would "remove the enemy's strongest incentive to end the war sooner by negotiation."[4]

Despite all the previous setbacks, Nixon and Kissinger still believed they had a fifty-fifty chance of ending the war in the summer of 1971, and they searched for some way to break the deadlock with North Vietnam. In late April Nixon learned that China's leaders would welcome a visit either from the president himself or his special envoy, and in May the United States and the Soviet Union signed an agreement designed to protect intercontinental ballistic missile launch sites. The overture by China, and the relaxation of tensions with the Soviet Union, raised the prospect that these two Communist powers would pressure Hanoi to make concessions at the bargaining table. At the end of May, in an effort to move the negotiations forward, Kissinger offered, for the first time, to set a date for the final withdrawal of U.S. forces from South Vietnam without demanding a mutual withdrawal of the NVA. But leaders in Hanoi still refused to give up their demand for the removal of President Thieu.

In mid-summer Nixon revealed to the American public that Kissinger had just returned from a trip to China, and that Chinese leaders had invited him to visit sometime in 1972. Now Nixon cast himself as a world statesman devoted to peace; "I will undertake," he proclaimed, "a journey for peace, peace not just for our generation but for future generations on this earth we share together."[5] This reaching out to America's enemy—part of Nixon's diplomatic grand design—blurred former distinctions between friends and foes and undercut the earlier rationale of American leaders for their commitment to South Vietnam. The war now seemed more of a local struggle rather than a grand Cold War confrontation.

But the president's troubles at home mounted. On June 13 he was stunned to read in the *New York Times* an account of what became known as *The Pentagon Papers,* a classified study, based on government documents, of American involvement in the Vietnam War. The documents had been taken from the Pentagon and leaked to the press by Daniel Ellsberg, a young Defense Department analyst who had once studied under Kissinger at Harvard. Kissinger was outraged by the leak, convinced that Ellsberg was "the most dangerous man in America today [who] must be stopped at all costs."[6] The president agreed, ordering a White House staff member to set up a group—known as the "Plumbers"—to stop the leaking of government documents. It was a fateful decision.

The View from Saigon

Throughout 1971 U.S. forces continued to withdraw from South Vietnam until, by the end of the year, only 180,000 American troops remained. Some of them continued to hunt for the enemy, but, by and large, the NVA avoided contact and the breakdown in the morale and discipline of the American army in Vietnam continued. Many units functioned well right up to their withdrawal date; others paid a heavy price for their lack of vigilance. In late March 1971, at Fire Support Base Mary Ann in the southern part of I Corps, a battalion of the Americal Division failed to protect its perimeter, allowing NVA attackers to overrun the base, destroying artillery pieces, throwing satchel charges into the command bunker, knifing Americans in their sleeping bags, and killing or wounding nearly half of the 250 soldiers stationed there. After the defeat, a U.S. Army investigation found a clear dereliction of duty on the part of officers in change, six of whom where formally disciplined. As General Abrams told an aide, "I need to get this Army home to save it."[7]

By the end of 1971 most of the planned expansion and improvements of the South Vietnamese Army were complete; as American troops departed, ARVN took over more and more of the fighting. The

regular South Vietnamese army consisted of thirteen divisions total-
ing 450,000 troops, while Regional and Popular Forces added another 550,000 men. From 1964 to 1972, the total armed forces of
South Vietnam grew from 514,000 to 1,000,000; if dependents are
included, around one-third of the nation's population was involved in
the war effort.

Some U.S. officials were optimistic about the results of Vietnamization. John Paul Vann reported that "We are now at the lowest level
of fighting the war has ever seen. . . . This program of Vietnamization
has gone kind of literally beyond my wildest dreams of success." And
despite the mixed results of Lam Son 719, General Abrams told Secretary of Defense Laird that "I think the *truth* of the matter is the
[South] Vietnamese have stepped up to the plate."[8]

Other observers were more skeptical. In March 1971 the American diplomat Howard R. Simpson returned to Vietnam for his fourth
visit. Unconvinced by the upbeat press briefings about progress in the
war, he ended his stay by visiting a senior South Vietnamese commander, General Pham Van Dong. Dong described continued North
Vietnamese infiltration into the south and the paralyzing political in-
fighting in Saigon. As Dong shook hands with his old American friend
he said gravely, "Simpson, it is not good."[9]

As the American presence in South Vietnam decreased, various
groups expressed more openly resentment against their nation's ally.
One Saigon university student told a reporter how, as a high school
student in Central Vietnam, he had admired American soldiers, who
"seemed so carefree, so strong, I was moved to think they would have
come from so far away to die for something other than their own
country." But later he came to view them more critically, understanding how "they interfered at all levels in Vietnamese society. . . . I
began to feel that the American presence itself is the reason why the
Communists continue the war." Saigon newspapers also began to attack the United States more frequently, while some politicians spoke
of Americans as they had once spoken of the French. At a meeting of
retired generals, General Ky referred to the American ambassador as
"Governor General Bunker" and spoke of Americans as "colonial-
ists."[10] Resentment toward Americans was intertwined with depen-

dence on their government's aid, but as the flow of American assistance lessened and the Vietnamese economy weakened, more and more signs of a new mood among the South Vietnamese people appeared.

Discontent with Thieu's regime also grew, although the opposition seemed incapable of formulating any clear alternative to his rule. Students in Saigon often demonstrated, calling for the overthrow of the government, and some of Thieu's opponents hoped for a contested presidential election in October 1971. But Thieu had no interest in broadening his base of support, ignoring the advice of Ambassador Bunker. He used tactics of intimidation and bribery to consolidate his position and outmaneuver potential opposing candidates; in the end, Thieu was the only candidate on the ballot and received 94 percent of the vote. For the moment his hold on power was secure, but many people in South Vietnam were now waiting for the crisis that they were sure would one day engulf the regime.

Hanoi's Calculations

In the aftermath of Lam Son 719, leaders in Hanoi realized that their military, political, and economic situation was bleak. ARVN's thrust into Laos had brought heavy casualties, pacification remained a serious threat to the NLF, and years of war had turned North Vietnam's economy into a shambles. But with the American withdrawal continuing and ARVN overextended, North Vietnam's rulers favored one more major military offensive to break the stalemate. Some preferred to wait until all American forces had pulled out; most agreed with Le Duan, first secretary of the Communist party, that waiting involved too many risks. Given all of the uncertainties about the war and the shifting international scene, Hanoi's leaders concluded that it was better to strike in 1972 rather than in 1973.

For years North Vietnam's war effort had relied heavily on Chinese and Soviet economic and military aid. But by the early 1970s relations with both these Communist allies were troubled. China's leaders, worried about their nation's international isolation and sharp border clashes with the Soviet Union, now saw Russia as a more serious threat than America. As they pursued a new dialogue with Nixon and Kissinger, they sought to drive a wedge between North Vietnam and the Soviet Union and encourage a settlement of the war. In November 1971 Mao Zedong urged the North Vietnamese to delay the liberation of South Vietnam. "As our broom is too short," he told Premier Pham Van Dong, "to sweep the Americans out of Taiwan, so yours is too short to do the same in South Vietnam."[11]

As North Vietnam's ties with China weakened and its dependence on the Soviet Union grew—in 1969 it received half a billion dollars worth of Soviet aid—its leaders also worried about the growing dialogue between Russia and America and how it might affect the Soviet view of the war. While Soviet General Secretary Leonid Brezhnev resisted Nixon's demands for linkage, he wanted negotiations in Paris to continue and was unenthusiastic about North Vietnam's plans for another offensive. In 1971 Le Duan and his associates watched nervously as Nixon prepared to travel first to China and then to the Soviet Union, denouncing the president's forthcoming trip to Beijing as a "perfidious maneuver" and a "false peace offensive."[12]

In early 1971 Le Duan traveled to Moscow, where he received assurances of Soviet aid for a new offensive. Brezhnev and his associates—despite their misgivings about an intensification of the war—now wanted to draw North Vietnam away from China and transform it into a Soviet outpost in Southeast Asia. Soon Soviet arms shipments began to arrive in Haiphong—tanks, artillery pieces, antitank missiles, and shoulder-launched surface-to-air missiles. Moscow even offered advanced armor training to more than three thousand North Vietnamese tank crews. Over the course of 1971 North Vietnam prepared for a major offensive, and by the end of the year the politburo decided to launch an attack.

Hanoi's leaders hoped that a successful offensive would humiliate Nixon and impress China and the Soviet Union with the power of North Vietnam's fighting machine. Most of all, they sought to alter the military balance in South Vietnam, demonstrate the futility of pacification and Vietnamization, and undermine the American position in negotiations. Once again, the old revolutionary leaders in Hanoi had grown impatient and determined to end the war in the south with one decisive blow.

Nixon's Maneuvers

In the fall of 1971 Nixon sought to reinforce his newly forged image as a world statesman. In October he announced that he would travel to the Soviet Union in May 1972 to conclude arms talks; a month later he announced that he would travel to China in February. "International affairs," he told one aide, "is *our* issue."[13] With two critical trips approaching, Nixon continued to play for time in Vietnam, now hoping that he would be able to exploit triangular diplomacy to end the war on favorable terms.

Nixon's dramatic diplomatic initiatives seized the imagination of the nation, and at a news conference in mid-November, he offered the public more good news, promising to withdraw another 45,000 troops by the end of the year. But the president refused to make any commitment to begin the withdrawal of American air power and indicated that, without a negotiated settlement to the war, a residual American force of 40,000–50,000 men would stay in South Vietnam.

Despite his diplomatic successes, Nixon worried about his political prospects. In 1968 he had promised to end the war; but as the election year drew near no end was in sight, and his political opponents remained active. In September 1971 Senator McGovern, a leading Senate dove and a potential presidential candidate, traveled to Paris to talk with North Vietnamese negotiators. On his return, McGovern announced that North Vietnam would release all American POWs once the president set a date for a complete U.S. withdrawal. Although McGovern failed to deal with the question of the fate of postwithdrawal South Vietnam, his proposal appealed to many Americans and put additional pressure on Nixon to justify his prolongation of the war. In early 1972 Nixon's approval rating slipped below 50 percent, while another poll showed that the president and his most likely Democrat opponent, Senator Edmund Muskie (Democrat, Maine), were even at 42 percent of the vote, with the Independence party candidate George Wallace drawing 11 percent.

In mid-January 1972 Nixon announced that he would pull 70,000 more U.S. combat troops out of South Vietnam by May 1, leaving only 69,000 still in the nation. Ten days later he delivered another major address on the war, claiming that he had done everything possible to achieve a negotiated settlement and revealing that Kissinger, in secret talks with North Vietnamese diplomat Le Duc Tho, had already offered to set a date for complete withdrawal in exchange for a cease-fire and the return of POWs. "The only thing this [the American peace] plan does not do," Nixon concluded, "is to join our enemy to overthrow our ally, which the United States of America will never do. If the enemy wants peace, it will have to recognize the important difference between settlement and surrender."[14]

Critics of the war were not impressed. "Is the United States," Senator Fulbright asked, "willing to get out and leave the Thieu government to its own devices?"[15] And Senator Muskie, in a major speech on the war, called for a unilateral American withdrawal coupled with U.S. insistence that Thieu reach a political settlement with his Communist opponents. Nixon, however, had somehow managed to buy more time for his policies in Vietnam. In early February one poll showed that he had opened up a four-point lead over Muskie, while his approval rating had moved upward to 54 percent. But most Americans still felt that the president—if he was to fulfill his pledge to end the war—had to achieve a cease-fire by November.

On February 17 Nixon and his wife left for China. His week there, as he visited historic sites, attended ceremonial banquets, and talked with Mao Zedong and Zhou Enlai, was a spectacular event, offering fascinating glimpses to a worldwide television audience of a nation that few Westerners had visited for several decades. Nixon's visit did not spur any important diplomatic breakthroughs; it was more symbolic than practical. But his opening to China was a recognition of reality—that the U.S. must deal with the Communist regime there—and offered further confirmation of his role as world statesman.

The Easter Offensive

On March 30 North Vietnam launched the Easter Offensive, a massive invasion of South Vietnam with 120,000 troops, virtually all of its armed might. Five years earlier, during the Tet Offensive, the Viet Cong had quietly led the way into the cities; now the NVA led the way using tanks, artillery, and infantry in hard-hitting and fast-moving assaults. The resulting battles were of unprecedented fury and lasted into June, causing heavy military and civilian casualties.

The Easter Offensive was in fact a three-pronged attack. The first came across the DMZ toward Quang Tri City, the second across the Central Highlands toward Kontum and Pleiku and the coast, and the third aimed at An Loc, a provincial capital sixty-five miles northwest of Saigon. Any one of these attacks, if successful, had the potential of knocking ARVN and the South Vietnamese government out of the war.

While Allied intelligence knew that a major enemy offensive was imminent, it once again failed to predict the timing and the precise direction of the assaults. On the northern front, the NVA's attack surprised ARVN's Third Division guarding the DMZ; its troops soon panicked and joined the stream of refugees heading south. On May 1 Quang Tri City fell to the NVA, threatening Hué, forty miles to the south. A day later Thieu fired the incompetent I Corps commander and replaced him with Ngo Quang Truong, one of his best generals, who was able to reorganize his forces and at the end of June launch a counteroffensive. Not until mid-September, however, did they retake Quang Tri City.

On the central front, the NVA cut the highway running between Kontum and Pleiku and in mid-May launched an attack on Kontum that carried some of its units into the city. For a time the situation was critical, but ARVN defenders, aided by U.S. B-52 strikes, held off enemy forces and by the end of the month assured Kontum's defense, preventing the NVA from driving to the coast and splitting South Vietnam in half.

On the southern front the NVA overran Loc Ninh on April 6 and moved toward An Loc. While enemy forces waited for resupply, Thieu reinforced the beleaguered garrison and from April 13 to May 14 ARVN units, supported by American air power, fought tenaciously and threw back three enemy assaults.

For a time in early May, when South Vietnam had suffered serious reversals on all three fronts, General Abrams was worried. "As the pressure has mounted and the battle has become brutal," he reported to Washington, "the senior military leadership has begun to bend and in some cases to break. In adversity it is losing its will and cannot be depended on to take the measures necessary to stand and fight."[16] He was not sure Hué and Kontum would hold. At the height

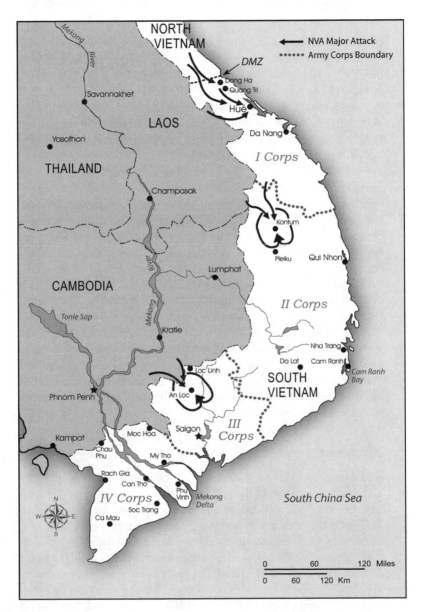

The Easter Offensive

of the battle Abrams and Bunker met with Thieu, both to offer their support and urge him to replace ineffective field commanders. With the fate of his nation hanging in the balance, Thieu made dramatic command changes and by mid-May the tide of battle had shifted. Abrams knew, however, that the network of American advisers, along with American air power, had been decisive. Some ARVN units had fought well, others had fled in panic; but without American support ARVN would surely have collapsed.

ARVN survived the Easter Offensive in part because North Vietnam's leaders had made critical mistakes in the deployment of their forces, scattering their troops over three fronts rather than concentrating them in one, and failing to realize that their field commanders had limited experience in coordinating artillery, infantry, and tanks. Nor did they appreciate the vulnerability of their troops and supply lines—if they fought a conventional war—to American air power. As a result, the NVA took appalling casualties and had not crushed ARVN or shattered the regime in Saigon.

Nevertheless, NVA troops stayed along the Laotian and Cambodian borders and near the DMZ, creating liberated zones within South Vietnam, and their commanders gained valuable experience for a future offensive. And the Easter Offensive had raised grave doubts about Vietnamization. All of those who were familiar with ARVN's response had to wonder what its fate would be if all American advisers and air power were one day withdrawn.

Nixon's Response

Nixon and Kissinger viewed the Easter Offensive as a test. If North Vietnam won the war in the spring of 1972, it would prove the ineffectiveness of Vietnamization and humiliate the United States. Although Nixon dared not reintroduce American ground-combat troops, he ordered an all-out counterattack by American air and sea power, removing many of the strike-free zones around Hanoi and Haiphong. As he brashly told several aides, "The bastards have never been bombed like they're going to be bombed this time." But, privately, the surge of violence in South Vietnam depressed Nixon, who found the prospect of a North Vietnamese victory "too bleak even to contemplate." Defeat, he told Kissinger, was "simply not an option"; and he confided to his diary that he would not be able to "survive politically" a failure in South Vietnam.[17]

In a televised address in late April, the president was belligerent, denouncing the North Vietnamese "invasion" of South Vietnam and warning his fellow Americans that "If the United States betrays the millions of people who have relied on us in Vietnam . . . it would amount to a renunciation of our morality, an abdication of our leadership among nations, and an invitation for the mighty to prey upon the weak all around the world." With a summit meeting scheduled in Moscow in late May, Nixon worried that a further escalation of the war might force Soviet leaders to cancel it. He calculated, however, "that the country can take losing the summit, but it can't take losing the war," and on May 8 announced his decision to mine waters off North Vietnamese ports and bomb its rail and road links with China. The only way to stop the killing, Nixon claimed, was "to keep the weapons of war out of the hands of the international outlaws of North Vietnam." Nixon told Kissinger that he was determined to "go for broke. . . . I intend to stop at nothing to bring the enemy to his knees. . . . What distinguishes me from Johnson is that I have the *will* in spades."[18]

The president's response inflicted serious damage on North Vietnam and demonstrated his determination not to abandon South Vietnam. He had already conceded North Vietnam's right to keep its troops in the south, but he would not remove Thieu or stand aside while the NVA crushed ARVN. Most Republicans supported the president's actions, while his leading Democratic critic, Senator McGovern, denounced the escalation as "reckless, unnecessary, and unworkable, a flirtation with World War III."[19] On May 20 Nixon left for a summit meeting in Moscow; when he returned on June 1 he had to reassess, once again, the ever-changing landscape of the Vietnam War.

After the Battle

By the early summer of 1972 General Abrams—who left Vietnam in late June—and Ambassador Bunker continued, as always, to be hopeful about the war. Abrams believed that ARVN, with American help, had beaten the enemy on the ground, while Bunker wrote that "There have been failures and weak spots but many units have fought heroically."[20] Both believed that South Vietnam—with proper American air and advistory support—could now defend itself.

But the mood in South Vietnam was subdued. Most South Vietnamese knew that their army had barely escaped defeat; according to one American adviser, "Now many are measuring sides and their commitments waiting for the winner."[21] President Thieu, sensing the uncertainty around him, became more repressive, demanding the power to rule by decree for six months and lowering the draft age. With both sides exhausted and serious negotiations now likely, Thieu felt deep anxiety about the future of his regime.

Leaders in Hanoi also faced a discouraging prospect. The Easter Offensive had been a disappointment; it had failed to crush ARVN and left the NVA exhausted and demoralized. One southern commander recalled that "Our cadres and men were fatigued, we had not had time to make up our losses, all units were is disarray. . . . The troops were no longer capable of fighting." Worse still, China and the Soviet Union—though they continued the flow of supplies—no longer found a prolongation of the war in their interests and pressured Hanoi to accept a compromise peace. "Let the Americans leave," Zhou Enlai advised Le Duc Tho, "as quickly as possible. In half a year or one year the situation will change."[22] The North Vietnamese now moved toward a position they had rejected for many years—a settlement that would force the Americans to go home but leave Thieu in power. Once America's withdrawal was complete, they could resume the struggle in South Vietnam.

Politics and Diplomacy

As Nixon pondered his campaign for reelection, he feared that the Democrats would nominate a mainstream candidate such as Senator Edmund Muskie and that Governor George Wallace would once again run as a third-party candidate, drawing off conservative votes. Neither of these fears materialized. In March Muskie lost a primary in Florida and dropped out of the race; in mid-May Wallace was shot and badly wounded, ending his bid for the presidency. By June it became clear that the nominee of the Democratic party would be Senator McGovern, one of the original opponents of the war and a representative of his party's left wing. In mid-July, at the Democratic National Convention in Miami, McGovern—a self-styled "prairie Populist"—issued a dramatic call for Americans to come home "From secrecy, and deception in high places. . . . From a conflict in Indochina which maims our ideals as well as our soldiers. . . . From military spending so wasteful it weakens our nation, come home America."[23] But the Democratic convention was a debacle, confused and undisciplined; in reaching out to women, African Americans, and liberals, McGovern neglected the urban bosses, labor leaders, and representatives of white ethnic groups who held the keys to the Democratic electoral coalition. They were outraged by his nomination and were inclined to sit out the election.

For his part, Nixon was exuberant over McGovern's nomination, using his campaign to attack his opponent's alleged extremism and court the traditionally Democratic groups alienated by the South Dakotan's campaign. In private the president claimed that "the issues are radicalism; peace-at-any price; a second-rate United States; running down the United States; square America versus radical America"; in public he warned that walking away from the war would result in a bloodbath in South Vietnam, "with perhaps at least a million marked for assassination. . . . That would be the height of immorality."[24]

Polls showed that most Americans strongly supported Nixon's basic position—that the United States should not agree to turn over the government in Saigon to the Communists and that some American forces should stay in South Vietnam until the POWs were returned. The president realized, however, that the frustration of the doves in the Congress was growing—they did not believe he wanted to end the fighting—and that he would soon face a crisis with the Democratic-controlled Congress, which was likely to cut off funds for a continuation of the conflict. Nixon knew that he must end the war; or as he told a journalist: "I'm sure of one thing. The war will be over. The war won't be holding over us in a second term."[25]

In late July, Kissinger set off for Paris for more talks with Le Duc Tho. The North Vietnamese were finally willing to compromise; though differences remained between the two sides, a settlement seemed within reach. Kissinger was eager to push ahead, and in mid-August he traveled to Saigon to persuade Thieu to also make concessions. But Thieu, while aware of the precariousness of his position, remained intransigent, hoping that American hawks would save his regime.

Kissinger believed that the United States was in a better bargaining position at this time than it would be after the elections, but Nixon was not so sure. The president had less faith in a negotiated settlement than his national security adviser and, confident of a victory over McGovern, was inclined to wait to deal with the North Vietnamese after his triumphal reelection. He reassured Thieu that "The United States has not persevered all this way, at the sacrifice of many American lives, to reverse course in the last few months of 1972."[26] The American people would not desert a brave ally.

In late August, at the Republican National Convention, also in Miami, the party showed unity and confidence. Police kept antiwar demonstrators from surrounding the convention hall and Nixon, when he arrived on August 23 to give his acceptance speech, received an enthusiastic welcome. He appealed to Democrats to "come home" to the Republican cause and promised that the United States, in its search for peace in Vietnam, would never abandon the POWs, impose a Communist government on Saigon, or stain America's honor.[27] At the end of the month, the Gallup Poll showed Nixon with a commanding lead of 64 to 30 percent (with 6 percent undecided) over McGovern. Confident of his reelection, the president prepared to get tough once again with North Vietnam.

The Election of 1972

In September Nixon stayed in the White House, while his surrogates denounced McGovern as the candidate of "acid, abortion, and amnesty."[28] In the middle of the month Kissinger returned to Paris, where, rejecting Le Duc Tho's demand for a coalition government, he now proposed the creation of a Committee of National Reconciliation that would oversee future elections in South Vietnam. But since this proposal, if accepted as part of the final peace, would give the Provisional Revolutionary Government legal status in the south, it was sure to meet with Thieu's bitter opposition.

By the fall of 1972 Thieu was more of an obstacle to the peace plan than were the leaders in Hanoi. In an attempt to win his consent, Kissinger sent his aide, General Alexander M. Haig Jr., to Saigon with still more assurances from President Nixon. In an emotional four-hour meeting, Thieu denounced the proposed terms and attacked Kissinger for his failure to take him into his confidence. Now Nixon grew impatient with his South Vietnamese allies; "I mean," he told Kissinger, "the tail can't wag the dog here." He advised Kissinger "to cram it [the agreement] down his [Thieu's] throat." Nixon was uncertain, however, about what he wanted, telling one aide "that the American people are no longer interested in a solution based on compromise, [and instead] favor continued bombing and want to see the United States prevail after all these years."[29]

Trailing badly in the polls, McGovern became frustrated, especially with Nixon's absence from the campaign trail. In early October he claimed that Nixon was the most deceitful president and the head of the "most corrupt administration in history." In a major Vietnam speech on October 10, McGovern announced that the day he was inaugurated he would stop the bombing of North Vietnam, begin the withdrawal all remaining American troops, and expect the return of American POWs in ninety days. "General Thieu," he declared, "is not worth one more American dollar, one more American prisoner, one more drop of American blood."[30] But Nixon was in closer touch with the mood of the American people than McGovern. At the end of the first week in October he had a two-to-one lead in the polls.

On October 8 Kissinger returned to Paris, where North Vietnamese negotiators produced a plan designed to bring a breakthrough. Soon the two sides agreed on the following five points:

1) An immediate cease-fire without waiting for the resolution of all political issues. In other words, the Thieu regime would remain in place in Saigon;
2) A unilateral withdrawal of all American forces from South Vietnam, while North Vietnamese troops would stay;
3) The return of all prisoners of war;
4) The right of the United States to continue to supply ARVN, and for Hanoi to continue to aid the NLF;
5) The creation of a National Council of Reconciliation that would organize elections. It would make decisions only by consensus

and would not replace the authority of the Saigon government or of the PRG, both of which would continue to administer the areas under their control.

For four years Kissinger had longed for this day; he recalled that the conclusion of the peace agreement was "my most thrilling moment in public service." Nixon was equally elated, describing the provisions of the accord—inaccurately—as "a complete capitulation by the enemy: they are accepting a settlement on our terms."[31]

On October 12 Kissinger returned to Washington, where he gave the president a personal report. Nixon was now less enthusiastic, noting that a settlement before the election "would not particularly help us" and asking: "Will it look like we've given in to Jane Fonda? [the film star and antiwar activist]"[32] But Kissinger sped ahead, oblivious to the president's reservations and Thieu's resistance. Without having informed Thieu in advance of the basic provisions of the agreement, on October 18 Kissinger left for Saigon to gain his consent, just five days before he was supposed to initial the pact in Hanoi.

These secret negotiations had aroused Thieu's greatest fear—that the United States would cut a deal with Hanoi behind his back and then impose it on him. He had learned of the details of the draft treaty through a captured Communist document, so from the moment Kissinger arrived in Saigon to begin discussions, the ensuing exchanges were bitter. "I wanted," Thieu recalled, "to punch Kissinger in the mouth." Kissinger issued threats, warning that "If you do not sign, we're going to go out on our own," but Thieu would not relent.[33] He and his advisers demanded twenty-three changes in the draft agreement, including the withdrawal of NVA forces and the elimination of the National Council. The showdown had finally come.

Kissinger wanted to go to Hanoi without Saigon's approval, but Nixon would not allow him to do so. While the president urged Thieu to accept, he did not want an open break. Nixon had always been ambivalent about a negotiated settlement, and in the fall of 1972 he felt pressure from the right wing of the Republican party to continue the war. General Westmoreland, along with many high-ranking officers, opposed the compromise, telling the president that he should "delay action on the new agreement and to hold out for better terms."[34] Westmoreland believed that more bombing of Hanoi and Haiphong would force the Communists to make further concessions, especially the withdrawal of North Vietnamese troops from South Vietnam. Nixon was inclined to agree. "Immediately after the election," he wrote in his diary, "we will have an enormous mandate . . . and the enemy then either has to settle or face the consequences of what we could do to them."[35]

In fact, Nixon did not know what he wanted; he had lost control of events. Kissinger cabled him that "His [Thieu's] demands verge on insanity," while the North Vietnamese insisted that the agreement was complete and soon began to broadcast its terms. Worse still, Kissinger, on his return to Washington, held a televised press conference in which he declared that "We believe that peace is at hand."[36] According to the national security adviser, only minor details remained to be worked out.

This declaration created great excitement, and most senators, whether Republican or Democrat, praised the administration's achievement. As critics of the war, however, scrutinized the terms, some asked what had been gained that could not have been achieved four years earlier. In early November Nixon, sensing his vulnerability, counterattacked, claiming that—while some details still had to be worked out—the agreement met major principles that he had laid down earlier and that "the most important thing is we are going to end this war and end it in a way that will lay the foundation for real peace in the years to come. This is what all Americans want."[37]

During the last week of the campaign, McGovern concentrated on Vietnam, declaring that the president had deliberately misled the nation into thinking that peace was at hand and asserting "The fact is that the war is now intensifying." Nixon defended his record, promising once again that he was "completely confident" that an agreement would soon be reached "which will end the war in Vietnam."[38] Most Americans accepted the president's portrayal of himself as a man of peace. In the election of 1972, he won one of the most lop-sided victories in modern American history, defeating McGovern by 60 to 37 percent and carrying every state except Massachusetts. Election night, however, found a subdued and angry Richard M. Nixon; Democrats had retained control of both houses of the Congress and he knew that he still had not delivered on his promise to end the war in Vietnam.

Peace at Last

In the aftermath of the election, Nixon continued to pressure Thieu, writing him that "You have my absolute assurance that if Hanoi fails to abide by the terms of this agreement it is my intention to take swift and severe retaliatory action."[39] But Thieu did not flinch, and on November 20 Kissinger returned to Paris to resume negotiations. He now proposed sixty-nine changes in the draft treaty requested by the South Vietnamese. Two were important, demanding that at least some NVA units leave South Vietnam and that the accord prohibit the movement of North Vietnamese troops back across the DMZ. When Le Duc Tho rejected the changes and presented some of his own, Nixon was incensed. He could not decide, however, what to do—whether to force the government in Saigon to accept the settlement or increase the bombing of North Vietnam. Thus he both threatened Thieu and asked the JCS to prepare contingency plans for the bombing of Hanoi and the mining of Haiphong harbor.

When, in early December, after a recess in the talks, Kissinger returned to Paris, he found that the North Vietnamese still rejected all of his demands. A deeply frustrated Kissinger condemned their conduct as "composed of equal parts of insolence, guile, and stalling"; after Le Duc Tho broke off the talks on December 13, the national security advisor returned to Washington and told the president that "They're just a bunch of shits. Tawdry, filthy shits." Nixon agreed that leaders in Hanoi were guilty of "cynicism and perfidy."[40]

Nixon was in a dilemma. He could not abandon the government in Saigon now or make further concessions to the North Vietnamese. He felt he needed to take some dramatic action that would induce Thieu to sign and also force the leaders in Hanoi to make at least cosmetic changes in the agreement. He concluded that more bombing was his only option. Thus he issued an order to send B-52s against Hanoi and reseed the mines; "the North Vietnamese," he recorded in his diary, "figure that they have us where the hair is short and are going to continue to squeeze us. That is why we had to take our strong action." But the president was unhappy over the choices he faced, over what Kissinger called "*his* last roll of the dice,"[41] and he refused to go on television to explain his decision. When OPERATION LINE

BACKER II, the "Christmas bombing," began, the uproar around the world was immediate and intense. "Not one NATO ally," Kissinger lamented, "supported us or even hinted at understanding our point of view." At home, some Republicans supported the president, but he was denounced in many editorial columns and the Democratic leader in the Senate, Mike Mansfield, termed the bombing a "stone-age tactic."[42]

For twelve days the attack—designed more for psychological rather than military purposes—continued. While U.S. B-52 losses were heavy (fifteen of the big bombers were shot down), the bombing devastated North Vietnam's air defense system and economy, destroying most of the progress of the last three years. And it raised the specter of what might happen if no agreement was reached. North Vietnam could not risk further bombing; revolutionaries in both the north and the south, one party leader wrote, "needed time to build up the country as well as our forces."[43]

On December 26, when North Vietnam proposed to resume talks in Paris on January 8, 1973, Nixon suspended the bombing north of the twentieth parallel. The president thought that leaders in Hanoi had made a "stunning capitulation," ignoring the fact that it was Saigon rather than Hanoi that had created the stalemate in the first place and that Thieu still refused to accept the agreement.[44] On January 5 Nixon once again assured South Vietnam's president of continued U.S. assistance; the next day, in discussions with Kissinger, Nixon pointed out that the war had to end or the new Congress would end it for him.

On his return to Paris, Kissinger found that he and Le Duc Tho were in agreement; both were prepared to sign a treaty that, with some minor changes, was the same as the one they had forged in October. Thieu, however, still held out, and Alexander Haig was once again dispatched to Saigon to deliver a mixture of promises and threats. Nixon was determined to force a settlement. "Brutality is nothing," he told Kissinger. "You have never seen it if this son-of-a-bitch doesn't go along, believe me."[45] With or without South Vietnam's acquiescence, he planned to initial the agreement on January 23, 1973.

In the eleventh hour, on January 22, Thieu, though he loathed the terms of the settlement, finally relented. The next evening Nixon went on television to announce that the formal signing of what became known as the Paris Peace Accords would occur in Paris on January 27 and that the cease-fire in Vietnam would begin at midnight of that day. Although Nixon believed that he had achieved peace with honor, he noted that he felt "sadness, apprehension, and impatience" on what should have been his hour of triumph.[46]

Over the course of his first term in office, Nixon had preserved the regime in Saigon, slowly withdrawn American troops, and avoided a right-wing revolt against America's retreat from Vietnam. Americans and Vietnamese, however, had paid a terrible price for the achievement of these goals. In four additional years of war, more than 20,000 Americans, 107,000 South Vietnamese, and perhaps half a million enemy troops were killed or wounded. Worse still, the Paris Peace Accords did not bring peace to Vietnam. Most Vietnamese expected the war to continue, while Nixon and Kissinger, although they desperately wanted the cease-fire to hold, realized that leaders in Hanoi might resume the struggle and were prepared to use American air power once again to avert defeat. They could only hope that the threat of American retaliation, along with pressure from China and the Soviet Union and the promise of American reconstruction aid, might restrain Vietnamese revolutionaries and lead to the permanent division of the nation. Four years earlier they had badly miscalculated the costs of achieving peace with honor; now it seemed likely that they had also miscalculated the balance of forces in Vietnam.

Notes

1 Quoted in Stephen E. Ambrose, *Nixon: Volume Two, The Triumph of a Politician, 1962–1972* (New York, 1989), 420, 421.

2 Ibid., 426, 429.

3 Quoted in Douglas Brinkley, *Tour of Duty: John Kerry and the Vietnam War* (New York, 2004), 11.

4 Ibid., 429.

5 Ibid., 453.

6 Quoted in Seymour M. Hersh, *The Price of Power: Kissinger in the Nixon White House* (New York, 1983), 385.

7 Quoted in Lewis Sorley, *A Better War: The Unexamined Victories and Final Tragedy of America's Last Years in Vietnam* (New York, 1999), 289.

8 Ibid., 282, 305–06.

9 *Tiger in the Barbed Wire: An American in Vietnam, 1952–1991* (New York, 1992), 243–44.

10 Quoted in Frances FitzGerald, *Fire in the Lake: The Vietnamese and the Americans in Vietnam* (Boston, 1972), 419.

11 Quoted in Qiang Zhai, *China and the Vietnam Wars, 1950–1975* (Chapel Hill, N.C., 2000), 205.

12 Ibid., 197.

13 Quoted in Ambrose, *Nixon: Volume Two,* 478.

14 Ibid., 509.

15 Ibid., 510.

16 Quoted in Lewis Sorley, *Thunderbolt: General Creighton Abrams and the Army of His Times* (New York, 1992), 322.

17 Quoted in Ambrose, *Nixon: Volume Two,* 529.

18 Ibid., 533, 537, 539, 540.

19 Ibid., 540.

20 Quoted in Sorley, *A Better War,* 348; quoted in Howard B. Schaffer, *Ellsworth Bunker: Global Troubleshooter, Vietnam Hawk* (Chapel Hill, N.C., 2003), 239.

21 Quoted in Dale Andradé, *America's Last Vietnam Battle: Halting Hanoi's 1972 Easter Offensive* (Lawrence, Kans., 2001), 486.

22 Quoted in Pierre Asselin, *A Bitter Peace: Washington, Hanoi, and the Making of the Paris Agreement* (Chapel Hill, N.C., 2002), 156; quoted in Zhai, *China And The Vietnam Wars,* 206.

23 Quoted in George McGovern, *An American Journey: The Presidential Campaign Speeches of George McGovern* (New York, 1974), 23.

24 Quoted in Ambrose, *Nixon: Volume Two,* 557, 591.

25 Ibid., 594.

26 Quoted in Nguyen Tien Hung and Jerrold L. Schecter, *The Palace File* (New York, 1986), 68.

27 Quoted in Melvin Small, *The Presidency of Richard Nixon,* (Lawrence, Kans., 1997), 263.

28 Quoted in Ambrose, *Nixon: Volume Two,* 605.

29 Quoted in Henry Kissinger, *White House Years* (Boston, 1979), 1339–40; quoted in Isaacson, *Kissinger: A Biography* (New York, 1992), 447.

30 Quoted in McGovern, *An American Journey,* 52, 114.

31 Kissinger, *White House Years,* 1345–46; Richard Nixon, *RN: The Memoirs of Richard Nixon* (New York, 1978), 692.

32 Ibid., 694; quoted in Ambrose, *Nixon: Volume Two*, 629.

33 Quoted in Hung and Schecter, *The Palace File,* 88; quoted in Isaacson, *Kissinger,* 456.

34 Quoted in Samuel Zaffiri, *Westmoreland: A Biography of General William C. Westmoreland* (New York, 1994), 366.

35 Quoted in Nixon, *RN,* 701.

36 Quoted in Isaacson, *Kissinger,* 457, 459.

37 Quoted in Ambrose, *Nixon: Volume Two,* 646.

38 Ibid., 648.

39 Quoted in Nixon, *RN,* 718.

40 Quoted in Stephen E. Ambrose, *Nixon: Volume Three, Ruin and Recovery, 1973–1990* (New York, 1991), 37.

41 Quoted in Nixon, *RN,* 732; Kissinger, *White House Years,* 1449.

42 Kissinger, *White House Years,* 1453; quoted in Ambrose, *Nixon: Volume Three,* 41.

43 Quoted in Asselin, *A Bitter Peace,* 157.

44 Quoted in Nixon, *RN,* 741.

45 Kissinger, *White House Years,* 1469.

46 Nixon, *RN,* 757.

*Top: Carpet
bombing by
B-52 bombers.
U.S. Air Force
Photo.
Bottom: Operation
RANCH HAND.
A C-123 on a
defoliation mission
over the South
Vietnamese jungle.
U.S. Air Force
Photo.*

Top: President Nixon shaking hands with troops in Vietnam, 1969. Courtesy of the National Archives. ARC 194650. Bottom: General Creighton Abrams in I Corps. U.S. Army Center of Military History.

Street execution of a Viet Cong officer by South Vietnamese Police Chief Brig. Gen. Nguyen Ngoc Loan, 1968. AP/Wide World.

Above: A large demonstration against the Vietnam War in Washington in October 1967. Library of Congress. LC-U9-18187.

Top: Aftermath of the My Lai massacre—bodies of women and children. U.S. Army Photo.
Bottom: American POW being given first aid while guarded by captors in North Vietnam, 1966. National Archives.

Top: Villagers run from a napalm attack, 1972. The girl is Kim Phuc, who survived and now lives in the United States. AP/Wide World. Bottom: ARVN restrain a Khmer Rouge, 1971. AP/Wide World.

Top: President Nixon with Henry Kissinger, discussing cease-fire negotiations. U.S. Army Center of Military History.
Bottom: Evacuation of siege-stricken refugees from Saigon, 1975. Courtesy of the National Archives. ARC 542335.

Top: South Vietnamese civilians surge on embassy in a desperate attempt to evacuate Saigon, April 30, 1975. AP/Wide World.
Bottom: U.S. helicopter leaves embassy during the evacuation of Saigon, 1975. AP/Wide World.

CHAPTER NINE

The Fall of South Vietnam, 1973–1975

By 1973 the Vietnam War had taken a terrible toll, not just on American lives and resources, but also on the American spirit. Looking back on the conflict James Carroll—in the early 1970s a young Catholic priest—remembered that "the death-littered valleys of Vietnam . . . changed the way I thought of my family, my nation, my faith, and myself." The son of a high-ranking government official, Carroll had grown up with "a vivid and continuous sense of connection" with America. As a two-year-old he had been present at Franklin D. Roosevelt's last inauguration, and in the post–World War II years, as he attended one presidential inaugural after another, he realized that they were "like a sacrament of the streets to me, rituals of rebirth, the one true American gala, a quadrennial instance of Jefferson's 'peaceful revolution.'" But the Vietnam War had transformed Carroll and his sense of America, until on January 20, 1973, at Richard Nixon's second inauguration, Carroll shook his fist in the air and "cursed the president of the United States"—an act that measured the distance he had come from his "youthful worship of these men."[1]

Nixon Turns Inward

In February and March 1973 the North Vietnamese released 591 American POWs. Most of these men had been held captive for years, and their emaciated and broken bodies revealed the harshness of their ordeal. As they returned and began to describe the torture to which they had been subjected, many Americans felt a sense of revulsion toward their enemy mixed with a sense of relief that the war was finally over. On March 29 President Nixon addressed the nation, reporting that "for the first time in 12 years, no American military forces are in Vietnam. All our American POW's are on their way home. . . . We have prevented the imposition of a Communist government by force on South Vietnam." Boasting of the tough decisions he had made, Nixon claimed that because the majority of Americans had "stood firm against those who advocated peace at any price," one American POW had been able to tell him, "Thank you for bringing us home on our feet instead of on our knees."[2]

Nixon knew, however, that the nation was tired of the Vietnam War and disillusioned with its ally in Saigon. As North Vietnamese violations of the cease-fire accumulated, Kissinger sent a series of notes to Hanoi warning of consequences that "would be most grave," and he traveled to Hanoi, then to Paris in an effort to strengthen the peace agreement.[3] He also urged a resumption of the bombing of trails in Laos. But his negotiations with Le Duc Tho failed and Nixon, although he initially ordered a one-day retaliatory strike on portions of the Ho Chi Minh Trail, soon changed his mind. The president had reluctantly concluded that South Vietnam was on its own: it no longer mattered to most Americans.

In early April, when Nixon fulfilled a long-standing obligation to bring Thieu to the continental United States—earlier meetings had been held on Guam, Hawaii, or Midway Island—he entertained him at his personal retreat at San Clemente, California, rather than run the risk of facing protests in the nation's capital. After stopping in San Clemente, Thieu traveled to Washington, where Vice President Agnew found that, at the arrival ceremony, only one member of the cabinet joined him. Nor were many senior members of the administration willing to attend the dinner given in honor of South Vietnam's president. As Kissinger remarked, it was a "shaming experience" to discover that the leader of an allied nation was treated like a pariah.[4]

In his meetings with Thieu, Nixon assured him that the United States would resist blatant violations of the peace agreement. "You can," the president told his South Vietnamese ally, "count on us." Thieu still had faith in Nixon, although he found him "preoccupied and absent-minded" and knew that support in the United States for South Vietnam's cause was weakening.[5]

As Vietnam faded from American newspapers and television screens, the nation's attention focused on Washington, where the Watergate crisis had reached a new stage. The investigation of the break-in at Democratic-party headquarters by the Plumbers (a group set up by Nixon in July 1971) on June 17, 1972, and the cover-up of this crime, implicated many of the president's closest advisers, leaving him isolated and confronting an aggressive special prosecutor and a select Senate committee headed by Sam Ervin (Democrat, North Carolina). The public hearings of the Ervin committee, which began on May 17, brought one spectacular disclosure after another, weakening Nixon's hold on power and fueling the mounting congressional assault on presidential authority. Many in Congress, nervous about the war in Cambodia and Vietnam, moved to cut off funding for any further U.S. combat operations. Bowing to mounting pressure from Congress, at the end of June Nixon agreed to a compromise in which, after August 15, all military activities throughout Indochina were banned. Antiwar members of Congress had at long last prevailed. As Kissinger remarked, "No one had the stomach to refight the Vietnam debate in the midst of Watergate."[6]

War without End

In the aftermath of the Paris Peace Accords, Thieu knew that the war had not ended, that neither he nor leaders in Hanoi had any interest in a political solution to the conflict. He publicly declared his policy of "Four No's"—no coalition government, no recognition of the enemy, no surrender of territory to the enemy, and no neutralization of South Vietnam.[7] In February he ordered ARVN on the offensive, seizing enemy controlled areas in the Mekong Delta and near the Cambodian border.

But Thieu did little to prepare for the inevitable showdown. He continued to rule through guile and repression, relying on the South Vietnamese Army and the U.S. alliance as the twin foundations of his regime. The military administered the country, while aid from the United States confirmed his hold on power. Thieu's American connection was vital to his survival, but it also branded him as a vassal of foreigners and undercut the legitimacy of his government. And over the years the sheer weight of the American presence had overwhelmed the South Vietnamese on all levels, inducing a kind of passivity in their ranks. To many South Vietnamese, it seemed as if the United States was responsible for the fate of their nation.

South Vietnam's president had mixed feelings toward his American benefactors. He resented all of the indignities to which he had been subjected, but he continued to believe that if real trouble came, Nixon would intervene to save his regime. Thieu had only a limited understanding of American politics, especially of the role of Congress and of the unfolding Watergate crisis. From his perspective, it seemed inconceivable that the United States, having made such a vast commitment of men and resources over so many years, would now simply abandon its ally.

On March 29, 1973, the sixtieth day of the truce, the last of the 5,200 U.S. troops in South Vietnam departed. At a small ceremony in the courtyard of the American military's huge headquarters building near Tan Son Nhut Airport, Military Assistance Command Vietnam was formally deactivated. General Frederick C. Weyand, the last American commander, announced that "Our mission has been accomplished."[8] The only U.S. military personnel left in South Vietnam were 159 Marine embassy guards and 50 members of the Defense Attaché Office, whose staff was to coordinate military aid requests. In addition, 9,000 American civilian contract workers stayed on to help maintain the equipment of the South Vietnamese Army.

At Camp Alpha, the processing barracks for departing American soldiers, a few Americans worked hard to prepare the site for international truce observers. On the day the last American troops left, Vietnamese workers and off-duty soldiers looted the camp, carrying away fixtures, furniture, and food, and smashing whatever they did not take with them. Concerned only with their own survival, they lacked any sense of being part of a larger cause.

Despite the American withdrawal, Thieu and his top commanders behaved as if the United States was still running the war. The Vietnamese Joint General Staff, chaired by General Cao Van Vien, was supposed to assume the functions of MACV, but it remained passive, failing to adjust to the new reality. Vien viewed its role as advisory, while Thieu, insecure and irresolute, often bypassed the Joint General Staff and communicated directly with his corps commanders. As the final crisis of the war approached, the leaders of the South Vietnamese military lacked any effective way to direct the war.

In early July 1973 the last American ambassador arrived in Saigon. Graham A. Martin, a career diplomat who had served in Italy and Thailand, was still inspired by the crusade to save Southeast Asia from communism. Emotionally involved in the war—his adopted son had died in combat there—he saw his task as a defender of the Saigon regime and dispatched a series of reports to Washington that played down its weaknesses. Soon after his arrival he informed Kissinger that "The level of corruption currently existing in South Vietnam corresponds roughly to that in the state of Massachusetts and the city of Boston during the first decades of the century. That problem was eliminated and . . . perhaps even more rapid progress may be made in Vietnam."[9] Martin thought he knew South Vietnam well; in fact, he rarely traveled outside of Saigon and never saw beneath the surface of events.

Ambassador Martin sought to prevent the erosion of U.S. economic and military aid, but he faced an uphill fight in Congress, where disillusionment with the war had grown widespread. ARVN needed about $3 billion a year to sustain itself, but Congress provided only $2.3 billion in 1973, $1 billion in 1974, and $700 million in 1975. As the Watergate crisis continued to unfold, it riveted the attention of the nation. By mid-summer, the testimony of one White House aide raised the issue of Nixon's participation in the obstruction of justice, while the testimony of another revealed the existence of tapes the president had secretly made of conversations between himself and others in the Oval Office. The mounting evidence of presidential improprieties and illegal behavior lowered Nixon's approval rating to a dismal 39 percent. The imperfections of the cease-fire in South Vietnam and concerns about the fate of that nation were all but irrelevant to most Americans.

Hanoi Prepares for War

The North Vietnamese government proclaimed the Paris Peace Accords a stunning victory, one that would bring a "great leap forward" in the world revolt against imperialism. "For the first time in one hundred years," General Giap announced in a radio address, "all foreign aggressor troops will have left Viet Nam."[10] Despite their florid rhetoric, however, leaders in Hanoi were in no rush to resume the war. NVA and Viet Cong forces in the south were worn down and demoralized, and party leaders—although they remained convinced that the path to victory lay through revolutionary violence—preferred to respect the cease-fire and, for a time, continue the struggle in South Vietnam through political means. Thus they sought to undermine the Thieu regime and seek a legitimate role for the Provisional Revolutionary Government.

A lull in the fighting would also ease the strain on the people of North Vietnam. Truong Nhu Tang, a high-ranking PRG official who drove north to Hanoi in early 1974, had last seen the city thirty years earlier, when it was still occupied by the French. Nothing had been built since then; he was now struck by the "dreariness and poverty" of this once graceful colonial city. Bomb damage had been unrepaired, and even the grand French-built public buildings were falling apart—"the vista was one of crumbling facades and peeling paint with only a hint of bygone dignity."[11] The streets were crowded, but Hanoi had none of the bustle of Saigon. Its people seemed sad and preoccupied, exhausted by the sacrifices of over a generation of war.

While the war let up in the south, North Vietnamese leaders once again sought to rebuild and reinforce their forces there. Hanoi had to motivate its soldiers—to convince them at long last that the end of the war was in sight—even while engaging in massive preparations for a new offensive. Throughout 1973 huge convoys rolled down the Ho Chi Minh Trail carrying troops, tanks, artillery pieces, and anti-aircraft weapons. The NVA expanded its logistical network, building new base areas, roads, airfields, a modern radio net, and even a fuel pipeline running deep into South Vietnam. By the end of the year 170,000 NVA regulars and 60,000 VC troops prepared to resume the struggle. As one Communist general remarked: "strong ropes inching gradually, day by day, around the neck, arms, and legs of a demon, awaiting the order to jerk tight and bring the creature's life to an end."[12]

The remarkable transformation of the Ho Chi Minh Trail revealed the extent of this North Vietnamese effort. In 1959 traveling from North to South Vietnam was an arduous, dangerous journey that took six months. By the end of 1973 the journey took eleven days. The "trail" had become an interlocking system of two-lane roads with a hard stone surface maintained by 100,000 soldiers and work battalions. Some workers had lived on the trail for eight to ten years without seeing their homes in the north. Bomb craters had been continuously repaired so that, over the years, an elaborate system of bypasses and cutoffs had made the thoroughfare invulnerable to air attack. At long last, the NVA possessed a logistical pipeline that could supply its highly mechanized forces in the south.

Throughout 1973, as the low-level struggle over territory continued, leaders in Hanoi remained cautious. ARVN seemed to retain the upper hand, the danger of American intervention remained, and Moscow and Beijing, while they continued to aid North Vietnam, urged patience in Hanoi's quest for unification. The North Vietnamese, Zhou Enlai advised Secretary General Le Duan, should "relax" and stop fighting in the south for five or ten years. While the NVA stepped up military operations in the fall, Le Duan warned that revolutionary forces still faced "difficulties and hardships"; the path to victory was still obscure.[13]

Crisis in South Vietnam

By the early months of 1974 an economic crisis had enveloped South Vietnam. Over the course of the war millions of refugees had fled from the countryside into the cities, where they had survived and even prospered catering to Americans. But most Americans were now gone, as were all of the jobs that their presence had generated, leaving about one-fifth of the civilian work force unemployed. The reduction in

American spending and economic and military aid, combined with rampant inflation, produced hardship nearly everywhere. In Can Tho, the largest city in the Mekong Delta, one U.S. official reported that "some school teachers have been seen driving pedicabs. . . . Government services are frequently sold and absentee rates are high."[14]

The collapsing economy and cutback in aid quickly affected army morale. Life in the ARVN had never been easy for ordinary soldiers, but by the summer of 1974 it had become even more difficult. Nor was the officer corps prepared for adversity. Heavily dependent on American aid and advice, most senior commanders had an ingrained sense of inferiority and feared the NVA. Panic had always lain just beneath the surface.

The South Vietnamese had been taught to fight a war the American way, with the heavy use of artillery, armored vehicles, transport helicopters, and air power. The new austerity brought cutbacks in training and mobility; ARVN suffered from a wide range of shortages, ranging from spare parts to fuel and ammunition stocks to clothing and food allowances. The use of helicopters and large aircraft decreased by half, and soldiers found their boots were replaced every nine months instead of every six, that evacuations of the wounded were often delayed, and that, when the injured did arrive at a hospital, medical supplies were sometimes in short supply. The head of the U.S. Defense Attaché Office, General John E. Murray, angrily complained that aid cuts had left ARVN on a "starvation diet."[15]

While congressional cuts in military aid no doubt affected ARVN's performance, the sufficiency of American support remains shrouded in confusion. American observers felt, for example, that ARVN's expenditure of ammunition before 1974 was wildly excessive and needed to be cut back. But no one knew how much ammunition was in South Vietnamese depots, or the extent to which ARVN was exaggerating its consumption, or what was, in fact, a reasonable level of expenditure. Aid reductions, in short, accentuated—but did not cause—longstanding weaknesses in ARVN's leadership and organization. Once it was forced to fight a poor man's war, a paralysis spread through the South Vietnamese military, where many senior officers clung to the illusion that American intervention would once again save the regime.

Throughout the American phase of the war, corruption had been a way of life in the South Vietnamese government, but in 1974, as fear and defeatism spread, it exceeded all previous bounds. Some commanders embezzled from the payrolls of their own troops, while others in quartermaster units often insisted on bribes for delivering food and ammunition, even to soldiers engaged in combat. Corruption reached all the way to the top, where Thieu's wife and the wives of his associates, seemingly indifferent to the dangers confronting their nation, made fortunes in real estate and other business deals. They set an example of official misconduct visible to all.

One province chief in the lower Mekong Delta, a cousin of Thieu, became famous for his greed. He taxed almost every commodity sold in his province, fired thousands of rounds of artillery unnecessarily so that he could sell the brass shell casings, and used the Phoenix program to blackmail innocent people, even as he let members of the NLF buy their way out of jail.

Well before 1974, some U.S. officials had become alarmed by the extent of this venality and tried to fight it. They compiled dossiers on corrupt South Vietnamese officials and had them delivered to Thieu. On seventy-eight occasions Ambassador Bunker raised corruption cases with President Thieu; "Corruption is a cancer," he warned in January 1971, "which will, unless checked, sap the strength of [Vietnamese] society."[16] But the American protests settled into a meaningless ritual. An official might be removed from his position as province or district chief and for a time given a staff job. Sooner or later, however, the same person would end up as the chief of another district or province. Saigon's officials rode a revolving wheel of corruption.

Despite his many years in power, Thieu had never inspired the South Vietnamese people, neither those in the cities nor those in the countryside. As South Vietnam's crisis deepened, his critics grew bolder and denounced his government. Buddhists demanded peace and reconciliation with the Communists; even some Catholics, disgusted by the extent of the graft, attacked the "present rotten, dictatorial family regime" in a "People's Anticorruption Movement";[17] and many in the urban elite dismissed Thieu's government and argued that a Communist victory would at least bring peace and autonomy to the south. Everywhere he turned, Thieu faced challenges to his authority.

Confronted with such a wide range of protest, Thieu was uncertain how to respond. He dismissed some cabinet members and fired three of his four corps commanders. But he had no way of conferring legitimacy on his regime. By the end of 1974 soldiers in ARVN were tired and demoralized. And while protests subsided in Saigon, many South Vietnamese now sensed that their nation was doomed.

Washington's Response

Early in 1974, as the Watergate crisis intensified, Nixon's ability to govern further weakened. His approval rating fell to 29 percent—down from 39 percent in the last year—and the Congress was in rebellion against his foreign policy. In May the Senate rejected the president's request to increase military aid to South Vietnam, despite the pleas of John Stennis (Democrat, Mississippi) that the extra money was "an obligation to an ally." Edward M. Kennedy (Democrat, Massachusetts), reflecting the mood of the majority, responded: "How long are we going to hear that argument? We have heard it long enough."[18] By the end of July, when the House passed the first impeachment resolution, the end of the Nixon presidency was near. On August 9 Nixon resigned in disgrace.

Thieu and his close advisers—who had never really understood the seriousness of Nixon's political situation—were shocked by his resignation. When Thieu received the news in his office at Independence Palace, he closed his eyes, bit his lips, and ground "his right fist into the palm of his left hand."[19]

Throughout 1974 the staffs of the American embassy in Saigon and the CIA station there played down the decline in ARVN's morale and the growing insecurity of Thieu's government. Neither Ambassador Martin nor CIA station chief Thomas Polgar could bring himself to believe that South Vietnam might soon be lost. A novice in Vietnam, Polgar told his agents that "I want you to know that everything is going OK. We don't see any major problems in 1975. Our reading is that the situation is under control."[20]

Nixon's successor, Gerald R. Ford, had served in Congress for many years before becoming vice president in December 1973. Ford had supported Johnson's escalation of the war, although he criticized him for "pulling our best punches in Vietnam," and throughout Nixon's presidency he backed the administration's Vietnam policy. On his first day as president, Ford wrote Thieu that "the existing commitments this nation has made in the past are still valid and will be fully honored by my administration."[21] Although Ford knew firsthand the mood in Congress—in September it reduced the administration's request for military aid to South Vietnam—he continued throughout the fall to assure Thieu that his administration had control of its foreign policy and would continue to fight for higher levels of aid. Until the end of 1974 President Ford seemed to believe that the United States could somehow save South Vietnam.

The Great Spring Offensive

Over the course of 1974 North Vietnamese rulers completed the rebuilding of the NVA and the modernization of its logistical network; they also conducted a series of military operations to prepare for an eventual all-out offensive. Leaders in Hanoi, however, were slow to pick up on signs of the disintegration of the South Vietnamese government and initially decided on a conservative strategy in 1975—putting off a general offensive until the following year. This time they overestimated ARVN, with vivid memories of earlier military failures, and they still feared U.S. intervention. But General Tran Van Tra, a southerner who commanded COSVN, argued for a bolder approach, urging northern leaders to authorize an assault on Saigon in 1975. Although the General Staff remained skeptical, Tran won enough concessions to unleash his forces on Phuoc Binh, the capital of a remote province eighty miles north of Saigon. While ARVN units fought hard in defense of the city, the NVA had massive superiority. On January 6, 1975, Phuoc Binh fell.

The fall of a provincial capital, along with Soviet assurances of increased aid, made North Vietnamese leaders bolder. Secretary General Le Duan concluded: "Now the Americans have withdrawn, we have our troops in the South, and the spirit of the masses is rising.

This is what marks an opportune moment."[22] They now focused NVA divisions on the Central Highlands, a large area in which ARVN was thinly spread. By early March the NVA closed in on the largest city in the highlands, Ban Me Thuot; soon armored units and assault troops attacked down the main highways into town, seizing the center of the city. The next day, March 12, resistance in Ban Me Thuot ended.

These losses stunned Thieu and his commanders, who were shocked by the lack of any U.S. reaction and confused by their inability to see the military situation clearly. The head of South Vietnamese forces in the Central Highlands, General Phan Van Phu, was incapable of maneuvering his troops in such a fluid situation. In mid-March, as the NVA moved toward Kontum and Pleiku, Thieu finally decided that his army could not hold everywhere; in a series of confused meetings, the president and his senior commanders decided to redeploy ARVN to the south—"lighten the top, keep the bottom"[23]— so that it could defend a truncated South Vietnam consisting of Saigon and the Mekong Delta. But Thieu's enclave concept was poorly developed. He mistrusted his generals, relied on his own maps, and issued orders without regard for battlefield realities. As South Vietnam edged toward collapse, Thieu had lost the confidence of his people and of his army.

General Phu—having been ordered to withdraw his forces from Kontum and Pleiku to the coast—was nervous and demoralized; he had fought with the French at Dien Bien Phu and had no desire to be captured again. The best road had already been cut by the NVA, so he decided to use an old road, Route 7B, that had not been maintained for years. On March 16 the chaotic withdrawal of ARVN units began, and soon panicked civilians and dependents joined what became known as the "column of sorrow."[24] CIA operated aircraft—flying several thousand feet above the column took photos showing hundreds of army vehicles intermingled with civilian trucks and buses jamming up at bridges and desperately searching for an escape route. As the NVA closed in to attack, the column came to a halt and ARVN's Second Corps dissolved: in its wake lay dead bodies, burning vehicles, and abandoned weapons on the roadside. Of the 60,000 troops who had begun the withdrawal, only 20,000 made it to the coast (and they were no longer fit for combat); of the 400,000 civilians who left, only 100,000 reached safety. The debacle was complete.

In I Corps—the area covering the northern third of South Vietnam—the retreat was, if anything, even worse. Earlier Thieu had pulled out one of his two best divisions to strengthen the defense of Saigon, leaving the able field commander General Ngo Quang Truong with badly outnumbered defending forces. As refugees streamed first toward Hué, then Da Nang, chaos and disorder spread and most ARVN units collapsed. On March 25 Hué fell; five days later Da Nang, the second largest city in South Vietnam and the site of major military bases, was occupied by enemy troops, slightly more than ten years after the U.S. Marines had landed on the nearby beaches. In a few weeks a total of eight provinces had fallen, all of ARVN in I and II Corps had been wiped out, and the South Vietnamese Army had lost half of its troops and half of its aircraft. Thieu had set in motion one of the worst planned and executed withdrawals in military history.

The mood among leaders in Hanoi was exuberant; they now realized that victory was possible in South Vietnam in 1975 and that the dream of a lifetime was within their grasp. They knew that—whatever the United States might do—there was no turning back. On April 2 most NVA divisions were ordered to turn south, to prepare for the attack on Saigon, the "Ho Chi Minh Campaign." Soon they were poised, in the words of their commander, like a "divine hammer" held aloft,[25] waiting for the order to launch the final battle of the war. The NVA hoped to capture Saigon before the rainy season began in May and before the remainder of ARVN could regroup to defend it.

The Fall of Saigon

In the early months of 1975, as the North Vietnamese offensive gathered momentum, Ambassador Martin and CIA Station Chief Polgar seemed paralyzed. Their emotions were so engaged with the cause of South Vietnam that they could not admit that all they had worked for was about to disappear. They resisted accurate briefings by their subordinates, delayed planning for an evacuation, and argued that it was still possible for ARVN to regroup and establish an enclave around Saigon. Both Americans now claimed that the key to South Vietnam's survival was $722 million in supplemental U.S. aid that could be used to mobilize fresh ARVN units.

The Great Spring Offensive. Adapted from Stanley Karnow, *Vietnam: A History* (Penguin Books, 1997) p. 677. Used by permission of WGBH Educational Foundation.

In Washington, Ford and Kissinger, who became secretary of state in September 1973, were aware that the end was near, but they were concerned about the way in which South Vietnam fell. "We are facing a great tragedy," Kissinger argued, "in which there is involved something of American credibility, something of American honor, something of how we are perceived by other people in the world."[26] On April 10 Ford appeared before a joint session of Congress to ask for additional aid, claiming that "we cannot . . . abandon our friends while our adversaries support and encourage theirs." He received no applause from either side of the aisle. Finally on April 23, in an address at Tulane University, Ford sought to distance himself from the war. "Today," he told 4,500 students, "America can regain the sense of pride that existed before Vietnam. But it cannot be achieved by re-fighting a war that is finished as far as America is concerned."[27] Before he spoke these final words, a roar went up from the crowd as students celebrated the end of the conflict. The president had correctly sensed the mood of the nation.

As the end of South Vietnam drew near, Lon Nol's Khmer Republic in Cambodia collapsed. Soon after Lon Nol had taken power in March 1970 the Cambodian Army suffered a series of defeats, and over the next five years—despite heavy U.S. bombing and military aid in excess of $1 billion—it steadily lost ground to a combinaton of Vietnamese Communists and an indigenous revolutionary force, the Khmer Rouge. Gradually these Cambodian insurgents, under the leadership of Pol Pot, took over most of the fighting; as they expanded their control of the countryside, they imposed their violent and fanatical doctrines on the population. With Lon Nol's resignation of April 1, and the American evacuation of Phnom Penh eleven days later, the Khmer Rouge occupied the capital city on April 17 and began their reign of terror, evacuating urban residents to work camps in the countryside and beginning the systematic killing of real or imagined opponents of their regime.

After the fall of Phnom Penh, in late April North Vietnamese divisions converged on Saigon, engaging badly outnumbered ARVN units. The only true engagement of this last phase of the war occurred at Xuan Loc, forty miles east of Saigon. In a fierce battle that lasted two weeks, South Vietnamese soldiers bravely held their ground until finally overwhelmed by superior enemy forces. Xuan Loc was ARVN's last stand. On April 21, the day before the battle, President Thieu addressed the nation. In a bitter, emotional address that lasted an hour and a half, Thieu blamed everyone but himself for the collapse of South Vietnam. Pouring out his resentment against America, he denounced aid cuts as "an inhuman act by an inhuman ally,"[28] declared his resignation as president, and announced that Vice President Tran Van Huong, ill and nearly blind, would replace him. A few days later, when Thieu learned that he would not be welcome in the United States, he responded: "It is so easy to be an enemy of the United States, but so difficult to be a friend."[29]

On the night of April 29 NVA forward columns reached the outskirts of Saigon; the next morning long lines of tanks and trucks filled with troops moved into the city. The lead tank of one armored unit burst through the high steel gate in front of the grounds of Independence Palace, coming to a halt near the bottom of its ceremonial staircase. Troops arrested the palace guards and raised the red and blue flag of the PRG from the rooftop flagpole. Two hours later President Duong Van Minh—Huong's successor—called on all South Vietnamese soldiers to lay down their arms. The war was finally over.

When officials in Washington realized that the end was near, Kissinger put intense pressure on the embassy in Saigon to accelerate the withdrawal of important personnel. On April 20 the final push began. Around 50,000 Americans and South Vietnamese had already left the nation, but many still remained. Nine days later the NVA began shelling Tan Son Nhut Airport; now only helicopters could complete the task.

On April 29 the U.S. military began the largest helicopter evacuation in history. Over the course of eighteen hours, helicopters carried more than 1,000 Americans and 6,000 Vietnamese from Saigon to aircraft carriers forty miles off the southern coast of Vietnam. In the original plan, Americans and Vietnamese designated for departure were to be picked up by bus at appointed locations and delivered to helicopter pads. But this plan quickly broke down as crowds of hysterical Vietnamese blocked the buses and thousands more surged toward the walls surrounding the American Embassy compound clamoring to be saved.

The chaos grew so great that evacuees could not be properly screened; some well-connected Saigon bar girls got out, while Vietnamese who had worked for years for various U.S. agencies did not. In the haste, many intelligence files were left undestroyed—making it easy for the North Vietnamese to identify collaborators—and a massive amount of military equipment was abandoned. Stuart A. Herrington, an American intelligence adviser, remembered, as his helicopter lifted off, all of the Vietnamese who had been left behind. "I know of no word in any language," he later wrote, "that can describe the sense of shame that swept over me during that flight." And Orrin DeForest, a CIA officer whose helicopter landed on the deck of an aircraft carrier in the South China Sea, looked at the chaos around him and thought: "So this is how it happens . . . this is how the United States bugs out."[30]

Vietnamese Perspectives

The fall of Saigon, which was soon renamed Ho Chi Minh City, was full of paradoxes. North Vietnamese troops had been fighting for years, hiding in jungles and remote sanctuaries, absorbing a steady diet of Marxist ideology and Communist propaganda. They were told that no sacrifice was too great for the liberation of their oppressed comrades in the south. But the soldiers who marched into Saigon on April 30 found that their welcome was far different than that Viet Minh troops had received when they entered Hanoi in August 1945. The Viet Minh had been greeted by banners and cheering crowds; the NVA found that initially the people of Saigon stayed indoors, only gradually venturing out to mingle with these legendary warriors. As northern soldiers settled in, they became aware of the great differences between the north and the south that had emerged in the twenty-one years since the division of Vietnam. They had grown up in an impoverished country where a watch or a radio was a prized possession; now they confronted an urban society that had adopted many aspects of the American lifestyle. As one American journalist remarked, Saigon "wore the veneer of a desert vacation boom town with flashy motorcycles, sporty cars, perfume, hair spray and sharp differences on the streets between the rich and poor."[31] It was a bewildering, new world for the "liberators" of South Vietnam, who now had to deal with the gap between their stereotypes of life in the south and the reality produced by two decades of the infusion of American money.

On May 15 a great victory celebration was held at Independence Palace Square in Saigon. Communist leaders gathered on a reviewing stand, with a huge crowd stretched out before them, to commemorate the end of thirty years of war and revolution. After the obligatory speeches, a victory parade began, led first by representatives of various mass organizations followed by NVA troops, wearing their distinctive olive-colored pith helmets. Finally a few Viet Cong units appeared, looking unkempt and disorganized and carrying the North Vietnamese flag. Truong Nhu Tang, the PRG's Minister of Justice, turned to the North Vietnamese general standing next to him and asked: "Where are our divisions one, three, five, seven, and nine?" General Van Tien Dung smiled slightly and replied: "The army has already been unified." "Since when?" Tang persisted, "There's been no decision about anything like that."[32] Without bothering to answer, Dung turned his eyes back to the parade.

Leaders in Hanoi had already put their own people in power and quickly imposed an authoritarian regime on the south. They made no allowances for all of the differences that had grown up between the peoples of the north and the south during years of separation. Nor did they allow any role for the PRG: northern officials became the wardens of the people they had allegedly liberated, placing 1 million South Vietnamese soldiers and civilians in so-called re-education camps, extending no forgiveness to those who had believed in the cause of the Saigon government.

After three decades of struggle, the late Ho Chi Minh's vision of a unified nation, one free of Western imperialism, had become a reality. It was, by any measure, an extraordinary triumph, this transformation of several generations of Vietnamese into a lethal revolutionary force and the outmaneuvering of first France and then the United States. But it had come at an enormous cost. Perhaps as many as 4 million north and south Vietnamese had lost their lives (1.5 million soldiers, 2.5 million civilians), while the physical destruction (in terms of infrastructure as well as environmental damage) in both the north and the south had been vast. Now that the war had ended, the nation desperately needed reconciliation and reconstruction, but leaders in Hanoi knew how to make war far better than they knew how to make peace. As Premier Pham Van Dong later recalled, "Waging war is simple, but running a country is very difficult."[33] They imposed a tyranny so harsh, and mismanaged the economy so badly, that in the years after 1975 1.5 million South Vietnamese risked their lives in fleeing their homeland, many of them, the so-called Boat People, taking to the open sea in small fishing boats. Looking back on these events, one disillusioned revolutionary concluded that "the Communist road to national liberation is in fact a road to national desolation."[34]

American Perspectives

During the final phase of the war, the U.S. government made many of the same mistakes that had drawn it into South Vietnam in the first place. It was as if, over all the years of the conflict, American leaders had learned nothing. After the signing of the Paris Peace Accords, many American officials in Washington and Saigon were careless and complacent, unwilling to concede defeat and admit that this time the United States would not prevail. Yet they continued to endow the conflict with symbolic importance and resist coming to terms with reality, refusing to listen to subordinates who had a better understanding of the bleak prospects for South Vietnam. When the end came, they left behind thousands of South Vietnamese who had served the United States loyally, even though American officials knew their fate would be a cruel one. In May 1975, reflecting on the collapse of South Vietnam, no less than Henry Kissinger admitted that "we probably made a mistake" by being too concerned about the "domino effect" when dealing with Vietnam. "We perhaps might," he conceded, "have perceived the war more in Vietnamese terms rather than as the outward thrust of a global conspiracy."[35]

For most Americans the outcome of the Vietnam War seemed almost beyond understanding. How had the conflict become a quagmire? How had the architects of the war, the best and brightest of their generation, miscalculated so badly? Why had the United States fought so long and so hard—a fight that took the lives of 58,000 American soldiers and cost American taxpayers $167 billion—in such a strange and distant place? And why, in the end, had the United States and its ally in Saigon suffered such a humiliating defeat? The fall of Saigon, with its final tragic scenes of panic and desperation, stunned Americans at home. They had not been prepared to witness this sort of flight. As helicopters reached the American fleet in the South China Sea, some of them flown by South Vietnamese pilots crash-landed in the water while others made unauthorized landings on the aircraft carriers. In order to make room for all the American helicopters to land, many had to be swept off the decks into the sea, floating, as one American war correspondent observed, "briefly before sinking out of sight. It was as if the war had been given a burial at sea, and that's when I knew it was over."[36]

The loss of South Vietnam left U.S. foreign policy in disarray, weakening all of those Cold War assumptions that had guided American leaders from the late 1940s through the late 1960s and bringing a bitter public reaction against two decades of crisis diplomacy and intervention. Weary of the costs and burdens of the Cold War, Americans became skeptical about the use of force as an instrument of foreign policy and acquired a new sense of the limits of U.S. power abroad. Some concluded that the Vietnam War revealed deep flaws in American society and foreign policy; they urged the nation to accept a reduced role in world politics. Reflecting on the fall of Saigon, George F. Kennan, the author of the containment doctrine, asked his fellow Americans to consider "whether the great miscalculations which led us into the folly of Vietnam were not something more than just the shortsightedness of a few individuals—whether they did not in fact reflect a certain unfitness of the system as a whole for the conceiving and executing of ambitious political-military ventures far from our own shores."[37]

Other public figures disagreed, arguing that the war was lost at home, not in Southeast Asia, and that the final collapse of the Saigon government came only because the United States sharply reduced aid to South Vietnam and thereby allowed the North Vietnamese Army to carry out a conventional military offensive. Convinced that the subsequent harshness of North Vietnam's rule vindicated the moral soundness of America's intervention, they were angry over the outcome. Supporters of the American war effort were determined to rebuild the confidence, moral resolve, and military strength of the nation, so that the United States could resume its rightful primacy in world affairs. "For too long," presidential candidate Ronald Reagan declared in August 1980, "we have lived with the Vietnam Syndrome. This is a lesson for all of us in Vietnam. If we are forced to fight, we must have the means and the determination to prevail, or we will not have what it takes to secure peace. And while we are at it, let us tell those who fought in that war, that we will never again ask young men to fight and possibly die in a war our government is afraid to let them win."[38]

Those who served in Vietnam, whether in high-level policy positions or in ground combat units, were frustrated by the way in which the war ended. General Westmoreland blamed his political superiors for the defeat. "Had the president allowed a change in strategy and taken advantage of the enemy's weaknesses," he maintained, "the North Vietnamese doubtless would have broken." William E. Colby, who directed important CIA programs in Vietnam, believed that a counterinsurgency strategy would have won the war. Over the final evacuation efforts from Saigon, he remembers, "hung the tragedy of this waste of lives and the years of effort of both Vietnamese and Americans who had hoped that Vietnam might develop in freedom."[39]

Severely wounded soldiers were especially disillusioned. Ron Kovic, the author of *Born on the Fourth of July*, suffered a terrible wound that left the lower half of his body paralyzed. After returning home, he lost his faith in the nation and its leaders, which he had once revered. Bitterly he wrote, "I have given my dead swinging dick for America. I have given my numb young dick for democracy. . . . Yes, I gave my dead dick for John Wayne." Lewis Puller Jr., also seriously wounded, had been apolitical before leaving Vietnam in the summer of 1968, accepting the judgment of leaders in Washington. Returning to America, he concluded that the war was a mistake and "began to feel that my own sacrifice and that of all of us who had fought the war were meaningless."[40] Many other veterans who had fought in what had become a lost cause were also unable to find meaning in their sacrifice, or to understand what had gone wrong to deprive the nation of victory.

Vietnam veterans received a mixed homecoming. In contrast to veterans of World War II, the 2,150,000 men and 6,431 women who served in the military in Vietnam did not enjoy victory parades or thanks for their service, and the government provided less help than veterans needed to deal with drug abuse, physical disabilities, health problems stemming from exposure to the chemical herbicide Agent Orange, or post-traumatic stress disorder (PTSD). Having fought in a morally ambiguous, divisive conflict, the Vietnam veterans found themselves denounced by both opponents and supporters of the war. Gradually, as the nation's wounds healed, most Americans realized that the veterans, like the nation itself, were victims of the misguided policies of America's leaders. The dedication of the Vietnam Veterans' Memorial in Washington, D.C., on November 23, 1982, symbolized the growing acceptance of Vietnam veterans and their sacrifice; it soon became one of the most frequently visited of the many monuments in the nation's capital.

Americans had entered the Vietnam War with the expectation that a distinctively American story would emerge. The escalation of the Vietnam War in 1965 came only twenty years after the end of World War II, a culminating event in the nation's history. The defeat of the Axis powers breathed new life into old American myths, confirming a whole cluster of beliefs about America's destiny, innocence, and invincibility deeply rooted in the nation's past. But the Vietnam War developed in unexpected ways; America's Vietnamese allies seemed venal and corrupt, while its Vietnamese enemies fought with skill and dedication. Those Americans who served in Vietnam were confused by the elusiveness of the enemy and the difficulty of measuring progress. Many felt—even early in their stay—that the war made no sense. As one Vietnam veteran recalls, "everything I'd been raised to believe in was contrary to what I saw in Vietnam."[41] As the war lengthened with no end in sight, it raised questions about Americans' explanation of their past and their vision of the future. And the final collapse of South Vietnam left many people with a sense of loss and betrayal, as if some vital piece of America's vision of itself had disappeared there.

After the Vietnam War, most Americans sensed that their nation had entered a new period of division, uncertainty, and moral confusion, both at home and abroad. Neither the powerful rhetoric of President Reagan in the 1980s, nor the stunning success of the Persian Gulf War in 1991, nor the collapse of the Soviet Union and the end of the Cold War in 1991 could restore the old sense of national self-confidence. Reagan, for all of his tough anti-Soviet rhetoric, never asked the American people to make any painful sacrifices in order to achieve his foreign policy goals; President George H. W. Bush, although he declared after the liberation of Kuwait that "By God, we've kicked the Vietnam syndrome," did not allow U.S. forces to advance on Baghdad and occupy Iraq;[42] and the breakdown of the Soviet Union and its empire brought few celebrations in the United States, where the length and cost of the immense struggle known as the Cold War had worn down the American people.

And the end of the Cold War—while it removed the nation's major enemy—brought a new and confusing era in U.S. foreign policy. For more than forty years the Cold War had been the organizing principle of American life and diplomacy; within the space of a few years it was gone. In the 1990s the United States emerged as the world's last superpower, with no serious challenges from any other nation and faced with no urgent, short-term dangers abroad. Uncertain how to respond to a series of regional crises, American leaders proceeded cautiously, reluctant to use force and eager to develop new international arrangements to keep the peace.

This decade of drift in U.S. foreign policy came to a sudden end on September 11, 2001, when terrorists brutally hijacked four American commercial aircraft, using two of the airplanes to destroy both towers of the World Trade Center in New York City and another to seriously damage the Pentagon in Washington. The fourth hijacked airplane, meant to destroy another target in Washington, crashed into farmland in Pennsylvania because some brave passengers on board interrupted the hijacker's plans. The attack claimed the lives of nearly three thousand people, most of them Americans.

President George W. Bush responded to the events of "9/11" decisively, declaring a "war against terror" and pursuing an assertive, unilateralist policy toward governments that appeared to sponsor it. In late 2001 the United States attacked the Taliban (fundamentalist Muslim) regime in Afghanistan, and in March 2003 invaded Iraq and brought down the regime of the dictator Saddam Hussein. President Bush, convinced that Americans had been "called to defend our nation and to lead the world to peace," focused the nation's diplomacy on what he deemed the "axis of evil"—rogue states and their terrorist allies.[43] This war on terror, still in its early stages as the twenty-first century began to unfold, seemed likely to take the place of the Cold War and become the central idea around which U.S. domestic and foreign policy would be organized for the foreseeable future.

The legacy of the Vietnam War was woven through all of these events. As the historian Arnold R. Isaacs writes, Vietnam "lingers in the national memory, hovering over our politics, our culture, and our long, unfinished debate over who we are and what we believe."[44] Four years into the new century and twenty-nine years after the fall of Saigon, memories of the Vietnam War continue to preoccupy many Americans. Evidence of the turmoil and controversy surrounding the war lies virtually everywhere. Aging policymakers continue to argue over the conduct of the war and its lessons for U.S. foreign policy. Memories of the Vietnam War had a powerful effect on the way in which President George H. W. Bush and his advisers approached the crisis in the Persian Gulf in 1990 and 1991, while the legacy of the war has surfaced in every presidential campaign from 1992 to 2004, reminding Americans of the immense gap between those who served in World War II and those who had to deal with Vietnam, and raising the question of the relevance of military service to presidential leadership.

And the growing debate over the war in Iraq and the occupation there have pulled Americans back to the controversies surrounding the Vietnam War, deeply dividing the nation. Issues familiar to those who lived through the Vietnam era have now returned, such as the credibility of American leaders, their inability to understand a distant society and culture, the paucity of international support for a foreign intervention, the conduct of American troops, and the lack of an exit strategy from a bloody and troubled occupation. As Senator John F. Kerry, at the time of this writing the Democratic nominee for president in 2004, notes, Vietnam "seems to be the war that won't ever go away."[45] Americans are now pondering the contrasts and comparisons between Iraq and Vietnam, and wondering if their leaders have learned from the Vietnam War and will manage the current crisis with more insight and wisdom than did their predecessors forty years ago.

Notes

1 James Carroll, *An American Requiem: God, My Father, and the War that Came Between Us* (Boston, 1996), 15, 32–33.

2 Quoted in Stephen E. Ambrose, *Nixon: Volume Three, Ruin and Recovery, 1973–1990* (New York, 1991), 94–95.

3 Quoted in Nguyen Tien Hung and Jerrold L. Schecter, *The Palace File* (New York, 1986), 185.

4 Henry Kissinger, *Years of Upheaval* (Boston, 1982), 311.

5 Quoted in Hung and Schecter, *The Palace File,* 163.

6 Kissinger, *Years of Upheaval,* 359.

7 Quoted in Hung and Schecter, *The Palace File,* 36.

8 Quoted in Arnold R. Isaacs, *Without Honor: Defeat in Vietnam and Cambodia* (Baltimore, Md., 1983), 124.

9 Quoted in Frank Snepp, *Decent Interval: An Insider's Account of Saigon's Indecent End Told by the CIA's Chief Strategy Analyst in Vietnam* (New York, 1977), 76.

10 Quoted in William J. Duiker, *The Communist Road to Power in Vietnam,* 2nd ed. (Boulder, Colo., 1996), 329; quoted in Cecil B. Currey, *Victory At Any Cost: The Genius of Viet Nam's Gen. Vo Nguyen Giap* (Washington, D.C., 1997), 292.

11 Truong Nhu Tang, *A Vietcong Memoir* (New York, 1985), 243.

12 General Van Tien Dung, *Our Great Spring Victory: An Account of the Liberation of South Vietnam* (New York, 1977), 15.

13 Quoted in Qiang Zhai, *China and the Vietnam Wars, 1950–1975* (Chapel Hill, N.C., 2000), 207; quoted in Duiker, *The Communist Road,* 333.

14 Quoted in Isaacs, *Without Honor,* 300.

15 Ibid., 315.

16 Quoted in Howard B. Schaffer, *Ellsworth Bunker: Global Troubleshooter, Vietnam Hawk* (Chapel Hill, N.C., 2003), 226.

17 Ibid., 322–23.

18 Quoted in Robert Mann, *A Grand Delusion: America's Descent into Vietnam* (New York, 2001), 718.

19 Quoted in Hung and Schecter, 238.

20 Quoted in Orrin DeForest and David Chanoff, *Slow Burn* (New York, 1990), 271.

21 Quoted in David L. Anderson, ed., *Shadow on the White House: Presidents and the Vietnam War, 1945–1975* (Lawrence, Kans., 1993), 186; quoted in John Robert Greene, *The Presidency of Gerald R. Ford* (Lawrence, Kans., 1995), 132.

22 Quoted in Duiker, *The Communist Road,* 339.

23 Quoted in Hung and Schecter, *The Palace File,* 266.

24 Quoted in Phillip B. Davidson, *Vietnam at War: The History, 1946–1975* (New York, 1991), 778.

25 Quoted in Duiker, *The Communist Road,* 345, 348.

26 Quoted in Walter Isaacson, *Kissinger: A Biography* (New York, 1992), 641–42.

27 Gerald R. Ford, *A Time To Heal* (New York, 1979), 254; quoted in Greene, *Presidency of Gerald R. Ford,* 140.

28 Quoted in Isaacs, *Without Honor,* 420.

29 Quoted in Hung and Schecter, *The Palace File,* 333.

30 Quoted in Isaacs, *Without Honor,* 476; DeForest, *Slow Burn,* 304.

31 Peter Arnett, *Live from the Battle Field: From Vietnam to Baghdad, 35 Years in the World's War Zones* (New York, 1994), 277.

32 Tang, *Vietcong Memoir,* 264–65.

33 Quoted in Stanley Karnow, *Vietnam: A History* (New York, 1990), 9.

34 Doan Van Toai and David Chanoff, *The Vietnamese Gulag* (New York, 1986), 347.

35 Quoted in Isaacson, *Kissinger,* 648.

36 Philip Caputo, *Means of Escape* (Guilford, Conn., 2002), 296.

37 George F. Kennan, *The Cloud of Danger: Current Realities of American Foreign Policy* (Boston, 1977), 4–5.

38 Quoted in James Reston, Jr., *Sherman's March and Vietnam* (New York, 1984), 263–64.

39 *A Soldier Reports* (New York, 1976), 542; *Lost Victory: A Firsthand Account of America's Sixteen Year Involvement in Vietnam* (Chicago, 1989), 6.

40 Ron Kovic, *Born on the Fourth of July* (New York, 1976), 98; *Fortunate Son: The Autobiography of Lewis B. Puller, Jr.* (New York, 1991), 132–35.

41 Quoted in Christian G. Appy, *Patriots: The Vietnam War Remembered from All Sides* (New York, 2003), 161.

42 Quoted in Richard A. Melanson, *American Foreign Policy since the Vietnam War: the Search for Consensus From Nixon to Clinton* (New York, 1996), 231.

43 Quoted in Ivo H. Daalder and James M. Lindsay, *America Unbound: The Bush Revolution In Foreign Policy* (Washington, D.C., 2003), 89, 99, 120.

44 Arnold R. Isaacs, *Vietnam Shadows: The War, Its Ghosts, and Its Legacy* (Baltimore, 1997), ix.

45 The *New York Times,* April 14, 2004.

GUIDE TO ACRONYMS

APC   Armored Personnel Carrier
ARVN   Army of the Republic of Vietnam (South Vietnamese Army)
CIA   Central Intelligence Agency (U.S.)
COSVN Central Office for South Vietnam (headquarters for Communist operations in South Vietnam)
DMZ   Demilitarized Zone (at seventeenth parallel)
DRV   Democratic Republic of Vietnam (North Victnam)
ICC   International Control Commission (watchdog body established to oversee the implementation of the Geneva Accords)
JCS   Joint Chiefs of Staff (of U.S. Armed Forces)
MAAG Military Assistance and Advisory Group (U.S. Army group, forerunner of MACV)
MACV Military Assistance Command, Vietnam (U.S. Army command)
NATO North Atlantic Treaty Organization
NLF   National Liberation Front (known derisively as Viet Cong)
NSC   National Security Council (of the United States)
NVA   North Vietnamese Army
OSS   Office of Strategic Services (U.S. agency, forerunner of CIA)
POW   Prisoner-of-War
PRG   Provisional Revolutionary Government (formed late in the war to serve as the political voice of all insurgents in South Vietnam)
RVN   Republic of Vietnam (South Vietnam)
SEATO Southeast Asia Treaty Organization
VC   Viet Cong (slang for NLF)

TABLE: COMPARATIVE MILITARY CASUALTY FIGURES

Year	Killed in Action		Wounded in Action*	
	U.S.	RVNAF	U.S.	RVNAF
1960	----	2,223	----	2,788
1961	11	4,004	2	5,449
1962	31	4,457	41	7,195
1963	78	5,665	218	11,488
1964	147	7,457	522	17,017
1965	1,369	11,242	3,308	23,118
1966	5,008	11,953	16,526	20,975
1967	9,377	12,716	32,370	29,448
1968	14,589	27,915	46,797	70,696
1969	9,414	21,833	32,940	65,276
1970	4,221	23,346	15,211	71,582
1971	1,381	22,738	4,767	60,939
1972	300	39,587	587	109,960
1973	237	27,901	24	131,936
1974	207	31,219	----	155,735
Total	46,370	254,256	153,313	783,602

*Required hospitalization.
Source: Jeffrey J. Clarke, *Advice and Support: The Final Years, 1965–1973,*
   p. 275

BIBLIOGRAPHICAL ESSAY

General Works

The literature on the Vietnam War is vast and rapidly changing. The most recent guide to it is David L. Anderson, *The Columbia Guide to the Vietnam War* (New York, 2002), while Lester H. Brune and Richard Dean Burns, *America and the Indochina Wars, 1945–1990* (Claremont, Calif., 1992), is older but more comprehensive. Three encyclopedias are invaluable, containing entries on a wide range of people and events: William J. Duiker, *Historical Dictionary of Vietnam,* 2d ed. (Metuchen, N.J., 1997); Stanley I. Kutler, *Encyclopedia of The Vietnam War,* 2d ed. (New York, 2005); and Spencer C. Tucker, *Encyclopedia of the Vietnam War* (New York, 2000).

Many volumes—often a mix of historical analysis and memoir— survey the whole of the American encounter with Vietnam. Neil Sheehan, *A Bright Shining Lie* (New York, 1988), is a brilliant biography of John Paul Vann as well as a study of many of the broader themes of the war; Stanley Karnow, *Vietnam: A History,* 2d ed. (New York, 1991), is a comprehensive, highly readable history of the French and American wars; A. J. Langguth, *Our Vietnam: The War, 1954–1975* (New York, 2000), focuses on individual personalities and emphasizes the futility of the American commitment.

Many books trace particular themes in the American involvement in Vietnam. Myths of American culture are examined in Loren Baritz, *Backfire* (New York, 1985), while American policy from 1945 to 1966 is traced in George McT. Kahin, *Intervention: How America Became Involved in Vietnam* (New York, 1986), and in William J.

Duiker, *U.S. Containment Policy and the Conflict in Indochina* (Stanford, Calif., 1994). Gabriel Kolko, *Anatomy of War: Vietnam, the United States, and the Modern Historical Experience* (New York, 1985), views from a left-of-center perspective the deeper social forces that shaped the conflict; Robert J. McMahon, *The Limits of Empire: The United States and Southeast Asia Since World War II* (New York, 1999), places the war in the context of American policy in Southeast Asia; and David L. Anderson, ed., *Shadow on the White House* (Lawrence, Kans., 1993), analyzes the policies of American presidents from Harry S. Truman through Gerald R. Ford. America's mythic heritage and its relationship to the war is studied in John Hellmann, *American Myth and The Legacy of Vietnam* (New York, 1986), and in Tom Engelhardt, *The End of Victory Culture* (New York, 1995). The connection between gender and class and the war is traced in Robert D. Dean, *Imperial Brotherhood* (Amherst, Mass., 2001). Robert Mann, *A Grand Delusion: America's Descent into Vietnam* (New York, 2001), focuses on the role of Congress from 1949 to 1975, while Phillip B. Davidson, *Vietnam at War: The History, 1946–1975* (New York, 1991), is a superb, wide-ranging military history, and Spencer C. Tucker, *Vietnam* (Lexington, Ky., 1999), is a briefer, more recent one. Shelby L. Stanton, *The Rise and Fall of an American Army: U.S. Ground Forces in Vietnam, 1965–1973* (San Rafael, Calif., 1985), covers military operations. Marc Jason Gilbert, ed., *Why the North Won the Vietnam War* (New York, 2002), includes essays with both American and Vietnamese perspectives.

A handful of memoirs convey a vivid sense of the French and American wars. Robert Shaplen, *The Lost Revolution* (New York, 1966), covers the years from 1945 to 1965. Four accounts by mid-level policymakers combine descriptions of decisionmaking in Washington with impressions of events in Vietnam: Chester L. Cooper, *The Lost Crusade* (New York, 1970), moves from the Geneva Conference to the early Nixon years; Paul M. Kattenburg, *The Vietnam Trauma in American Foreign Policy, 1945–75* (New Brunswick, N.J., 1980), provides a diplomat's perspective; Howard R. Simpson, *Tiger in the Barbed Wire* (New York, 1994), contains remarkable descriptions of both Vietnam and French and American leaders; and George W. Allen,

None So Blind (Chicago, 2001), records the keen observations of an intelligence professional.

Various documentary collections allow students to analyze the decisionmaking process within the American government. The Department of State's *Foreign Relations of the United States* volumes on Vietnam, published through 1966, are an exhaustive and authoritative source, and *The Pentagon Papers: The Defense Department History of United States Decision Making on Vietnam: The Senator Gravel Edition,* 5 vols. (Boston, 1971–72), are still useful. George C. Herring, ed., *The Secret Diplomacy of the Vietnam War: The Negotiating Volumes of the Pentagon Papers* (Austin, Tex., 1983), includes previously unpublished sections of the papers that deal with peace initiatives. A wide range of documentary material on U.S. policymaking is collected in William Conrad Gibbons, *The U.S. Government and the Vietnam War: Executive and Legislative Roles and Relationships,* 4 vols. (Princeton, N.J., 1986–1995).

Controversy over the Vietnam War has spawned a large polemical literature, one that extends all the way to the present. Arthur M. Schlesinger Jr., *The Bitter Heritage* (Boston, 1966), argues that American leaders did not realize that Vietnam would become a quagmire; David Halberstam, *The Best and the Brightest* (New York, 1972), claims that the architects of the war were arrogant and overly optimistic; Daniel Ellsberg, *Papers on the War* (New York, 1972), denounces American leaders for their immorality; Norman Mailer, *Why Are We in Vietnam?* (New York, 1967), probes the destructive aspects of the American psyche; and Leslie H. Gelb and Richard K. Betts, *The Irony of Vietnam: The System Worked* (Washington, D.C., 1978), contends that American presidents knew where they were heading. Frances FitzGerald, *Fire in the Lake: The Vietnamese and the Americans in Vietnam* (Boston, 1972)—while it romanticizes Vietnamese revolutionaries—is a brilliant exploration of the enormous gap between Vietnamese and American culture. Three books defend America's role in Vietnam: Guenter Lewy, *America in Vietnam* (New York, 1978), denies that American troops committed war crimes; Norman Podhoretz, *Why We Were in Vietnam* (New York, 1982), argues that American intervention sought to spare the South

Vietnamese the horrors of communism; and Michael Lind, *Vietnam: The Necessary War* (New York, 1999), asserts that the war was an international struggle that the United States had to fight.

Our knowledge of the North Vietnamese side of the war remains limited. Leaders in Hanoi—still promoting their own revolutionary mythology—have allowed only limited access to archives on the war. Even so, Western researchers have pieced together accounts of the other side. Three path-breaking books by William J. Duiker are invaluable: *The Communist Road to Power in Vietnam,* 2d ed. (Boulder, Colo., 1996), traces the history of Vietnamese revolutionaries from 1900 to their triumph in 1975; *Sacred War: Nationalism and Revolution in a Divided Vietnam* (New York, 1995), is a briefer account of the Vietnamese revolution; and *Ho Chi Minh* (New York, 2000), is a first-rate biography of this legendary revolutionary leader. Ho's military commander, Vo Nguyen Giap, offers his own version of events in *Unforgettable Days,* 3d ed. (Hanoi, 1974), and two biographies attempt—with limited success—to evaluate Giap's celebrated military career: Peter Macdonald, *Giap: The Victor in Vietnam* (New York, 1993), and Cecil B. Currey, *Victory at Any Cost: The Genius of Viet Nam's Gen. Vo Nguyen Giap* (Washington, D.C., 1997). Hanoi's version of the war, first published in 1988, has been translated into English. *Victory in Vietnam: The Official History of the People's Army of Vietnam, 1954–1975* (Lawrence, Kans., 2002), written by a committee of senior Vietnamese military officers, offers some insights into the thinking of North Vietnamese leaders. In the aftermath of victory in 1975, a few high-ranking revolutionaries became disillusioned with postwar policies and fled to the west. Truong Nhu Tang, *A Vietnam Memoir* (New York, 1985), explains why some prominent southerners joined the NLF; Doan Van Toai, *The Vietnamese Gulag* (New York, 1986), argues that the Vietnamese Communist party betrayed the revolution; and Bui Tin, *Following Ho Chi Minh* (Honolulu, 1995), describes his long military career and, in *From Enemy to Friend* (Annapolis, Md., 2002), reflects on the French and American wars. Finally, Neil L. Jamieson, *Understanding Vietnam* (Berkeley, Calif., 1993), attempts to convey to Americans a deeper understanding of Vietnamese culture and society.

The collapse of South Vietnam in 1975 brought an end to that nation's short history, and made it difficult for discredited South Vietnamese officials to tell their stories. Even so, a number of books have added to our knowledge—still thin—of America's ally. Nguyen Cao Ky, *How We Lost the Vietnam War* (Briarcliff Manor, N.Y., 1976), offers scattered insights into the mentality of South Vietnam's ruling elite, and his *Buddha's Child* (New York, 2002), covers the whole of his life. Bui Diem, *In the Jaws of History* (Boston, 1987), is the wide-ranging memoir of South Vietnam's ambassador in Washington, while Tran Van Don, *Our Endless War* (San. Rafael, Calif., 1978), records the memories of another top South Vietnamese official. Only a few of South Vietnam's army and navy officers have written memoirs. Lam Quang Thi, *The Twenty-Five Year Century* (Denton, Tex., 2001), describes his early life and military service with the French and later with ARVN; Kiem Do and Julie Kane, *Counterpart* (Annapolis, Md., 1998), is the story of a navy captain who fled South Vietnam in 1975. Finally, Anthony James Joes, *The War for South Vietnam, 1954–1975* (Westport, Conn., 2001), emphasizes the South Vietnamese perspective.

The end of the Cold War has brought a new wave of scholarship on the international dimensions of the Vietnam War. Older works that remain useful include: Douglas Pike, *Vietnam and the Soviet Union* (Boulder, Colo., 1987), and R. B. Smith, *An International History of the Vietnam War,* 3 vols. (New York, 1984–90). Newer books, however, move deeper into the thinking of former enemies. Ilya V. Gaiduk, *The Soviet Union and the Vietnam War* (Chicago, 1996), covers Soviet policy from 1964 to 1973, and his sequel, *Confronting Vietnam* (Washington, D.C., and Stanford, Calif., 2003), deals with the period from 1954 to 1963. Two first-rate books explain China's crucial relationship to the war: Chen Jian, *Mao's China and the Cold War* (Chapel Hill, N.C., 2001), and Qiang Zhai, *China and the Vietnam Wars, 1950–1975* (Chapel Hill, N.C., 2000). And three volumes include a wide range of essays on international aspects of the conflict: Peter Lowe, ed., *The Vietnam War* (London, 1998); Lloyd C. Gardner and Ted Gittinger, eds., *International Perspectives on Vietnam* (College Station, Tex.,

2000); and Andreas W. Daum, Lloyd C. Gardner, and Wilfried Mausbach, *America, the Vietnam War, and the World* (Washington, D.C., and Cambridge, Eng., 2003).

The First Indochina War, 1945–1954

The origins of the Vietnamese revolution are explored in David G. Marr, *Vietnamese Anticolonialism* (Berkeley, Calif., 1971), *Vietnamese Tradition on Trial* (Berkeley, Calif., 1982), and *Vietnam 1945: The Quest for Power* (Berkeley, Calif., 1995). Revolutionary politics are studied in Kim N. B. Ninh, *A World Transformed: The Politics of Culture in Revolutionary Vietnam* (Ann Arbor, Mich., 2002). Two older works remain useful: John T. McAlister Jr., *Vietnam: The Origins of Revolution* (New York, 1971), and William J. Duiker, *The Rise of Nationalism in Vietnam, 1900–1941* (Ithaca, N.Y., 1976). France's understanding of its role in Indochina is analyzed in Nicola Cooper, *France in Indochina: Colonial Encounters* (New York, 2001).

The outbreak of the first Indochina war is traced in Martin Shipway, *The Road to War: France and Vietnam, 1944–1947* (Providence, R.I. and Oxford, Eng., 1996), while Ellen Hammer, *The Struggle for Indochina, 1945–1954* (Stanford, Calif., 1966), remains the best account of the politics and diplomacy of this conflict. Three studies chronicle French military operations: Bernard B. Fall, *Street Without Joy* (Mechanicsburg, Pa., 1961); Lucien Bodard, *The Quicksand War* (Boston, 1967); and Edgar O'Balance, *The Indochina War: 1945–1954* (London, 1964).

America's involvement with Vietnamese revolutionaries has been controversial. Archimedes Patti, *Why Vietnam? Prelude to America's Albatross* (Berkeley, Calif., 1980), claims that the United States could have worked with Ho Chi Minh; R. Harris Smith, *OSS* (Berkeley, Calif., 1972), contains details of the American intelligence operation in Indochina; and Mark Philip Bradley, *Imagining Vietnam and America: The Making of Postcolonial Vietnam, 1919–1950* (Chapel Hill, N.C., 2000), is an ambitious attempt to explore cultural differences between Americans and Vietnamese.

The Franco-American relationship is described in Roland E. Irving, *The First Indochina War* (London, 1975), and Irwin M. Wall, *The*

United States and the Making of Postwar France, 1945–1954 (New York, 1991). Four books deal with the evolution of American policy in East and Southeast Asia: Robert M. Blum, *Drawing the Line* (New York, 1982), analyzes the origins of containment policy; Gary R. Hess, *The United States' Emergence as a Southeast Asian Power, 1940–1950* (New York, 1987), focuses on Southeast Asia; Ronald L. McGhothlen, *Controlling the Waves* (New York, 1993), deals with Acheson's role as secretary of state; and Lloyd C. Gardner, *Approaching Vietnam* (New York, 1988), emphasizes the ideas behind American policy from 1941 to 1954. Finally, Melvyn P. Leffler, *A Preponderance of Power* (Stanford, Calif., 1992) studies the evolution of the Truman administration's national security policies, while Alonzo L. Hamby, *Man of the People: A Life of Harry S. Truman* (New York, 1995), and Arnold A. Offner, *Another Such Victory: President Truman and the Cold War, 1945–1953* (Stanford, Calif., 2002), recreate the larger context for Truman's policies.

Two books set the stage for Eisenhower's approach to Indochina: Stephen E. Ambrose, *Eisenhower: Volume Two, The President* (New York, 1984); and Chester J. Pach Jr., and Elmo Richardson, *The Presidency of Dwight D. Eisenhower* (Lawrence, Kans., 1991). David L. Anderson, *Trapped by Success* (New York, 1991), traces Eisenhower's policies toward Vietnam, and Ronald H. Spector, *Advice and Support: The Early Years of the United States Army in Vietnam, 1941–1960* (New York, 1985), contains fascinating information on the activities of U.S. Army advisers.

The Battle of Dien Bien Phu brought a crisis in Franco-American relations. For the battle itself, Bernard B. Fall, *Hell in a Very Small Place* (Philadelphia, 1967), provides a vivid account, while Vo Nguyen Giap, *Dien Bien Phu* (Hanoi, 1962), gives a Vietnamese perspective. Three volumes study Eisenhower's decision not to intervene: Melanie Billings-Yun, *Decision against War* (New York, 1988); John P. Burke and Fred I. Greenstein, *How Presidents Test Reality: Decisions in Vietnam, 1954 and 1965* (New York, 1989); and John Prados, *"The Sky Would Fall": Operation Vulture, the U.S. Bombing Mission, Indochina, 1954* (New York, 1983).

Robert F. Randle, *Geneva 1954* (Princeton, N.J., 1969), is a detailed account of the Geneva Agreements; Francois Joyaux, *La Chine et le reglement du premier conflit d'Indochine* (Paris, 1979), and James Cable, *The Geneva Conference of 1954 on Indochina* (New York, 1986), add important details.

The Era of Ngo Dinh Diem and John F. Kennedy, 1954–1963

The history of South Vietnam during the Diem era needs further study. Robert Scigliano, *South Vietnam: Nation under Stress* (Boston, 1964) remains useful, and three newer works assess the nature of Diem's rule and the challenges that he faced: Ellen J. Hammer, *A Death in November: America in Vietnam, 1963* (New York, 1987); Philip E. Catton, *Diem's Final Failure* (Lawrence, Kans., 2002); and Robert J. Topmiller, *The Lotus Unleashed: The Buddhist Peace Movement in South Vietnam, 1964–1966* (Lexington, Ky., 2002). Edward G. Lansdale, *In the Midst of Wars* (New York, 1972) and Cecil B. Curry, *Edward Lansdale, The Unquiet American* (Boston, 1988), tell the story of Diem's most sympathetic American adviser, while Frederick Nolting, *From Trust to Tragedy* (New York, 1988), is the account of the American ambassador from 1961 to 1963. John Ernst, *Forging a Fateful Alliance: Michigan State University and the Vietnam War* (East Lansing, Mich., 1998), and Joseph Morgan, *The Vietnam Lobby: American Friends of Vietnam, 1955–1975* (Chapel Hill, N.C., 1997), study groups who supported Diem. Harvey Neese and John O'Connell, *Prelude to Tragedy: Vietnam, 1960–1965* (Annapolis, Md., 2001), contains essays by Americans and South Vietnamese who were involved in counterinsurgency operations.

The origins of the insurgency in South Vietnam are still difficult to assess. Douglas Pike, *Viet Cong: National Liberation Front of South Vietnam* (Cambridge, Mass., 1966), is a pioneering book. Jeffrey Race, *War Comes to Long An: Revolutionary Conflict in a Vietnamese Province* (Berkeley, Calif., 1972), and William Andrews, *The Village War: Vietnamese Communist: Revolutionary Activity in Dinh Truong Province, 1960–1964* (Columbia, Mo., 1980), are low-level studies that explain the persistence of the revolution in the south. A more recent work, Carlyle Thayer, *War by Other Means: National Liberation and Revolution in Vietnam, 1954–1960* (Boston, 1989), analyzes the origins of the insurgency. Robert K. Brigham, *Guerrilla Diplomacy: The NLF's Foreign Relations and the Viet Nam War* (Ithaca, New York,

1999)—an important book based on Vietnamese sources—traces tensions between southern and northern revolutionaries, while Le Ly Hayslip, *When Heaven and Earth Changed Places* (New York, 1989), reveals the appeal of the NLF to a peasant girl near Da Nang. Malcolm W. Browne, *The New Face of War* (New York, 1965), provides a vivid description of guerilla tactics.

Kennedy's brief presidency has been heavily studied. James N. Giglio, *The Presidency of John F. Kennedy* (Lawrence, Kans., 1991) provides a good introduction; Richard Reeves, *President Kennedy* (New York, 1993), adds important details; and Robert Dallek, *An Unfinished Life* (Boston, 2003), is a balanced, perceptive biography. More specialized studies include: Peter Busch, *All the Way with JFK? Britain, the U.S., and the Vietnam War* (Oxford, Eng., 2003); William J. Rust, *Kennedy in Vietnam* (New York, 1985); Anne E. Blair, *Lodge in Vietnam: A Patriot Abroad* (New Haven, Conn., 1995); and Francis X. Winters, *The Year of the Hare: America in Vietnam, January 25, 1963–February 15, 1964* (Athens, Ga., 1997).

The controversy continues to rage over Kennedy's plans for Vietnam if he had lived longer. John M. Newman, *JFK and Vietnam* (New York, 1992), argues that Kennedy planned to withdraw and advances an unconvincing conspiracy thesis, one embodied in Oliver Stone's film *JFK*. Howard Jones, *Death of a Generation: How the Assassinations of Diem and JFK Prolonged the Vietnam War* (New York, 2002), also contends that Kennedy opposed the commitment of ground combat troops and sought to pull back from Vietnam. Three recent studies reject a conspiracy thesis and add important information and perspectives: Fredrik Logevall, *Choosing War: The Lost Chance for Peace and the Escalation of War in Vietnam* (Berkeley, Calif., 1999), focuses on the period from August 1963 to late February 1965 and suggests that American policymakers could have made different choices; David Kaiser, *American Tragedy: Kennedy, Johnson, and the Origins of the Vietnam War* (Cambridge, Mass., 2000), claims that Kennedy resisted the more aggressive policies of his advisers; and Lawrence Freedman, *Kennedy's Wars: Berlin, Cuba, Laos, and Vietnam* (New York, 2000), agrees that Kennedy might have withdrawn after his reelection.

Many of Kennedy's advisers wrote detailed memoirs that have helped to shape interpretations of his presidency. Some of the best are: Arthur M. Schlesinger Jr., *A Thousand Days* (Boston, 1965); Theodore C. Sorensen, *Kennedy* (New York, 1965); Roger Hilsman, *To Move a Nation* (New York, 1967); Maxwell Taylor, *Swords and Ploughshares* (New York, 1972); Walt W. Rostow, *The Diffusion of Power* (New York, 1972); Dean Rusk as told to Richard Rusk, *As I Saw It* (New York, 1990); and Robert S. McNamara, *In Retrospect: The Tragedy and Lessons of Vietnam* (New York, 1995).

Scholars have also written extensively about Kennedy's foreign-policy advisers. Thomas J. Schoenbaum, *Waging Peace and War* (New York, 1988), and Thomas Zeiler, *Dean Rusk* (Wilmington, Del., 2000), cover Kennedy's and Johnson's secretaries of state; Deborah Shapley, *Promise and Power* (Boston, 1993), and Paul Hendrickson, *The Living and the Dead* (New York, 1996), try to understand Robert McNamara; Kai Bird, *The Color of Truth* (New York, 1998), deals with the Bundy brothers; John M. Taylor, *An American Soldier* (Novato, Calif., 1989) and Douglas Kinnard, *The Certain Trumpet* (Washington, D.C., 1990), follow Maxwell Taylor, a key military adviser; Rudy Abramson, *Spanning the Century* (New York, 1992), tells the story of W. Averell Harriman; and David L. DiLeo, *George Ball, Vietnam, and the Rethinking of Containment* (Chapel Hill, N.C., 1991), and James A. Bill, *George Ball* (New Haven, Conn., 1997), study a prominent dissenter.

American journalists played an important part in shaping images of the Diem regime. David Halberstam, *The Making of a Quagmire* (New York, 1964), and John Mecklin, *Mission in Torment* (Garden City, N.Y., 1965), convey a bleak picture of Diem and his family, while William Prochnau, *Once Upon a Distant War* (New York, 1995), describes the role of the press in the early 1960s.

Escalation and Stalemate, 1964–1968

Johnson's decision to escalate the war, and his management of it, have been thoroughly examined. His memoir, *The Vantage Point* (New York, 1971), is unrevealing, but Robert Dallek, *Flawed Giant: Lyndon Johnson and His Times, 1961–1973* (New York, 1998), is balanced and full of interesting detail, and two older studies, Doris Kearns, *Lyndon Johnson and the American Dream* (New York, 1976), and

Vaughn Davis Burnet, *The Presidency of Lyndon B. Johnson* (Lawrence, Kans., 1983), contain valuable insights. Michael R. Beschloss, *Taking Charge: The Johnson White House Tapes, 1963–1964* (New York, 1991) and *Reaching for Glory: Lyndon Johnson's Secret White House Tapes, 1964–1965* (New York, 2001), reveal Johnson's great political skill, while Lloyd C. Gardner, *Pay Any Price* (Chicago, 1995), assesses the whole of his Vietnam policy, and David M. Barrett, *Uncertain Warriors: Lyndon Johnson and His Vietnam Advisers* (Lawrence, Kans., 1993), claims that Johnson accepted dissent from his advisers. Two books deal with Johnson's approach to the world: Warren I. Cohen and Nancy Bernkopf Tucker, eds., *Lyndon Johnson Confronts the World* (New York, 1994); and H. W. Brands, *The Wages of Globalism* (New York, 1995). Thomas Alan Schwarz, *Lyndon Johnson and Europe* (Cambridge, Mass., 2003), argues that LBJ displayed great skill in dealing with European allies.

Historians have closely studied American escalation of the war. Edwin E. Moise, *Tonkin Gulf and the Escalation of the Vietnam War* (Chapel Hill, N.C., 1996), is a carefully researched monograph. Larry Berman, *Planning a Tragedy* (New York, 1982), focuses on 1965; Brian VanDeMark, *Into the Quagmire* (New York, 1991), covers the period from November 1964 to July 1965; Richard E. Neustadt and Ernest R. May, *Thinking in Time* (New York, 1986), and Yuen Foong Khong, *Analogies at War: Korea, Munich, Dien Bien Phu, and the Vietnam Decisions of 1965* (Princeton, N. J., 1992), analyze the role of historical analogies.

Many of Kennedy's advisers stayed on to work for Johnson. In addition to the memoirs and biographies cited in the section on the era of Diem and Kennedy, students should consult: George W. Ball, *The Past Has Another Pattern* (New York, 1982); Joseph A. Califano Jr., *The Triumph and Tragedy of Lyndon Johnson* (New York, 1991); Clark Clifford with Richard Holbrooke, *Counsel to the President* (New York, 1991); U. S. G. Sharp, *Strategy for Defeat* (Novato, Calif., 1978); William C. Westmoreland, *A Soldier Reports* (New York, 1976); and Victor H. Krulak, *First to Fight* (Annapolis, Md., 1984). Westmoreland deserves a better biography than Samuel Zaffiri, *Westmoreland* (New York, 1994), but Johnson's vice president is treated fully in Carl Solberg, *Hubert Humphrey* (New York, 1984), as is his army chief of staff in Lewis Sorley, *Honorable Warrior: General Harold K. Johnson and the Ethics of Command* (Lawrence, Kans., 1998).

Johnson's conduct of the war has been controversial. Larry Berman, *Lyndon Johnson's War* (New York, 1989), traces the decisions that led to a stalemated conflict; Wallace J. Thies, *When Governments Collide: Coercion and Diplomacy in the Vietnam Conflict, 1964–1968* (Berkeley, Calif., 1980), explains why the bombing of North Vietnam did not intimidate leaders in Hanoi; and George C. Herring, *LBJ and Vietnam: A Different Kind of War* (Austin, Tex., 1994), argues that Johnson's style of leadership was ill-suited for the conduct of limited war. Two polemical books explore the military's approach and civilian-military relations: Robert Buzzanco, *Masters of War* (New York, 1996), describes divisions within the military and claims that many officers were skeptical of success in Vietnam; and H. R. McMaster, *Dereliction of Duty* (New York, 1997), denounces the president and his military advisers for their flawed approach to the war.

Military strategy has also generated much debate. General Westmoreland argues that civilian restrictions prevented a military victory, but Harry G. Summers Jr., *On Strategy* (Novato, Calif., 1982), and Bruce Palmer Jr., *The 25-Year War* (Lexington, Ky., 1984), contend that military leaders misunderstood the nature of the conflict. Andrew F. Krepinevich Jr., *The Army and Vietnam* (Baltimore, 1986), and Larry Cable, *Unholy Grail: The U.S. and the Wars in Vietnam, 1965–68* (New York, 1991), suggest that a counterinsurgency strategy might have worked, while David H. Hackworth and Julie Sherman, *About Face* (New York, 1989), indict American commanders for their distance from the realities of ground combat, and James William Gibson, *The Perfect War: The War We Couldn't Lose and How We Did* (New York, 1986), indicts them for their overemphasis on technology. Three authors, D. Michael Shafer, *Deadly Paradigms: The Failure of U.S. Counterinsurgency Policy* (Princeton, N.J., 1988), Jeffrey Record, *The Wrong War: Why We Lost in Vietnam* (Annapolis, Md., 1998), and John Prados, *The Hidden History of the Vietnam War* (Chicago, 1998), doubt that anything would have worked.

Many books focus on more specialized military operations. The air war is covered in James Clay Thompson, *Rolling Thunder* (Chapel

Hill, N.C., 1980); Mark Clodfelter, *The Limits of Air Power: The American Bombing of North Vietnam* (New York, 1989); and Earl H. Tilford Jr., *Crosswinds: The Air Force's Setup in Vietnam* (College Station, Tex., 1993). Operation RANCH HAND is studied in William A. Buckingham Jr., *Operation RANCH HAND: The Air Force and Herbicides in Southeast Asia, 1961–1971* (Washington, D.C., 1982), and Paul Frederick Cecil, *Herbicidal Warfare* (Westport, Conn., 1986). Harold G. Moore and Joseph L. Galloway, *We Were Soldiers Once ... and Young* (New York, 1992), and Edward F. Murphy, *Dak To* (Novato, Calif., 1993), describe the battles of the Ia Drang Valley and Dak To. Richard H. Schultz Jr., *The Secret War against Hanoi* (New York, 1999), Timothy N. Castle, *One Day Too Long: Top Secret Site 85 and the Bombing of North Vietnam* (New York, 1999), and Kenneth Conboy and Dale Alldradé, *Spies and Commanders* (Lawrence, Kans., 2000), all deal with secret military operations.

An extraordinary number of books have been written about those who fought in Vietnam. Christian G. Appy, *Working-Class War* (Chapel Hill, N.C., 1993), describes the experiences of American soldiers; and Eric M. Bergerud, *Red Thunder, Tropic Lighting* (Boulder, Colo., 1993), examines the world of the Twenty-fifth Infantry Division, while Samuel Hynes, *The Soldiers' Tale: Bearing Witness to Modern War* (New York, 1997), and Peter S. Kindsvatter, *American Soldiers: Ground Combat in the World Wars, Korea, and Vietnam* (Lawrence, Kans., 2003), generalize about ground combat throughout the twentieth century. David Maraniss, *They Marched into Sunlight: War and Peace Vietnam and America, October 1967* (New York, 2003), juxtaposes the ambush of a battalion of the First Infantry Division with a bloody confrontation between student demonstrators and police in Madison, Wisconsin.

Personal memoirs—many of which are exceptionally moving and well written—capture the texture of combat and cover virtually every aspect of the war. Those worth reading include: Ron Kovic, *Born on the Fourth of July* (New York, 1976); Philip Caputo, *A Rumor of War* (New York, 1977); Stuart A. Herrington, *Silence Was a Weapon* (Novato, Calif., 1982); Robert Mason, *Chickenhawk* (New York, 1983); David Donovan, *Once a Warrior King* (New York, 1985); William Broyles Jr., *Brothers in Arms* (New York, 1986); Lewis B. Puller Jr.,

Fortunate Son (New York, 1991); Winnie Smith, *American Daughter Gone to War* (New York, 1992); and Tobias Wolff, *In Pharaoh's Army* (New York, 1994).

Vietnam veterans have also written many novels. Some of the best are: Tim O'Brien, *Going after Cacciato* (New York, 1978) and *The Things They Carried* (New York, 1990); James Webb, *Fields of Fire* (New York, 1978); John Del Vecchio, *The 13th Valley* (New York, 1982); and Larry Heinneman, *Close Quarters* (New York, 1977) and *Paco's Story* (New York, 1986).

Oral histories provide a different perspective on the war. A partial list includes: Mark Baker, *Nam* (New York, 1981); Al Santoli, *Everything We Had* (New York, 1981); Wallace Terry, *Bloods: An Oral History of the War by Black Veterans* (New York, 1984); Charley Trujillo, ed., *Soldados: Chicanos in Viet Nam* (San Jose, Calif., 1990); Otto J. Lehrack, *No Shining Armor: The Marines at War in Vietnam* (Lawrence, Kans., 1992) and Kathryn Marshall, ed., *In the Combat Zone* (New York, 1983). Myra McPherson, *Long Time Passing* (New York, 1984), uses oral history to explore the experiences of the Vietnam generation.

The domestic impact of the war and shifts in public opinion can be traced in a number of studies. Robert W. Stevens, *Vain Hopes, Grim Realities* (New York, 1976), and Anthony S. Campagna, *The Economic Consequences of the Vietnam War* (Westport, Conn., 1991), look at the economic effects of the war. Lawrence M. Baskir and William A. Strauss, *Chance and Circumstance* (New York, 1978), George Q. Flynn, *The Draft, 1941–1973* (Lawrence, Kans., 1993), and Michael S. Foley, *Confronting the War Machine* (Chapel Hill, N.C., 2003), unravel the workings of the draft and measure the influence of the draft-resistance movement. The growing doubts of the public about the war are analyzed in Samuel Lubell, *The Hidden Crisis in American Politics* (New York, 1971), Louis Harris, *The Anguish of Change* (New York, 1973), and John E. Mueller, *War, Presidents, and Public Opinion* (New York, 1973), which compares the conflicts in Korea and Vietnam.

The antiwar movement has received a great deal of attention. Charles DeBenedetti, *An American Ordeal* (Syracuse, N.Y., 1990), traces the changing nature of the movement; Todd Gitlin, *The Sixties: Years of Hope, Days of Rage* (New York, 1993), reflects on youthful protest; Tom Wells, *The War Within* (Berkeley, Calif., 1994), gives a detailed account of antiwar protests; Rhodri Jeffreys-Jones, *Peace Now!* (New Haven, Conn., 1999), looks at different segments of American society; and Melvin Small, *Johnson, Nixon, and the Doves* (New Brunswick, N.J., 1988) and *Antiwarriors: The Vietnam War and the Battle for America's Hearts and Minds* (Wilmington, Del., 2002), claim that opponents of the war had a substantial impact on official policy. Adam Garfinkle, *Telltale Hearts: The Origins and Impact of the Vietnam Antiwar Movement* (New York, 1995), argues that radical protests prolonged the war. Four books place the antiwar movement in the broader context of the 1960s: David Farber, *The Age of Great Dreams* (New York, 1994); David Burner, *Making Peace with the 60s* (Princeton, N.J., 1996); Terry Anderson, *The Movement and the Sixties* (New York, 1995); and Maurice Isserman and Michael Kazin, *America Divided: The Civil War of the 1960s* (New York, 2000).

Many antiwar protestors have written memoirs. Fred Halstead, *Out Now* (New York, 1978), Abbie Hoffman, *Soon to be a Major Motion Picture* (New York, 1980); Tom Hayden, *Reunion* (New York, 1988), and David Dellinger, *From Yale to Jail* (New York, 1994), all provide vivid accounts of the authors' activities. James Carroll, *An American Requiem* (Boston, 1996), chronicles his turn against the war, as does William Sloan Coffin Jr., *Once to Every Man* (New York, 1977). Daniel Ellsberg, *Secrets* (New York, 2003), gives his perspective, while Tom Wells, *Wild Man of the Left* (New York, 2001), is a study of Ellsberg's life. Two books chart the effect of the war on American intellectuals: Sandy Vogelsgang, *The Long Dark Night of the Soul* (New York, 1974); and Robert R. Tomes, *Apocalypse Then: American Intellectuals and the Vietnam War* (New York, 1998).

More monographic studies focus on specific groups and institutions. Books that deal with specific groups include: Michael K. Ball, *Because of Their Faith: CALCAV and Religious Opposition to the War in Vietnam* (New York, 1990); and Amy Swerdlow, *Women Strike for Peace* (Chicago, 1993). Andrew Runt, *The Turning* (New York, 1999), and Gerald Nicosia, *Home to War* (New York, 2001), follow veterans against the war. The war on the campuses is covered in: W. J. Rornbaugh, *Berkeley at War* (New York, 1989); Kenneth J. Heinemam, *Campus Wars: The Peace Movement at American State Universities in the Vietnam Era* (Albany, N.Y., 1993); and Marc Jason Gilbert, *The Vietnam War on Campus* (Westport, Conn., 2001).

On the role of Congress, Mann's *A Grand Delusion* (New York, 2001)—a comprehensive overview from 1949 to 1975—is the place to start. Randall B. Woods, ed., *Vietnam and the American Political Tradition* (New York, 2003), contains essays on senators who opposed the war; Terry Dietz, *Republicans and Vietnam, 1960–1968* (Westport, Conn., 1986), analyzes the position of congressional Republicans. J. William Fulbright, *The Arrogance of Power* (New York, 1966), challenges the nation's foreign policy, while George McGovern, *Grassroots* (New York, 1977), tells the story of his opposition to the war and of his presidential campaign. Books dealing with individual senators include: William C. Berman, *William Fulbright and the Vietnam War* (Kent, Ohio, 1988); Randall Bennett Woods, *Fulbright: A Biography* (New York, 1995) and *J. William Fulbright, Vietnam and the Search for a Cold War Foreign Policy* (New York, 1998); Gilbert C. Fite, *Richard B. Russell Jr., Senator trom Georgia* (Chapel Hill, N.C., 1991); Gregory Allen Olson, *Mansfield and Vietnam* (East Lansing, Mich., 1995); and Don Oberdorfer, *Senator Mansfield* (Washington, D.C., 2003).

On the North Vietnamese side of the war—aside from those books listed in the first section—Jon M. Van Dyke, *North Vietnam's Strategy for Surival* (Palo Alto, Calif., 1972), is based on published North Vietnamese sources, while *Vietnam: The Anti-U.S. Resistance for National Salvation, 1954–1975* (Hanoi, 1980), is an official history. Tran Van Tra, *Ending the Thirty-Year War* (Washington, D.C., 1983), explores North Vietnamese and NLF strategy; David Chanoff and Doan Van Toai, *Portrait of the Enemy* (New York, 1986), Michael Lee Lanning and Dan Cragg, *Inside the VC and the NVA* (New York, 1992), and Tom Mangold and John Penycate, *The Tunnels of Cu Chi* (New York, 1985), use interviews and captured documents to recreate the world of enemy soldiers. The history of the NVA is traced in Greg Lockhart, *Nation in Arms: The Origins of the People's Army of Vietnam* (Boston, 1989), and Douglas Pike, *PAVN: People's Army of Vietnam* (San Rafael, Calif., 1986). Sandra C. Taylor, *Vietnamese Women at War* (Lawrence, Kans., 1999), and Karen Gottschang Turner, *Even the Women Must Fight* (New York, 1998), analyze the important role of women in the North Vietnamese war effort. The story of the Ho Chi Minh Trail is told in Richard L. Stevens, *The Trail* (New York, 1993), and John Prados, *The Blood Road* (New York, 1999). Finally, works of fiction offer many insights into the human side of the North Vietnamese war machine. Some of the best novels include: Bao Ninh, *The Sorrow of War* (New York, 1993); Duong Thu Huong, *Paradise of the Blind* (New York, 1993), *Novel Without a Name* (New York, 1995), *Memories of a Pure Spring* (New York, 2000), and *Beyond Illusions* (New York, 2002).

In recent years international aspects of the war have been carefully analyzed. Many general studies are listed in the first section. Three books describe various peace initiatives: Allan E. Goodman, *The Lost Peace* (Stanford, Calif., 1978); Gareth Porter, *A Peace Denied: The United States, Vietnam, and the Paris Agreements* (Bloomington, Ind., 1975); and Janos Radvanyi, *Delusion and Reality* (South Bend, Ind., 1978). Robert S. McNamara, et al., *Argument without End* (New York, 1999), is a muddled search for missed opportunities to end the war.

America's Asian allies—with the exception of Australia—displayed little commitment to the conflict. Glen St. J. A. Barclay, *A Very Small Insurance Policy* (New York, 1988), Peter Edwards, *Crisis and Commitments* (Sydney, 1992), and John Murphy, *Harvest of Fear* (Boulder, Colo., 1994), deal with Australia's involvement; Thomas R. H. Havens, *Fire Across the Sea* (Princeton, N.J., 1987), explains Japan's reaction; and Robert M. Blackburn, *Mercenaries and Lyndon Johnson's "More Flags"* (Jefferson, N.C., 1994), focuses on Korean, Filipino, and Thai participation.

Many books cover the origins and impact of the Tet Offensive. Don Oberdorfer, *Tet!* (Garden City, N.Y., 1971); James J. Wirtz, *The Tet Offensive: Intelligence Failure in War* (Ithaca, N.Y., 1991); Ronnie E. Ford, *Tet 1968* (Portland, Ore., 1995); and Marc Gilbert and William Head, eds., *The Tet Offensive* (Westport, Conn., 1996), look at different aspects of the offensive. Its impact in Washington is analyzed in Townsend Hoopes, *The Limits of Intervention* (New York, 1970); and in Herbert Y. Schandler, *The Unmaking of a President: Lyndon Johnson and Vietnam* (Princeton, N.J., 1977). Robert Pisor, *The End of the Line* (New York, 1982), and John Prados and Ray W.

Stubbe, *Valley of Decision* (Boston, 1991), seek to understand the pivotal battle of Khe Sanh, while Ronald H. Spector, *After Tet: The Bloodiest Year in Vietnam* (New York, 1993), follows military operations throughout the rest of 1968. Finally, two memoirs, Bruce E. Jones, *War without Windows* (New York, 1987), and Sam Adams, *War of Numbers* (South Royalton, Vt., 1994), deal with the puzzling order of battle controversy.

The role of the media—especially during the Tet Offensive—remains controversial. Michael Arlen, *The Living Room War* (New York, 1969), analyzes television coverage, Peter Braestrup, *Big Story,* 2 vols. (Boulder, Colo., 1977), argues that the reporting of Tet was misleading, and Kathleen Turner, *Lyndon Johnson's Dual War: Vietnam and the Press* (Chicago, 1985), assesses Johnson's strained relationship with reporters. Three studies refute the claim that the press was responsible for the loss of the war: Daniel C. Hallin, *The "Uncensored War"* (New York, 1986); William M. Hammond, *Reporting Vietnam: Media and Military at War* (Lawrence, Kans., 1998); and Clarence R. Wyatt, *Paper Soldiers* (New York, 1993). *Reporting Vietnam: American Journalism, 1959–1975* (New York, 1998) is a compilation of some of the finest writing on the war. Many reporters have written memoirs. Among the best are: Morley Safer, *Flashbacks* (New York, 1990); Malcolm W. Browne, *Muddy Boots and Red Socks* (New York, 1993); Peter Arnett, *Live from the Battlefield* (New York, 1994); Philip Caputo, *Means of Escape* (Guilford, Conn., 2002); and John Laurence, *The Cat from Hué* (New York, 2002).

On the My Lai massacre, Seymour Hersh, *My Lai 4* (New York, 1970), is an early account; Michael Bilton and Kevin Sill, *Four Hours in My Lai* (New York, 1992), deals with the incident and its aftermath; David L. Anderson, ed., *Facing My Lai* (Lawrence, Kans., 1998), contains wide-ranging reflections, and Michael R. Belknap, *The Vietnam War on Trial* (Lawrence, Kans., 2002), describes the court-martial of William Calley.

A number of books capture the high drama of the 1968 presidential campaign. Allen J. Matusow, *The Unraveling of America* (New York, 1984), focuses on the decline of liberalism; James T. Patterson, *Grand Expectations* (New York, 1996), covers the years from 1945 to 1974; Lewis L. Gould, *1968: The Election that Changed America*

(Chicago, 1993), deals with the turbulent campaign; and David Farber, *Chicago '68* (Chicago, 1988), describes the Democratic convention. Books that cover the presidential candidates include: Arthur M. Schlesinger Jr., *Robert Kennedy and His Times,* 2 vols. (Boston, 1978); Ronald Steel, *In Love with Night: The American Romance with Robert Kennedy* (New York, 2000); Evan Thomas, *Robert Kennedy* (New York, 2000); Joseph A. Palermo, *In His Own Right: The Political Odyssey of Senator Robert F. Kennedy* (New York, 2001); William Chafe, *Never Stop Running: Allard Lowenstein and the Struggle to Save American Liberalism* (New York, 1993); Dan T. Carter, *The Politics of Rage: George Wallace, The Origins of the New Conservatism, and the Transformation of American Politics* (New York, 1997); and Dominic Sandbrook, *Eugene McCarthy: The Rise and Fall of Postwar American Liberalism* (New York, 2004). Jeff Shesol, *Mutual Contempt* (New York, 1997), explores the feud between Johnson and Robert Kennedy.

Nixon, Kissinger, and Withdrawal, 1969–1973

Both Nixon's and Kissinger's memoirs contain much information on their approach to the war. Nixon, *RN* (New York, 1978), quotes from his diaries and private papers, while Kissinger, *White House Years* (Boston, 1979), *Years of Upheaval* (Boston, 1982), and *Years of Renewal* (New York, 1999), cover his years of service under Nixon and Ford in nearly four thousand pages. His *Ending the Vietnam War* (New York, 2003), brings together material dealing with the war from his earlier books. Howard B. Schaffer, *Ellsworth Bunker* (Chapel Hill, N.C., 2003), traces the career of America's ambassador to South Vietnam from 1967 to 1973. Interesting memoirs on the Nixon years include: William Safire, *Before the Fall* (New York, 1975); U. Alexis Johnson, *The Right Hand of Power* (Englewood Cliffs, N.J., 1984); Vernon Walters, *Silent Missions* (Garden City, N.Y., 1978); and Alexander M. Haig Jr., *Inner Circles* (New York, 1982). H. R. Haldeman, *The Haldeman Diaries* (New York, 1994), conveys the tone of the Nixon White House.

Of the many biographies of Nixon and Kissinger, Stephen E. Ambrose, *Nixon,* 3 vols. (New York, 1987–1991), is the place to start;

but Richard Reeves, *President Nixon: Alone in the White House* (New York, 2001), adds valuable material, as does Anthony Summers, *Arrogance of Power: The Secret World of Richard Nixon* (New York, 2000). Joan Hoff, *Nixon Reconsidered* (New York, 1994), emphasizes Nixon's domestic rather than his foreign policy achievements; Stanley I. Kutler, *Abuse of Power: The New Nixon Tapes* (New York, 1997), contains transcripts of White House tapes. Seymour M. Hersh, *The Price of Power: Kissinger in the Nixon White House* (New York, 1983), is highly critical; Robert D. Schulzinger, *Henry Kissinger* (New York, 1989), is more balanced; and Walter Isaacson, *Kissinger* (New York, 1992), tells the story of his life.

The assumptions behind Nixon's and Kissinger's foreign policy are assessed in John Lewis Gaddis, *Strategies of Containment* (New York, 1982), but William Bundy, *A Tangled Web* (New York, 1998), is more skeptical of their achievements. Melvin Small, *The Presidency of Richard Nixon* (Lawrence, Kans., 1999), assesses the whole of Nixon's White House years; Jeffrey Kimball, *Nixon's Vietnam War* (Lawrence, Kans., 1998), gives a detailed account of Vietnam policy, and his *The Vietnam War Files: Uncovering the Secret History of Nixon-Era Strategy* (Lawrence, Kans., 2003), challenges Nixon's and Kissinger's version of events. Larry Berman, *No Peace, No Honor* (New York, 2001), and Pierre Asselin, *A Bitter Peace* (Chapel Hill, N.C., 2002), focus on the negotiations leading to the Paris Peace Accords. Nguyen Tien Hung and Jerrold L. Schecter, *The Palace File* (New York, l986), provides a valuable South Vietnamese perspective. Keith L. Nelson, *The Making of Détente* (Baltimore, 1995), deals with Soviet-American relations; Gordon H. Chang, *Friends and Enemies* (Stanford, Calif., 1990), deals with China, the Soviet Union, and the United States.

Military operations from 1969 to 1973 are covered in: James L. Collins Jr., *The Development and Training of the South Vietnamese Army, 1950–1972* (Washington, D.C., 1975); Jeffrey J. Clarke, *The United States Army in Vietnam: Advice and Support, The Final Years, 1965–1973* (Washington, D.C., 1988); and James H. Willbanks, *Abandoning Vietnam* (Lawrence, Kans., 2004). Lewis Sorley, *Thunderbolt* (New York, 1988), is a sympathetic biography of Creighton Abrams, while his, *A Better War: The Unexamined Victories and Final Tragedy of America's Last Years in Vietnam* (New York, 1999), covers the period from 1968 through 1975 and claims that the war had, in fact, been won by the end of 1972. Dale Andradé, *America's Last Vietnam Battle* (Lawrence, Kans., 2001), is a fine study of the Easter Offensive; G. H. Turley, *The Easter Offensive* (Annapolis, Md., 1985), is the memoir of an American adviser to the Third ARVN Division. David H. Hackworth, *Steel My Soldiers' Hearts* (New York, 2002), explains his transformation in 1969 of an American battalion stationed in the Mekong Delta.

Studies of the CIA and of pacification programs provide fascinating glimpses into the other war in Vietnam. John Ranelagh, *The Agency* (New York, 1986), and Christopher Andrew, *For the President's Eyes Only* (New York, 1995), are excellent histories of the agency, while John Prados, *Presidents' Secret Wars* (Chicago, 1996), has chapters on Laos and Vietnam, and his *Lost Crusader* (New York, 2003), is the first biography of William Colby. Thomas Powers, *The Man Who Kept the Secrets* (New York, 1979), analyzes the career of Colby's predecessor, Richard Helms; David Corn, *Blond Ghost* (New York, 1994), deals with another top CIA official. Memoirs by Robert Komer, *Bureaucracy at War* (Boulder, Colo., 1986), William Colby, *Lost Victory* (Chicago, 1989), Richard Helms, *A Look over My Shoulder* (New York, 2003), offer high-level perspectives; Orrin DeForest, *Slow Burn* (New York, 1990), and Sedgwick D. Tourison Jr., *Talking with Victor Charlie* (New York, 1991), offer the perspectives of officers working in the field.

Douglas S. Blaufarb, *The Counterinsurgency Era: U.S. Doctrines and Performance* (New York, 1977), and D. Michael Shafer, *Deadly Paradigms: The Failure of U.S. Counterinsurgency Policy* (Princeton, N.J., 1988), are good general studies; Richard A. Hunt, *Pacification* (Boulder, Colo., 1995), focuses on the whole of Vietnam, Eric M. Bergerud, *The Dynamics of Defeat* (Boulder, Colo., 1991), focuses on Hau Nghia province, and Francis J. West, *The Village* (New York, 1972), describes the Marines' efforts in one area. The Phoenix Program remains controversial; books by Dale Andradé, *Ashes to Ashes* (Lexington, Mass., 1990), Douglas Valentine, *The Phoenix Program*

(New York, 1990), Zalin Grant, *Facing the Phoenix* (New York, 1991), and Mark Moyar, *Phoenix and the Birds of Prey* (Annapolis, Md., 1997), offer different assessments of it.

William Shawcross, *Sideshow* (New York, 1979), deals with Nixon's and Kissinger's policy in Cambodia, while Ben Kiernan, *How Pol Pot Came to Power* (London, 1985), analyzes the tragic aftermath there. Studies of the war in Laos include: Timothy N. Castle, *At War in the Shadow of Vietnam* (New York, 1993); Jane Hamilton Merritt, *Tragic Mountains: The Hmong, the Americans, and the Secret Wars for Laos, 1942–1992* (Bloomington, Ind., 1993); and Roger Warner, *Backfire* (New York, 1995) and *Shooting at the Moon* (New York, 1997).

The Fall of South Vietnam, 1973–1975

Gerald R. Ford, *A Time To Heal* (New York, 1979), John Robert Greene, *The Presidency of Gerald R. Ford* (Lawrence, Kans., 1995), and P. Edward Haley, *Congress and the Fall of South Vietnam and Cambodia* (East Brunswick, N.J., 1982), describe the perspective of leaders in Washington during South Vietnam's final years. Frank Snepp, *Decent Interval* (New York, 1977), Stuart, A. Herrington, *Peace with Honor?* (Novato, Calif., 1983), and James E. Parker Jr., *Last Man Out* (New York, 1999), give the perspective of Americans stationed in South Vietnam. Stephen T. Hosmer, et al., *The Fall of South Vietnam* (New York, 1980), records the reflections of South Vietnamese leaders. Arnold R. Isaacs, *Without Honor* (Baltimore, 1983), is a superb account of South Vietnam from January 1973 through the fall of Saigon. General Tran Van Tra, *Ending the Thirty Years' War* (Washington, D.C., 1983), and Van Tien Dung, *Our Great Spring Victory* (New York, 1977), provide a North Vietnamese view.

The many books dealing with the fall of Saigon include: John Pilzer, *The Last Day* (New York, 1976); Alan Dawson, *55 Days: The Fall of South Vietnam* (Englewood Cliffs, N.J., 1977); Tiziano Terzani, *Giai Phong! The Fall and Liberation of South Vietnam* (New York, 1985); David Butler, *The Fall of South Vietnam* (New York, 1985); and Olivier Todd, *Cruel April* (New York, 1990).

Legacies of the War

The impact of the war in Vietnam and America has been intense and longlasting. The legacy in postwar Vietnam is discussed in Gabriel Kolko, *Anatomy of Peace* (London, 1997), Robert Templar, *Shadows on the Wind* (New York, 1998), and Nayan Chanda, *Brother Enemy* (New York, 1986). Neil Sheehan, *After the War Was Over* (New York, 1992), tells the story of his return to Vietnam in 1989. On the American side, Michael Shafer, ed., *The Legacy: The Vietnam War in the American Imagination* (Boston, 1990), Arnold R. Isaacs, *Vietnam Shadows* (Baltimore, 1997), and Charles E. Neu, ed., *After Vietnam* (Baltimore, 2000), offer general assessments of the impact of the war. Many books assess the way in which the war affected American foreign policy. Among the best are: William Head and Lawrence E. Grinter, eds., *Looking Back on the Vietnam War* (Westport, Conn., 1993); Timothy J. Lompeis, *From People's War to People's Rule* (Chapel Hill, N.C., 1996); and Richard A. Melanson, *American Foreign Policy since the Vietnam War* (Armonk, N.Y., 2000). H. Bruce Franklin, *M.I.A. or Mythmaking in America* (New Brunswick, N.J., 1993), explores the M.I.A. myth, James Reston Jr., *Sherman's March and Vietnam* (New York, 1984), compares the Civil War and Vietnam, and Gloria Emerson, *Winners and Losers* (New York, 1976), and Myra MacPherson, *Long Time Passing* (Garden City, N.Y., 1984), trace the impact of the war on individual Americans. Vietnamese who fled to the United States are dealt with in Paul James Rutledge, *The Vietnamese Experience in America* (Bloomington, Ind., 1992), and in Hien Duc Do, *The Vietnamese Americans* (Westport, Conn., 1999), while Jonathan Shay, *Achilles in Vietnam* (New York, 1994), follows the reintegration of combat veterans back into society, and Eric T. Dean Jr., *Shook over Hell* (Cambridge, Mass., 1997), compares the combat experience in the Civil War and Vietnam.

The cultural legacy of the war has been immense. Linda Dittmar and Gene Michard, eds., *From Hanoi to Hollywood* (New Brunswick, N.J., 1990) studies films on the war, while John Carlos Rowe and Rich Berg, eds., *The Vietnam War and American Culture* (New York, 1991), contains wide-ranging essays. Jerry Lembcke, *The Spitting Image: Myth, Memory, and the Legacy of Vietnam* (New York, 1998), examines images associated with the war, and Fred Turner, *Echoes of Combat* (New York, 1996), views the war in the nation's collective memory. Robert Glen Butler, *A Good Scent from a Strange Mountain* (New York, 1991), explores cultural tensions between Vietnamese and Americans, James Webb, *Lost Soldiers* (New York, 2001), traces the legacy of the war in contemporary Vietnam, and Christian G. Appy, *Patriots: The Vietnam War Remembered from All Sides* (New York, 2003), collects the moving recollections of 135 men and women.

INDEX

America's Lost War: Vietnam, 1945–1975
Developmental Editor and Copy Editor: Andrew J. Davidson
Production Editor: Lucy Herz
Proofreader: Claudia Siler
Cartographer: Jason Casanova, Pegleg Graphics
Indexer: Margie Towery
Printer: McNaughton & Gunn, Inc.